Teaching and Learning Through Modules

Edited by

David Warwick

Basil Blackwell

First published 1988
© David Warwick 1988

Published by Basil Blackwell Ltd
108 Cowley Road
Oxford OX4 1JF
England

British Library Cataloguing in Publication Data

Teaching and learning through modules.
  1. Curriculum planning ——— Great Britain
  I. Warwick, David, 1936–
  375'.001'0941   LB1564.G7

  ISBN 0-631-16168-6
  ISBN 0-631-15772-7 Pbk

Typeset in Great Britain
by Photo-graphics, Honiton, Devon
Printed in Great Britain
by T. J. Press Ltd, Cornwall

Contents

Introduction: cafeteria curriculum
David Warwick   1

PART ONE: PREPARATION AND PLANNING

1 Preparing a module   *Richard Dunn, Clive Marshall, David
                        Sharp and Geoffrey Wilby*   9

2 Primary approaches   *Susan Bourne*   26

3 Problems of planning   *Terry Brown*   42

4 Starting from scratch   *Glynis Weller and James Williams*   69

PART TWO: MODULAR ISSUES

5 Extending the core   *Michael Jones*   80

6 Negotiated pathways   *Bruce and Susan Pyart*   101

7 Modular development and the pastoral curriculum
  Edward Goodhew   122

8 Industrial links   *Sidney Slater*   137

PART THREE: ASSESSMENT PROCEDURES

9 Modular accreditation   *Henry Macintosh*   154

10 Credit banking   *Christine Southall*   161

11 Profiling through computers   *Geoffrey Molyneux*   181

12 Consortia issues   *Adrian Booth, David Darwood, Julie
                       Wright*   196

13 Modules in management   *David Warwick*   207

14 Modular INSET   *Michael Phillips*   220

Notes on contributors   235

Index   240

Introduction: Cafeteria Curriculum

The institutionalised curriculum has always had a culinary look about it. In the good/bad old days it was served up rather like school dinners, complete in itself, delivered in front of you on a take-it-or-leave-it basis. Hot, wholesome and nourishing, such repasts were said to contain all that was required to fortify the inner man, and there were constant reminders of their efficacy in this respect: how to leave the greens, swop the spuds for peas or ask for a smaller portion might do irreparable damage. Someone out there in the culinary beyond knew what they were talking about: the food was 'good for you' and, if eaten up without complaint, one day we would thank them for it.

The problem was that, wholesome and sustaining though it might be, the food was neither interesting nor appetising. The changes were rung from day to day, but one soon came to know what to expect – 'if it's Friday it must be fish', etc. – and the menus had a grey sameness about them. School meals, far from being joyous, sociable occasions, degenerated into mere acts of nutrition. So, too, the curriculum. In those pre-1944 days it had the great benefit of being regarded as a whole and it did provide a broad and balanced diet. The problems of feeding young minds and the feeding of young bodies, however, were tackled in much the same way. The staple fare was seen as consisting of all those elements which together were required to sustain intellectual growth and enable one to hold one's own in the hurly burly of daily living. Such a curriculum had a long and honourable provenance, stretching back as it did to the *trivium* and *quadrivium* of the Middle Ages, but it responded neither quickly nor favourably to change and, as the pulse of society quickened in the immediate post-war era, difficulties began to emerge.

Schools were getting out of step with the world beyond their walls, but the methodology encouraged – didactic, subject-centred, segmented and elitist – was manifestly inappropriate for the fast-moving, democratic and self-service society that was coming into being. Openness, individual freedom and self-determination were seen as its major attributes and, just as canteen service was transforming the nature of mealtime in schools, similar changes modified their curriculum. In true British manner, though, this was done in an evolutionary fashion; it was a revolution in retrospect only!

The introduction of GCE, and later of CSE, were manifestations of this greater openness and wider choice. Selection there now was between subjects and one no longer had to take these all at the same time, but methodology changed very little and – as HMI have recently pointed out[1] – attempts to encompass the maximum range of possibilities have resulted in an overcrowded timetable and, for many, a paradoxical narrowing of the curriculum. The *set menu* approach might have given way to *table d'hôte* offerings, but waiter-service remained the order of the day, there was very little interchangeability bewteen items and the managers did not seem to realise that many of their customers were leaving the restaurant before they had finished the complete meal. As this was often merely part-way into the main course, and sometimes at the hors d'oeuvre stage only they were departing, some chronically under-nourished, others suffering from diet deficiency brought about through a lack of vital curricular trace elements.

Modular planning, a transition from the *à la carte* to a *cafeteria* approach, attempts to combat all these weaknesses. In essence, it breaks down the total curricular offering into units very much smaller than teachers have ever felt possible, puts each of these clearly on display – so that one can see precisely what it is that one is buying – and invites the customer to 'pick 'n mix' between them. For accreditation purposes, the value of each item is marked – in canteen style – and there is no set time for the duration of the meal. The system begins with the individual tastes of those making the choice, who are more likely to be predisposed towards a menu they themselves have had a hand in constructing. Supervision is, of course, still required but this function becomes somewhat different from traditional waiter-service. It relates far more to the management of the style, environment and presentation of what is available than to the serving up of what one was supposed to have ordered, in a manner over which one has no control, in the management's own sweet time!

Once having been prepared, it is quite common these days for dishes that have proved popular to be deep frozen and served at a later date, either by those who have cooked them or by others: even to be transported to different establishments for inclusion on their menus. A short time in the micro-oven and they are ready to serve as good, or

---

[1] See HMI *Aspects of Secondary Education* (HMSO, 1979)

almost as good, as when they were first made. In modular terms, this fast-food process is called *banking* and refers either to the content of a particularly successful or innovative unit, or to its accreditation for examination purposes.

There are obvious weaknesses about the modular approach to curricular planning and a careful eye needs to be kept on these. The whole process might have been introduced through economic necessity, which is a mistaken view of things, or insufficient thought may have been given to the various components that go to make up the scheme. One aspect could be over-represented, another hardly present at all, or insufficient attention might have been paid to the customer's response to the change in approach. The menu may cease to reflect his changing needs, which would be a pity as a cafeteria approach is able to respond with greater speed and more precision than any other. When applied directly to a school or a college, this type of curriculum may lead to intellectual indigestion through the encouragement of an ill-assorted grouping of modules, to cranial constipation if a series of 'easy-options' are permitted, or plain biliousness should students be allowed to feast too freely on a diet over-rich in units which are basically similar. The besetting sin of the cafeteria approach is that it may become an unappetising diet of continual curricular *smorgasbord*. Unless seen as part of an overall menu this will be the fate of any modular scheme.

But what – in clear, unambiguous language – is a module and how might such a fate be obviated?

Any definition will have to be broad enough to encompass the full range of permutations possible – from modules which are viewed as sequential units leading progressively to the mastery of a subject, to those having more of a complementary function within the cafeteria concept; from the ones placed within a national curriculum[2] to provide important elements which the HMI claim might otherwise slip through the epistemological net[3] to those which allow for different vocational pathways through a mass of material which is common to all.

The brief definition supplied within an earlier book is as good as any. It has a *module* as being:

> A **short** unit, **complete** in itself, which may be **linked** to further units towards the achievement of **larger tasks** or **long term** goals[4]

The terms in bold type require further elaboration:

---

[2] DES *The National Curriculum 5–16: a Consultation Document* (HMSO, 1987), para. 18.
[3] HMI *The Curriculum from 5–16* (HMSO, 1985) paras. 13–15.
[4] See Warwick, D, *The Modular Curriculum* (Blackwell, 1987) p. 4.

1 Complete units

One of the most commonly ascribed attributes of the module is that, like a sentence in the English language, it is an entity complete in itself. Just as every sentence must, by definition, have one or more verbs, so each module must have clearly-defined goals. Verb and goal both tell you where the action is, give shape to the unit as a whole and differentiate it from others around it. Without them it could not be regarded as a totality.

Different types of modules will require their goals to be spelt out in different ways – some will have a distinctly empirical look ('this module sets out to *show* . . .'), some are more behavioural ('at the conclusion of this unit you *will be able to* . . .') and some are more expressive by nature, the distinction between *process* and *product* not always being clear ('over the next five weeks you will be *experiencing* . . .'). Sometimes a combination of differing goals are incorporated into a single unit but, however they are derived or whatever form they take, it is from them that its content emerges and towards their fulfilment that it inexorably moves. Goals are the alpha and omega of the modular process.

2 Short units

Linked very closely to the setting of goals is the need for these to be short-term and shared with those who are to learn through them. These goals are essentially achievable ones – they take weeks rather than months to reach and thus the motivation of all concerned, teachers and taught, will be strong.

There is no delayed gratification here. Possibly for the first time, pupils are told exactly what is expected of them; they experience the satisfaction of frequently succeeding rather than continually failing to meet nebulous and ever-receding targets. Those who might otherwise have been consigned to lowly 'differentiated' streams from the outset may now be introduced to GCSE criteria in a more gradual fashion through a careful arrangement of the material in modular format. Indeed, there are intrinsic benefits in re-examining all the subjects that we teach in this way. Decisions over specialisation, examination entry or vocational choice may also be delayed, and so facilitated, while in no way interfering with the progress of others in the group or year. CPVE uses modules in precisely this fashion and many TVE schemes have adopted them in order to add a specific dimension to the curriculum as a whole. At sixth-form level, self-directed study is facilitated through modular approaches, as are important cross-curricular elements of study-skills at every stage in an individual's scholastic career.

In all these, and in many other ways, our students are given greater access to decisions which affect them. They are permitted to have some say in their education, to see that they are getting somewhere. All this can be achieved through the orchestration of self-contained, short units into a larger and coherent curricular totality.

3 Long-term goals

Important though these short-term goals may be, modules should not be regarded as ends in themselves. They always form part of some larger curricular scheme or are used with the attainment of much longer term objectives in mind. Unless this is the case, the end product is likely to resemble the intellectual smorgasbord referred to earlier!

These long-term objectives are either externally imposed, as is the case when examination boards set restrictions on the combination of modules for assessment purposes, or stem from internal considerations relating either to the course being followed or the meeting of individual need. If it is the structuring of the course which is regarded as having precedence, then the modules will be ordered in such a manner that there is a progression towards its ultimate goals and each individual part is fully understood in sequential relation to all the others. In other words, a utilisation of the classic division into *aims* and *objectives*.

On the other hand, if the ultimate aim is the meeting of the individual needs of each and every student, very little pre-structuring is possible. The controlling influence here is likely to be tutorial guidance linked to carefully kept records of progress, probably along *profiling* lines.

4 Linked units

How modules are individually linked will, then, depend on factors beyond the internal objectives that each was designed to reach. Clear links between individual modules there have to be, but their relationship one with the other must clearly be seen as an outcome, or product, of such an overview and not vice-versa. It is surprising how frequently this important yet elementary fact is overlooked.

As has been seen, in some cases a specific sequence, progression or order will have been built in from the outset. The method of linking modules here is directional and the approach is almost always a *stratified* one, entailing a series of *levels*. Stage One leads to Stage Two, Stage Three cannot be attempted until both the previous ones have been understood, and so on. Modules here represent a succession of base-camps by which individuals are enabled to scale their way up the epistemological summit.

The second broad approach – in which modular choice is in the students' hands and each such selection may have a coherence of its own – may be termed *complementary* as the modules in the programme are not arranged in any particular order. However, it may become *sequential* if a minimum of structure is introduced. All students opting for it may, for example, be required to cross the same terrain, but there is no set route by which they must do so. Modules may be taken in any order and, if the going gets too rough or manifestly unsuitable, others are available which allow individuals to branch out in slightly different directions. Stratified schemes are largely closed-circuit and really designed for those who opt for them from the outset. The others are far more open-ended and their individual components could well form sections *complementary* to or *sequential* within other courses.

If combinations of both these basic approaches are required, this is possible through the use of *key/core* and *optional* modules (the *concentric* approach) or by following units of different kinds *concurrently*. Nor should it be forgotten that, at each level, *stratified* units may also be *complementary*, or open to selection, and that – if the modules have been carefully planned – once such a pre-specified course has been entered into, the possibility always remains of branching off in other directions. The flexibility given to curriculum developers once the balance between long-term goals and short-term objectives has been grasped, is enormous.[5]

5 Larger tasks

Modules have been introduced to facilitate schemes that have wider outcomes and involve long-term planning. Unless they do so, curricular disintegration will occur. But these schemes are themselves part of a broader process – the education of each individual within the context of a specific school or college. Through them each unit owes a wider allegiance, and this relates to the aims of the institution as a whole. If attention is not paid to such broader, all-embracing concepts, the resulting fragmentation may not be so immediate; it may take place on a much grander scale, but it will – just as surely – occur.

The setting of such aims should not devolve upon the Head or any central management team alone. As all staff are involved in the process of translating aims into practice, each and every one of them needs to have a say in the setting of these aims. Once this is done, in whichever manner is most appropriate for the institution concerned, such aims

---

For full discussion of these modular links see Warwick, *op. cit.*, pp. 83–99.

may readily be converted into expressive objectives, or guiding principles, for the conduct of its work at each level. These are the attitudes, skills and behaviours basic for anyone hoping to take their place in society, make some contribution towards it, question its ideology or actively struggle against its values. It is not the function of an educator to prescribe the use to which learning is put – that way lies indoctrination. Rather, he must ensure that, once they leave him, his charges have the opportunity of reaching their potential in whatever direction this may take them; that they have the opportunity at least of being heard, however distasteful their views may be. Too liberal or too open an education works precisely *against* these precepts if it undermines or devalues basic socialisation of this kind. Modular planning, when handled in all the ways referred to above, places at an institution's disposal a certain method of ensuring that such broad aims are translated into practice; of converting educational aspirations into reality.

Within the school or college itself structures of various kinds will be required if such schemes are to be satisfactorily introduced. These will be inter-related and consist, first and foremost, of fairly *large blocks of time* in which all staff involved in the programme are available and a sufficient number of modules may be run, both concurrently and consecutively, for the scheme to be effective. *Control mechanisms* will also be needed to ensure that curricular coherence is, in fact, achieved. These will probably consist either of the kind of pre-structuring of the material already described, strong tutorial guidance or the careful monitoring of individual progress – possibly through the use of computers. The last two of these controls are frequently combined.

In schemes which involves a large element of student choice, an effective method of *communication* not only of the titles of the modules but of their 'vital statistics' – content, objectives, length, approach, etc – is crucial. Such details may be produced in tabulated and easily understandable format through the production of *modular specification* sheets. These need to be available to all students within the scheme, their parents and those responsible for advising on the uptake of such units.

Finally, *evaluation* of both the scheme and the learning it encourages are features of any curricular innovation. Here, two of the differentiations within such processes made by Robert Stake[6] are of particular interest to those involved in modular planning. These consist of *formative* and *summative* assessment. The first is conducted whilst the programme is

---

Stake, R, *Evaluating Educational Programmes: The Need and the Response* (CERI/OECD, Paris, 1976), pp. 18–28.

in progress and is of assistance in keeping students on course or modifying their aspirations, and the latter is conducted at its conclusion, usually for accreditation or profiling purposes. As Stake says: 'When the cook tastes the soup it is formative evaluation and when the guest tastes the soup it is summative!' Second, he points out the important difference between *preordinate* studies, which set out to meet prescribed objectives, and *responsive* ones, which 'are organized around phenomena encountered – often unexpectedly – as the programme goes along'. It can be seen how these relate to the two broad types of modular planning referred to throughout this chapter and entail rather different assessment procedures.

All the aspects of modular planning briefly outlined in the above pages are explored far more extensively in the individual chapters that follow. These have been written by those active in this field, most of them currently engaged in the running of modular projects of their own. The majority of the contributions also take the form of *case studies* of individual schools which have been eminently successful in developing such schemes. Although the issues addressed, then, are broadly similar and the structures adopted relate closely one to another, no attempt has been made to cajole the authors into the adoption of a uniform approach, nor would I wish to do so. It will be quite obvious in reading through the pages that follow that, whilst there is broad agreement over the opportunities offered through modules to 'break the mould'[7] of the English educational system, there remains a lively debate over the precise nature of the modular planning that is required. The rich variety of possibilities that are thus opened up is, to my mind, one of the most interesting features of *Teaching and Learning through Modules*.

David Warwick
Farnham, September, 1987

See Moon, R, *The Modular Curriculum: Remaking the Mould* (Harper and Row, 1987)

1 Preparing a module

*Richard Dunn, Clive Marshall, David Sharp,
Geoffrey Wilby*

*Hemsworth is a bustling village which combines two societies, the
mining and the rural. A number of smaller villages also lie within
the school catchment area. Some are characterised by decline and
deprivation, others by relative prosperity and expansion and this
provides a truly comprehensive intake. The style of the curriculum
adopted, within the broad areas outlined below, is very much a
response to the local community and the nature/ability of our
students.*

*Hemsworth High was formed in 1968 by the amalgamation on
one campus of a grammar school and two secondary modern
schools. It is now a well established and successful mixed
comprehensive school (13–18) with good buildings in attractive
grounds. At present, it enjoys the resources and staffing associated
with a roll of almost 1300 students and a sixth form of 150 but
there is likely to be a decline in numbers over several years to an
estimated low of 900.*

*Pastorally, the school is organised into 'half-year' divisions, with
a Division Head responsible for 150 to 180 students and the
coordination of a team of six or seven tutors. The pastoral
structure, a natural extension of a year system, was a direct
response to the increasingly modular form of curriculum being
developed for many of our students. It was felt that a more secure
yet active pastoral base was essential if the many advantages of a
modular curriculum were not to be undermined by frequent
changing of teachers and courses.*

*Hemsworth is departmentally arranged, although the adminis-
tration and development of the curriculum is undertaken by a
number of coordinators. These senior staff are responsible for
groups of departments and are actively involved in making both
practical and philosophical sense of our modular schemes.*

The intake year (third year) is taught in tutor groups. In the fourth and fifth years, students follow a variety of GCSE, unit accreditation or City and Guilds courses, depending upon ability and individual choice. Within this framework, all students must take English, Maths, at least one subject from the humanities, a creative subject and 20% science/technology. French and German are available for those with an interest in and aptitude for modern languages.

Staff at Hemsworth High have produced, implemented, reviewed and rewritten more than 200 modules. Some are 18-week courses (of two 50 minute lessons per week) designed to meet the requirements of particular subjects, but most are nine weeks long, in order that they can meet the requirements of our rotational scheme. Some staff have planned in teams to produce shared modules (or a number of modules with common objectives) whilst others have worked in isolation to create a single course that represents a unique contribution to an option package.

The preparation and 'ownership' of modules by individual staff within broad subject guidelines has been the key element in our planning, and for this reason it was felt that it would be more appropriate to offer a corporate view which tries not to generalise, but attempts accurately to portray the range of processes that lead to modules being created. This chapter has therefore been completed by four staff, each offering a view of how individual preference or departmental need can lead to a contrast of styles and approaches.

A propos of a discussion on curriculum problems comes the suggestion, 'Why don't you write a series of modular courses?'. Blank response, uneasy shifting of position, averted gazes. 'You could tackle one for starters and see how things go'. The parties go their separate ways. Nothing to show, one might be tempted to think, but the wheel has begun to turn and the thought processes to work.

Does a module appear out of thin air? Does it gradually materialise and take shape out of a dim mist? Does it grow out of barren soil where nothing has been planted and where nothing has grown before?

There are those who suggest that modular courses do just that and so are addenda to what is familiar, well-tried, tested, comfortable and expedient. Modules have no foundation, no ancestral line and no pedigree. Because of this they are regarded, by some, as a troublesome academic exercise whose end result contributes little to the educational status quo. Our own view is that modules are not planned in a vacuum but are a natural extension of the work going on in all curricular areas. The material that constitutes a module is no new thing, even though the concept of the module may be.

All of us must be able to look back on our schooldays and remember weeks and weeks spent on 'The apostrophe', 'South America', 'The causes of the French Revolution' and any amount of other such topics; even the examination papers were conveniently sectionalized. This was, of course, the splitting up of material for convenience, but this sub-division of a syllabus into manageable sections is not the same as creating a modular course. In order to create a module, we must be prepared to look critically at the educational process and identify the essential elements of experience involved.

Thus one of the main advantages of a module is its property of encapsulation. The attention is concentrated into a smaller sphere of activity and the field of vision is narrowed; objectives are seen in sharper focus. It might be thought that this would restrict possibilities but narrowing the immediate field of vision is no bad thing as long as a wide field of vision has been used to establish the main principles of the basic syllabus.

Planning

Preparing modules is in many ways no different from any other form of curriculum planning. The debate continues about the appropriateness of declaring specific or even explorative aims as the first step for planning. Our experience at Hemsworth is that initiatives have arisen as a result of the evaluation of existing practice. Malcolm Skilbeck[1] outlines the curriculum development process as a cyclical process that can begin at any point but will involve some form of situational analysis prior to the formation of goals or planning.

The first step to the individual planning of modules was taken corporately when, early in 1983, a full appraisal of the existing school curriculum was undertaken, basically as a response to difficulties being experienced with a large number of students. Concern had been expressed by a number of staff about the appropriateness of CSE courses for many of our students. We established that up to 50% of our students could be classified as having moderate learning difficulties (in addition to 7% with severe learning difficulties). At that time this represented up to eight teaching groups per year in which it was felt that motivation was poor and that learning styles created underachievement and friction between staff and students. Add to this the disincentive

---

Skilbeck, M 'The curriculum development process: a model for school use' from *School-based curriculum development and teacher education.* (mimeograph, 1975) in Bolam, M and Prescott, W *Supporting Curriculum Development* Open University Press, 1976, p. 96.

of high unemployment and poor social conditions for many students and the need for radical change was obvious.

Our school-based initiative was the establishment of a cross-curricular modular programme where the main emphasis was to be the learning process. In addition to this, the Science Department, followed by the Humanities Department, also devised their own modular schemes.

In Science, for example, members were invited to develop a nine or 18 week course, based upon two out of 30 lessons per week, which would be repeated with different groups of students on a rotational basis. Each student would therefore have six lessons per week and would cover three separate modules every nine weeks; twelve per year.

Scientific modules

Science, Humanities and Creative Studies, working independently, each adopted distinctly different ways of establishing the purpose of a module. In Science, the initial brief given to participating staff was to:

- devise a unit of work which was relevant to the demands of today's technological society;
- ensure that the course was practically biased;
- choose a topic in which they themselves were particularly interested;
- write a module which the students would find interesting, thus increasing motivation.

Science staff were also advised that each module should be coherent and autonomous but must adhere to the general aims and objectives of the department, as follows,

1   To develop an atmosphere in which both staff and students enjoy working together.
2   To provide, through well-designed studies of experimental and practical science, a worthwhile educational experience.
3   To develop abilities and skills that are relevant and useful in everyday life.
4   To stimulate curiosity, interest and enjoyment in science.
5   To develop knowledge and understanding of scientific phenomena and scientific and technological applications with their social, economic and environmental implications.

The modules were put together in a coherent package which ensured a meaningful, broad and balanced scientific contribution to the curriculum.

This was achieved by considering proposed titles collectively prior to further development of each module, to avoid unnecessary overlap and ensure a range of content and approaches. Each member of staff provided a brief syllabus outline before embarking upon in-depth planning. Choice of module was largely dictated by personal interest, existing departmental resource materials and the availability of commercially published resources.

The humanities

Following the success of Science, the departments of History, Geography and Economics were brought together to prepare a number of Humanities modules. They began their planning process by establishing a series of 'points for consideration'. These were:

How might the module contribute towards the general aims and philosophy of the school? It was agreed that the objectives set for their students in their classroom activities should be consistent with, and work towards, the overall aims of the school.

What criteria should be used to help in the selection of content, concepts and experiences? Staff in the Geography, History and Economics departments were reminded of what were considered to be the major aims and objectives of their subjects and asked to write their modules with these in mind.

Does the content of the module help to develop skills and attitudes as well as concepts and knowledge? Too often courses are associated with covering facts and perhaps too little opportunity is given for students to think critically, solve problems, make judgements or analyse.

Which skills are critical to the module? Should there be a balance between general skills, common to all Humanities subjects, or skills specific to individual subjects?

Is it possible to build learning progression into each module? If so, how do we accomplish it? Do the concepts and ideas planned relate to the students' present understanding and knowledge? Can key ideas and skills be progressively developed and reinforced in a carefully constructed manner within each module or between modules?

Are appropriate teaching methods being considered? A variety of approaches, particularly those which encourage active learning, should be adopted.

What evaluation techniques, marking policies and forms of student assessment will be needed? Student as well as staff evaluation of modules should be considered.

Creative studies

The creative studies approach to planning modules focuses on the special contribution made by expressive and creative activities in the curriculum. It is important here to keep in mind the essential element of the experience – which, in turn, may be that which is simple and which may be approached almost as a skill to be acquired and developed by means of steps. In the Department of Art and Design, for example, it became apparent that all students must have a working knowledge of, and experience in, the manipulation of *line*. Line is the basic requirement of so much of the work undertaken in creative studies: it is a vehicle for expression, description, analysis and representation. Coupled with this, particularly with regard to design work, is the concept of *balance*, achieved through a working knowledge of scale, proportion and accurate placement.

With this in mind, it was decided to write a module entitled *Creative line drawing and construction*. The essential element is that the students must be able to use line effectively, so there must be some practical outcome, some example of line used creatively or – better still – several examples of line employed for different purposes. This might be regarded as putting the skill to the test, so we must then work backwards in order to establish and learn the skills.

The learning process begins with the following of simple instructions related to the choosing of suitable equipment and the various methods of handling that equipment. Once there is some positive outcome from this use of the equipment, accurate measuring may be introduced so that the practice pieces demonstrate some balanced form. While this is taking place, the teacher will be encouraging the students to experiment with the direction and movement of line and with its capacity to create or define shapes, and will also be demonstrating the possibilities in relation to scale and proportion. The more practice the student has, the more he or she will improve, and the whole process will be consolidated through recording the practice exercises by way of notes, sketches and diagrams.

It is necessary for the student to work as an individual but it is also necessary for the student to be able to resolve decisions and solve problems by testing possibilities in discussion with the teacher and fellow students. In this way the skill is perfected because only the right approach and the correct application will achieve the right result. It then remains for the student to produce the finished items. Thus, in the module the student has concentrated attention on a particular aspect of Art and Design; has absorbed a concept or essence; has learned a number of skills, practised them and become familiar with their characteristics; and has then come up with the finished product, an example of practical application.

In some areas of study, however, a different concept may serve to launch the module, not this time 'the essential element of an experience' but instead 'the elemental essence of an experience'. Seeking the essence in an experience is an exercise well known in the world of expressive arts, for example, where an experience in one artistic form may be crystallised and re-expressed in a different form. A piece of music may generate an emotion within an individual; that which has caused the emotional response, the pure essence, then becomes the centre point or stimulus for new expression which may spread outwards in concentric rings and the actual form may vary widely. A jazz musician will take an established line and rhythm, the key to the essence or mood of a piece; from then on he or she improvises new melodic or dynamic musical lines as a way of developing a personal statement. This statement, however, must have as its root the essence of the experience.

Modules which come about in this way are essentially personal to the teacher who devises the course. The reasons for establishing modular courses, however, may be varied and may arrive from outside rather than come about through a teacher's own searching for more effective methods. Whatever the starting point – modules fitting into the requirements of an external 'examination' course; those fitting into a scheme of cross-curricular work; those intended to provide a particular functional skill; those intended to make the greatest use of an individual teacher's particular skill, the school's specialist facilities or the locality's unique character, and so on – the teacher must recognise the potential offered by modules for the efficient promotion of material and seek for apt learning processes. The course will have its essential core, its basic purpose or, if we are to move into the grandiose, its 'truth'. Once that has been established then the *modus operandi* can be devised in the light of what is to be learned, how it is to be learned, what practices are to be employed and what practical application is to be made to achieve relevance.

Shared ownership

Modular structures are not new to the school. They have had a long, yet intermittent, history in the humanities area. In the early 1970s the departments comprising the Humanities devised a two-year Mode 3

CSE Social Studies course of a modular nature. In the minds of many people this course was not successful and it was eventually abandoned, the students reverting to mainly specialist History and Geography courses. The main reasons for this failure were identified as follows:

1 The modules, including resource materials, had been prepared by individuals, although they were to be taught by a team of staff.
2 There had been few meetings after the course was originally devised.
3 There was little sharing of ideas, specialisms and methodologies. The important feelings of 'ownership' were therefore missing when staff taught other teachers' modules. Resource materials intended to last for six lessons or more were 'consumed' in a single lesson. Sometimes teachers became more 'deliverers' of materials than educators.

In 1984 several important conclusions were drawn with regard to the Humanities. Most importantly, it was felt that the curriculum for the less able students lacked balance since they could opt for only one subject from History, Geography or Economics. As a result of our review, the time allocation given to Humanities was doubled and a new modular structure, covering all three subjects, was devised (Figure 1.1).

Teachers were to keep their groups for 18 weeks in which time they would normally study two modules (nine weeks, three lessons per week).

Figure 1.1

Group	18 wks Sept–Feb	18 wks Sept–Feb	18 wks Sept–Feb	18 wks Feb–July
A	History	Economics	Geography	Community studies
B	Economics	History	Geography	Community studies
C	Economics	Community studies	History	Geography
D	History	Geography	Economics	Community studies
E	Geography	History	Community studies	Economics

This structure allowed staff to teach their specialisms and reinforced the idea of ownership. At the same time it promoted a new integrated 'community studies' module which was to be prepared by all those involved in its teaching in an attempt to establish 'joint ownership' and so avoid previous problems of lack of staff motivation and commitment. The agreed aims which were developed for this module included a specific statement that the course should be made suitable for a range of staff. The module had therefore to be flexible enough to accommodate a variety of learning techniques and staff abilities and experiences.

Many course meetings were held and in the summer term, time was found during the school day to develop materials. It was thought vital that staff from all the three areas should be involved. Fieldwork was devised and piloted by staff and eventually the entire module was piloted by one teacher and a group of students. This enabled the module to be evaluated and modified before the bulk of the students embarked upon it. Meetings continued to be held and resources and methodologies improved and shared.

The concept of 'shared ownership' has become increasingly important in Humanities as more staff are expected to teach a module which lies outside their strict specialism. It is, we believe, a common experience that specialist subject teachers feel threatened when expected to teach unfamiliar courses or materials.

The preparation of the community studies module resulted in the best practice of each of the separate departments being accessible to all, as different expertise could be shared and built upon.

Multi-media resources

The extent to which one can generate totally new teaching materials in any curriculum development is governed by finance and the suitability of what already exists. At Hemsworth, we were attempting to establish a new style of course within an existing budget. Some additional resources were made available by the Headmaster but the scale of reform meant that a realistic appraisal of existing resources was vital. This presented few problems for most staff since the exercise involved a re-examination, prioritising, and enriching of existing good practice. Where courses represented a major change to the established curriculum, money was made available. Staff strongly identified with their modules and this helped reduce financial needs to a minimum as considerable time, energy and ingenuity were put into the gathering of appropriate but cheap resources.

Teaching approaches varied considerably between staff and departments but the process followed by the Physical Science department provides a typical example of how resources were planned.

Discussion took place on how the individual modules should be put together on paper. Some staff chose the conventional method, that is, the students using exercise books. Others produced worksheets which were kept in a folder and others made booklets of their worksheets which were given to the students at the start of the module. The production of booklets was by far the most successful method in that it allowed pupils to see the module as a coherent whole, it facilitated the 'catching up' process for students who had been absent and it encouraged individual learning programmes for students with learning difficulties or for students who quickly completed their particular task. The marking of students' booklets was also much easier!

Each module had a large practical component. Some practicals were designed to develop scientific skills such as following instructions or using scientific apparatus with due regard to safety; others attempted to develop problem-solving skills and experimental learning techniques. Practical work took up approximately two thirds of the course and the remaining time was spent on various research exercises, involving working from textbooks, questionnaires, and TV or video programmes. All these activities were intended to provide depth and support for the practical work.

Because each module could be taught four times within one year it soon became obvious to all staff that time spent in producing resource materials was worthwhile and soon overhead projectors, the micro computer and video cameras were in greater demand as aids to teaching.

When planning was completed, we found that all modules fully utilised the resources of the department and the school, and developed experimental learning techniques through practical investigations. Some courses required very little written work, some were based around teacher-prepared worksheets and others had, as previously stated, their own self-contained booklet. Preparing resource materials is often time-consuming and expensive but in the context of modules seemed well worth the effort in the long term.

Evaluation

One of the main advantages of the modular structure (at least from the staff point of view) is that staff are teaching to their strengths; devising and developing modules which they are interested in and thus passing on this interest to the students. Because the courses are taught continually in a rotational scheme, it has also meant that staff can, and do, review, modify and update their modules on a regular basis.

In conventional courses lasting one or even two years the problem of evaluation is exacerbated by the pressure 'to keep going' and the difficulty of matching general and elusive long-term goals to specific situations. There is always a sense of immediacy, if not urgency, when evaluating modules. The preparation and evaluation become one and the same process. The modular programme allows staff to identify problem areas or weaknesses with a view to making changes in content or methodology which can be implemented within a few weeks with the next group of students.

It is essential that evaluation is not regarded as an individual process and that staff as a group identify common problems which arise from the modular curriculum. Joint evaluation of some of our early modules has produced the following conclusions about our initial planning.

1   The key aspects of each module must be reinforced, by providing a series of opportunities for students to be involved in the essential elements (in whatever way they are defined by each teacher). This allows students to consolidate their experiences, makes the module more compact but also helps students who have been absent to understand the work and capture 'the mood' of the unit.
2   Time must be allocated during the later stages of a module for reflection, revision and catching up on work that has been missed, particularly if the module is to be externally accredited.
3   Inevitably students work at different rates and courses which are not heavily content-based will only be successful if extension materials are built into the programme.
4   Finally, the most frequent criticism! Some modules were unsuccessful because they were too ambitious. Staff who were not selective enough and attempted modules crammed with experiences, content or skills very quickly discovered that the completion of the course dominated the learning process to the exclusion of all else. In reality they had produced the equivalent of two units, and initial failures were quite often converted to successes when additional, sequel modules were established.

An example

The chapter would not be complete without at least one example of how a specific module was planned. I offer the following comments about my own thoughts and planning, with regard to a module entitled *Body performance*. This was a basic course in anatomy and physiology prepared as a contribution to the science scheme.

Situational analysis

As previously stated, the target group was clearly defined for me in terms of ability, attitude and social need. Further research, therefore, was aimed at the nature and availability of resources. Important factors were:

- *finance* – some additional money was available but ultimately courses on this scale would have to be affordable.
- *facilities* – like most deputies, I expect to lead a nomadic existence. Specialist facilities and equipment would have to be borrowed. Experiments needed to be simple and preferably portable.
- *published materials* – I considered a number of publications, looking for ideas since there seemed little point in re-inventing the wheel. At the same time, investing in expensive books for such a relatively short course also seemed extravagant. In the end, I decided to create my own small booklet which blended ideas and materials from a number of sources into what I hoped would be a cohesive form.

Purposes

Having created a clear picture of the context in which the module would be planned, the next step was to decide upon some general goals. I decided upon four.

1   Students of all abilities are conditioned in many schools to regard writing as the only legitimate form of 'real work'. This course would explicitly challenge this attitude not only by emphasising practical work, but also by discussing openly with each group the style of learning and learning outcomes.
2   The course's essential element, that is 'scientific practice', would be achieved by including a variety of simple experiments, involving measurement, observation, recording and basic conclusions.
3   The course would attempt to examine aspects of body performance that seem relevant to everyday life and student interest. To assist this objective, content would be minimised, so allowing time for me to develop ideas that either arose spontaneously from the class or were particularly topical.

4 The final goal was idealistic and probably unattainable but nevertheless underpinned all of the planning. I wanted to excite the students' imagination and give them a sense of wonder about their own bodies, a Herculean task with students not noted for their intellectual curiosity or creativity.

Content

With a maximum of 18 lessons, selection of appropriate areas to study was extremely difficult. The following content was used as the springboard for learning. It was not in any sense an attempt to produce a balance of cognitive elements or a logical exploration of anatomy.

Using our senses
Pain. Who needs it?
Seeing is believing. How to fool the senses.
Testing our senses.

Bones and breakages

Strength and fitness

Methodology

One of the disadvantages of modular courses can be a lack of time for staff to develop relationships and consolidate on concepts, skills or interests. Within each general 'content' area were to be opportunities to stress the same themes, ie scientific experiment, discussion, group work and practical activity.

The style of learning was also aimed at the development of positive attitudes and relationships. For example, lesson one would be devoted to sharing goals and informal discussion about the students' previous experiences.

We are all teachers of language but in this course writing would be kept to a minimum. This was not to be an abdication of language responsibility but rather an attempt to concentrate upon aural and oral work and the recording of information in more diagrammatic forms. Experience tells us that many less-able students are happy to record information in their books without it passing through their consciousness.

Students would each have an A5 sized booklet containing basic information, outlines of tests and experiments, word searches, anatomical diagrams and simple questions designed to stimulate discussion (Figure 1.2).

Figure 1.2 Extract from students' booklet

USING YOUR SENSES

Listen carefully to the following sounds and write down what you think they are:

1.
2.
3.
4.
5.
6.
7.
8.
9.
10.

Is it more confusing when you can only use one sense organ at a time?

The senses can be fooled. Think of how magicians work.

Look at the picture below. What can you see?

Now try to draw a star while looking at the paper **only** through a mirror. Why do you think this is difficult?

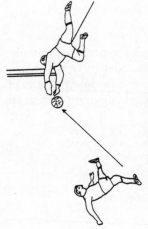

Question What is a reflex save?

Answer

Question What is the difference between a reflex save and a body reflex?

Answer

Question Can you name 3 reflex actions?

Answer 1.

2.

3.

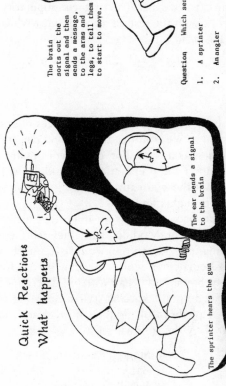

Quick Reactions
What happens

The sprinter hears the gun

The ear sends a signal to the brain

Quick reactions are brought about by the **NERVOUS SYSTEM**

The nervous system is made of:

1.

2.

3.

Each time we practice something, we improve. Practice helps the brain sort things out faster

The brain sorts out the signal and then sends a message, to the arms and legs, to tell them to start to move.

Question Which sense organs do the following people use?

1. A sprinter   A.

2. An angler   A.

3. A tennis player   A.

4. A typist   A.

5. A wine taster   A.

6. A cook   A.

7. A sculptor   A.

Question Why should we not 'DRINK AND DRIVE'?

Answer

OUTCOME 6

Wherever possible, I hoped to use familiar situations as analogies to demonstrate scientific principles and build upon the students' own experiences to illustrate key points. In addition, a range of visual aids and teaching materials were gathered together to help support the unit. The local hospital provided X-rays and the fire station offered the loan of a resuscitation dummy. The Biology Department made available a skeleton, hip replacement joint and eye test materials. I borrowed pins for repairing fractures and a spirit level to demonstrate the principle of balance. Tape recordings were made and conjuring tricks practised. (I hoped this would be a course to remember).

A nine-week module taught four times a year allows continual reassessment and refinement of the course. The unit has proved to be very successful and has never been taught in the same way twice since student interest takes us in different directions each time. Some aspects of the course have been removed because they were unsuccessful, whilst others paradoxically have been extracted because of their popularity. The most obvious case is the work with the resuscitation dummy which has spawned a new course in First Aid.

Conclusions

This chapter has attempted to share with readers the experiences of one school in the preparation of modules. We continue to learn and develop and therefore offer this contribution as a 'snapshot' of current practice. We hope that those embarking upon the preparation of modules will find the information useful and that those already involved in this style of course will recognise familiar thoughts and processes.

The preparation of modules has become for us an important aspect of both curriculum and staff development. Modules, since they represent an important aid to team building, provide an opportunity for staff to be creative and engage in cross-curricular work. Starting points for planning have varied considerably. Some staff began with pre-determined cognitive areas while others decided upon a specific style of learning as the foundation for their work. A plethora of modules now exists and the diversity of units is illustrated by the following list:

1 Orienteering
2 Community service
3 Laboratory skills
4 Personal budgeting
5 First aid
6 DIY
7 Stage set construction
8 Batik
9 Jewellery making
10 Forensic science
11 Pet care
12 Domestic electricity

13 Keeping warm
14 Graphical communications in science
15 Looking after an allotment

16 Meteorology
17 History of medicine
18 Letter writing
19 Rock climbing

Although some general guidelines for writing a module have emerged, we believe that the most successful modules reflect an individual, even idiosyncratic, approach to preparation.

Our modules were written originally to meet the needs of the lower half of the ability range and as such we were freed from many of the usual curricular constraints associated with examination work. Most GCSE courses, for example, follow a conventional two-year pattern and may not be designed in a way that facilitates division into a number of equal parts. For those staff who would like to re-structure existing courses into modules, or prepare accredited units that are compatible with GCSE work, the task will not be easy. We feel that it is essential to resist the temptation to revert to an almost mechanical division of content, since the impact and purpose of well prepared, meaningful modules may be lost.

2 Primary approaches

Susan Bourne

New Scotland Hill Primary School serves a dormitory area, predominantly of middle-class owner-occupiers. Parents are concerned, involved and knowledgeable. The school is always open to them, they work with the children and the PTA is a strong one. The open plan, team teaching structures have needed to be explained and justified from the outset, 17 years ago, as New Scotland Hill competes with the local church school, which is more traditional in its approach.

170 children are organised in infant, lower and upper junior teams which are vertically grouped. The roll has fallen from three to two-teacher teams. A lively, friendly outward-looking school, New Scotland Hill welcomes teaching-practice students each year, including Americans. The Headteacher, Mr H Gillings, is a computer enthusiast.

Primary teachers know only too well that there is never enough time in the working day to do everything they would like to. But there is one particular approach which helps with this problem and means that a teacher can fit in more initiatives, stay in command of the situation, and end up with a real sense of achievement.

This approach involves the teacher in the design, presentation and assessment of modules. These are units or sections of work organised with particular structural characteristics. A module is best described as a unit of work which is clearcut, usually short, very specific in its purpose and has a marked degree of feedback.

Many of the features of the modular approach already exist in primary schools – for example, formal schemes of work for mathematics and language teaching. However, such schemes can be either too rigid or too general in their approach. Modular approaches embody flexible, interactive work patterns which monitor, and are adapted to, the learner's needs and reactions – in the tradition of best primary school practice. The approaches are responsive to the concerns of those outside the school and, above all, are easily communicated and form the basis for dialogue and productive development.

Different kinds of modules

Modules can be one-off initiatives, quickly conceived and easily transmitted by an individual teacher. Alternatively, a teacher might consider the educational ground which is to be covered, cut it into bite-sized pieces, and clearly identify the constituent parts. Each part, or unit, is then dealt with, and a module or set of modules designed to cover the material. A third approach is to link modules into complex hierarchical structures, evolved either by an individual or by a group. The aim here is to produce a broad, varied and balanced set of modules, within which it should be possible to promote practical investigations and experience of all areas of the curriculum. Typical module titles are: *Elizabethans, Weather, Canals, Growing up, Famous people, Food.* Each module then has its own unique, carefully defined purposes and structures.

Such modules may be repeated, if required. This cuts down on the preparation time, utilises feedback, and exploits gained expertise and resources. Stored video material, familiar computer programmes and stimulating worksheets can be re-used. One particular module, *Growing up*, is utilised each summer, using different material for third and fourth years, as it links with work to prepare children for transfer to secondary school.

However, within this structure any unit can be replaced at will by an equivalent, to reflect immediate interests, priorities and resources. Just as in creating the initial programme the aims, resourcing and organisation of each initiative are considered, so similar care goes into any changes that are made.

Each module has a clearly defined purpose, beginning and end, with built-in feedback and evaluation procedures. It is characteristic of modular approaches that the purposes and procedures in each initiative are very clearly stated at the outset to everyone involved, even to very young children. Channels of communication are opened up in all directions as a result.

Modular case studies

Teachers' expertise is currently being challenged in a multitude of ways. Schools' standards of achievement and methods of assessing such achievement are under close scrutiny, which puts great pressure on the teacher, both as an individual and as a member of staff. More specifically, the classroom practitioner of 1987 is being asked to cope with:

- falling rolls, leading to organisation problems;
- new technology, notably computers and videos;
- curriculum evaluation, in particular the concern with standards of numeracy and literacy;
- growing awareness of the meaning and value of process-based learning;
- a wish to promote relevant and interactive learning at all levels;
- the drive to achieve the most effective organisation of teaching resources.

The modular approach has grown in response to these pressures. It is a dynamic response which offers teachers a promising way forward. The following case-studies illustrate how one school used the approach in a number of different ways.

Mini-enterprise – community teamwork

The mini-enterprise scheme is one in a set of modules designed to cover a two-year span. The modules are to be taught to third and fourth year juniors and are designed in detail, cooperatively, by several teachers and others who are to help transmit them. The responsibility for an overview of the structure lies with the team leader.

The general idea was to get 60 third and fourth year juniors to set up ten small companies, each of which would make a product or offer a service. The aims were:

- to help the children develop their skills in planning, testing and evaluating;
- to help them solve problems by identifying them and using a strategy for coping;
- to help them succeed in listening, contributing, deciding and taking responsibility as one of a group;
- to develop pupils' basic skills through practical, relevant, self-negotiated activity;
- to stimulate imaginative projection and individual enterprise;
- to see that all completed the activity with positive gain of some sort.

In order that the aims of the enterprise be met, additional resources were needed:

- Parents and the headteacher agreed to join the two teachers concerned and act as advisers to the groups of children.
- The sixth form from Edgebarrow, the local comprehensive, who had

just completed their own industry-sponsored scheme, came and made a presentation on the subject, explaining very clearly the trials and tribulations of going into business.

- Yately Industries, a sheltered workshop for the handicapped which runs a retail outlet in craft goods, visited and described all the planning they needed to do in order to succeed in their aims.
- Ilex Lubricants came up with a free gift of candle wax in the nick of time for one struggling group.
- The National Westminster Bank granted the children an initial loan of £30!

A range of basic work (in addition to time allocated to project work) was introduced to help with the ideas and vocabulary that were needed. This is the strength of integrated primary work. Basic skill development can be achieved through meaningful real activities. The children were introduced to the idea of a Management Team with allocated responsibilities. Consumers, market research, advertising, costing, resources and accounts were all discussed, and the ideas and skills that these involved were explored.

The first independent decision of many that the children were to make, was to reject the company groups suggested to them, and make out a good case for choosing their own groups. They were sure that co-operation would be easier and motivation improved. They accepted that all of them must agree to the suggested group, understood constraints on size, and organised themselves to produce suitable groups within minutes. Motivated children can make outstanding achievements.

The children were given handouts which explained that they had seven weeks in all for the project, and they were given starting and finishing dates. An hour a week could be spent with the adviser, who would help with their planning but not lead the event. One afternoon a week could be spent on development, and other times were open to negotiation by individual groups. The structure and its purposes were explained to the children in much the same terms used among the adults.

There would be three stages, and the completion of each would be marked with a suitable badge. To get the first badge, a plan, including costing, must be approved by the organisers. The WE PLANNED IT badge was followed by the WE TESTED IT and the WE MADE IT badges. (In the event, the first badge was the only one used because the badge-making machine broke down, but nobody seemed to mind. So much for badges!) The stages were very important as milestones for the children. All of the children had encountered *plan, make,* and *evaluate* ideas in CDT. Some had specifically been taught thinking skills designed to help them get results and solve problems (GRASP). The mini-enterprise scheme was introduced to these children as yet another useful vehicle for practising such approaches.

For seven weeks the groups and their advisers sustained the activity. They allocated jobs, did market research, planned, tested, advertised and kept going. They ran a bring and buy sale and video shows, and they made and sold cakes, candles, computer games, lavender bags, drinks, greetings cards, jewellery and a magazine.

They raised money for materials by selling shares, and negotiating loans from the school fund and from the bank loan. They negotiated rates for use of school materials and the photocopier. The advisers needed frequent liaison meetings to decide on responses to the many entrepreneurial initiatives. While encouraging ingenuity and initiative it was essential to steer children away from excessive parental support. The stated purposes of the enterprise were frequently referred to by both children and advisers, they were effective guidelines which helped show the way forward.

Individually many children showed strengths in this sustained practical activity which had not been so clearly seen before, and this was in a school which has justifiable pride in its child-centred, activity-based approaches.

The gain in motivation was marked in most children, and resulted in solid achievements. Ingenuity and initiative were seen throughout the ability range, while the most able children found their managerial skills challenged when their schemes had to be realised. Problems of co-operation, communication and planning became very real. The teachers and adult advisers identified their own shortcomings here and they too learnt a great deal. The children considered, in retrospect, that their greatest problems had been co-operation and planning. The badly advertised video show, the incomplete costings, the meeting that lost all sense of direction, were all useful experiences which contributed to a very effective learning situation.

The children had been previously introduced to a work programme on *Getting Results and Solving Problems*. They had been encouraged to use the GRASP techniques in the mini-enterprise and had been overheard using 'What?' and 'How?' approaches. Some of the children clearly turned to this specific teaching for help when challenged by a multiplicity of ideas and problems. The teaching of thinking skills in an abstract way, backed by real-life example and practice, was clearly productive.

When a general review of the whole project was held with those children who had been taught reviewing as a specific technique it was both productive and enjoyable. The children considered what had happened, what was achieved and whether they could have done better.

There were many anecdotes to share, and a great deal of thought had clearly taken place. The feeling amongst the children was similar to the exhilaration produced by the residential field study trips that they enjoy. In the subsequent year, when the mini-enterprise was not on the schedule, some of the children decided to try a similar attempt themselves.

The children's success led to donations to four charities of their choice (typically two children's charities and two animal charities), and the purchase of a microscope for the school, presented by the children of the third team.

If the design was right the aims should have been met, and to a large extent they were. The group size was about right. They worked well with six members each, and the adviser's role proved to be very important. Summer term was a good time for such a project. Preparatory teaching had taken place, the children knew each other well, outdoor activities were easy. The project was easily sustained for seven weeks and the three stages were very important to keep momentum going. Areas of difficulty, such as communication, sexist groups, and planning (we nearly trespassed on the PTAs fund-raising area), were identified for next time.

The project is well worth repeating, and has earned its place in the next two year programme. A successful project is always more than the sum of its stated aims. The mini-enterprise produced growth and development, in many unexpected ways, in both the adults and children who took part. It was real life experience, with the built-in safety net that a simulation always has.

The food project – linking primary and secondary schools

This module was a collaborative venture between Berkshire Local Education Authority and the Fulmer Research Institute. The general aims were:

- to promote team project work in class and among teachers;
- to create new teaching materials which drew out thinking skills, such as decision making and problem solving;
- to develop practical skills of the Design-Make-Test variety;
- to strengthen general awareness of the concerns of industry and technology.

The *Food project* was a very small development in the total scheme. Different initiatives within it emphasised different aspects. This one focused on primary/secondary liaison, development of teaching materials, and promotion of an interactive teaching style.

To initiate the *Food project*, the headteachers of five primary schools who sent children to the local comprehensive, the head of the comprehensive, local advisers, and the project coordinator from the Fulmer group, attended the first development meeting. This group needed to understand and endorse the aims of the project, and decide if it should go ahead in one form or another. Subsequent meetings involved the teachers doing the actual work, library support services, and advisers.

The unit involved the development of a junior science/home economics module, based upon diet, to be taught to fourth year junior children. The content would be evolved by primary and secondary teachers in liaison. It would be taught in each primary school concerned. Secondary teachers would be involved in the teaching of the material as much as possible. Schools might be reimbursed for any expenditure that was necessary and an amount of time was allowed for development meetings. Secondary school work schemes would reflect and extend the work done in the junior schools as the pupils moved on. Further developments towards the stated aim of helping liaison between primary and secondary school could then be made and primary teachers could work in the secondary school's classes.

The primary schools involved found it possible to go ahead with the project. The unit of work was self-contained, yet flexible enough to fit into their very different patterns and practices. The design was a success in this respect; and as the project progresses more experience of such initiatives is gained all round. This particular enterprise will aid the development of future ones.

The design was flexible. The problem areas got careful consideration during evaluations, which were built in at various stages. The interactive development style, with input and feedback from all those participating, helps to oil the wheels. Review procedures such as these are vital in complex situations where external factors can be so compelling that they force many a potentially good enterprise to the breaker's yard.

Curriculum development took place. Work materials were developed jointly by the teachers concerned. There was broad agreement on the main ideas such a topic would cover and the teachers, working in small groups, each contributed to a different section of an overall plan. Typically, this considered the time-scale and possible sequence in covering the material, but left all decisions to the teachers' discretion.

Living and growing – three kinds of modules

Mini-enterprise and *Food* are two modules from a set where each module takes on average six weeks to complete, and the entire set covers two years. The set aims at a broad and balanced input. *Mini-enterprise* is very heavy on *process* skills, while *Food* covers essential facts about health and nutrition, so has quite a lot of essential *content*. Modules are hierarchical so a set of smaller modules is often designed within a larger enterprise. The example given here describes the design within a six week scheme of work on *Living and growing*.

The scheme of work on *Living and growing* includes *content modules* with specific, directed input on plants, animals, and humans. Factual information about living things is transmitted at a level suitable for the children concerned. The scheme also includes *process modules*. These are directed at developing process and other skills, and use any suitable material, probably from the living things scheme, that the child cares to choose. In addition, there are *non-directed* areas, carefully timed and planned, where the child can demonstrate in his own way what he knows and can do as a result of the various inputs he has received. This is essential as it allows the child to practise and extend his skills, and allows the teacher to monitor his progress. It is tempting to consider the areas as content modules, process modules and non-directed modules.

Within *Living and growing* there is a specific content module which extends for fourth year juniors, a unit of work on giving birth which is covered with second year juniors each year. In the extended fourth year work the *physical changes* of adolescence are described. Both second year and fourth year inputs are content modules which have been used for some time, and have been evaluated and refined through experience. Both use television programmes, *Merry-go-round*, and *Living and growing*. Television, and subsequently video, has encouraged the development of modular approaches.

The work is carefully planned. Visitors from outside the school discuss child care and development. Parents are made aware of the ground to be covered and will be able to help the children to look back at their own birth and infancy. Feedback will be received from them as well as from the children.

Both inputs on human biology involve areas of experience for the child which are precisely timed and purposefully planned by the staff. Each is a describable unit. They are modules within a whole school programme of work on living things. Equivalent units for first and third years cover information about plant and animal life in general.

A process module within the *Living and growing* scheme for upper juniors is one where the teacher helps the children to develop and use skills of observation, description, analysis, synthesis, patterning, hypothesising and testing. These skills are closely linked to the science-related 'living things' scheme. Obviously it is impossible to focus on all process skills at once, and skills such as research, manipulative and presentation skills will be focused on in process modules in other schemes.

The teacher's role within the non-directed module is to observe and consider what use the child is making of the resources that are available to him to develop his own ideas. It is important to recognise these non-directed modules within schemes as they provide the teacher with clear feedback on the child's understanding and attainment. Such modules must also be specified as they require time allocation.

Description of these three types of module (the *content*, the *process* and the *non-directed*), and closer definition of each module, is made within the specific plans drawn up by the teacher or teachers. Implementation will vary considerably according to the age of the children, and the ethos of the teacher. Coverage of the material described in the plans might be ensured by timetabling in advance, or, in more informal settings, by checking back on the plans now and again. In either case the work undertaken will be highly directional and evaluated to provide insights for future initiatives.

Such planned experience is common in many primary schools. It can be described but such a description would not be restrictive. Work on the living world will be done throughout a child's primary schooling, and approached in many different ways. Fascinating facts will be encountered randomly, and investigated, and urgent questions immediately dealt with. However, a modular approach to the planning helps the teacher to hand a complex situation methodically.

Inferences drawn from examples

From the above three examples certain inferences may be drawn:

1   A modular approach does not necessarily mean block timetabling. It does mean that each planned initiative has a time scale designed into it. There are clear beginnings and endings.
2   Modular design can be used on large scale plans and smaller enterprises which are within these plans.
3   Modular design requires stated purposes. Therefore choices between alternative ways of fulfilling the same purposes can be made by both teacher and pupil.
4   Initiative, flair and creativity are not inhibited by modular design. Children flourish in the interactive learning situation and the teacher's professionalism is realised in the purposeful transmission of the curriculum.

The advantages of modular planning

More generally, the advantages of modular planning for the primary school emerge as:

1   Teachers are helped to focus on particular targets

Primary school concerns cover two particular areas. On the one hand there are those outside the school itself, for a primary school is the centre of a web of interested groups. In this web are the community, the parents, the governors, other primary schools, secondary schools, education advisers, employes, local and central government. All of these groups are rightly concerned with what the school is attempting and achieving – and the school must communicate with them, as it did through the *mini-enterprise* work described above. On the other hand, the school's major concern is to assess and prioritise the needs of each individual child; to start courses of action to meet those needs; and to transmit an appropriate curriculum to the child.

The primary school itself has a small staff and a great many concerns. One teacher is responsible for giving sufficient thought to the individual needs of about 30 children and to the whole curriculum. It is incredibly easy to get bogged down in such a complex situation. Modular approaches help the teacher to cover the input the children need. Modules can be short, punchy initiatives, quickly designed and easily transmitted, which allow a swift response to be made to problem situations. They are designed with specific aims, and measured against those aims so that they produce more information for future use.

In one particular classroom situation it was clear that the children needed to become more adept at mental arithmetic, though their grasp of basic mathematical ideas was very sound. A module was designed to meet this need. An intensive input of three sessions a week for three weeks was planned. The children's standard was monitored by testing at the beginning and end of the three weeks. These structures, and some of the content covered in the lessons, were the same as those used in a county trial of material useful for developing skills at mental arithmetic. The structures used in this particular instance can be contrasted with the regular sessions over a long-term approach, or more chancy, opportunistic approaches.

The teacher's modular approach is distinguished by the decisiveness and control it shows. At the conclusion of the unit there is clear information available, on which to base the next enterprise. Yet within the overall structure, the approach to each child is as individual as the teacher has time and ingenuity to devise, and the module itself is individually designed for the situation where it is implemented. With such an approach a teacher can feel secure about the nature of the achievement, whether it was a success or not! In practice, teachers tend to feel they have done more, done it better and profited from the evaluation involved.

2 Modules are based on commonly accepted primary school practice

Modular ideas are based in commonly accepted good teaching practice. Primary schools are already full of purposeful activity each and every day. The challenge for the teacher is to establish purposes, then consider the design features, and possibly constraints, of time, space, resources and group size. What tends to happen is that the constraints are so powerful that they dominate and change the original purposes.

The modular approach is one where design is very carefully considered. The purpose of the module is clearly stated. Time, space, resources and group size are juggled to optimise the chances of achieving the purpose. Procedures are written into the module to achieve feedback and evaluation, leading to growth and development.

In primary schools this approach stimulates ingenuity, initiative and flexibility, and enhances the best child-centred enterprises. Modular approaches, which are essentially dynamic and immediately responsive, encourage the fine tuning of the situation to the precise needs of the class, group or individual. Individual modules may well be repeated with other children but will fail to achieve their purpose as effectively if fossilised into standard practice and transmitted uncritically. For the possibilities of modular approach have not been fully exploited unless the characteristics of tailor-made, purposeful, self-conscious design are present.

3 Communication is improved

Modules are clearly describable units, with particular purposes, and if an enterprise is clearly described the channels for discussion are open. The school can communicate its purposes to all those other groups that are outside it but concerned with it, and communication within the school itself is improved. *Parents*, in particular, value enormously every effort that a school makes to communicate with them. Parents' concerns typically are that a child is happy at school, is encountering a curriculum which will benefit him, and is making progress. Maths schemes, language schemes and special projects have been welcomed by parents because they are clearly planned, describable areas which offer tangible and reassuring signs of purposeful development and enterprise. Modular approaches highlight these particular features.

Where modular initiatives are made it becomes simpler to communicate effectively to parents what is going on and why it is as it is. Modular planning also includes reviewing the outcomes of a designed event, with the result that the staff and the individual teachers who have designed the event are well equipped to speak with parents on the outcomes, and to indicate the progress their child has made. For example, parents who are anxious because their child's written work has many mis-spellings, which have not been corrected, will be reassured by an explanation of this as deliberate policy on the teacher's part since the work has been designed to serve a different purpose. They will also need to know what input is organised for the purpose of helping children to improve their spelling, with comment on their own child's progress.

The productive sharing of ideas and experiences among *staff* increases when specific areas are focused on and discussed, as they are when modular approaches are being described or designed. Groups achieve a sense of direction when they focus on purposes and means, and groups with a common purpose can be very potent.

The staff of the primary school featured in this chapter decided to respond to over-crowding in the infant areas in a particular way. A project called *Moving* was planned, to involve the whole school. For several sessions a week and for three weeks all teachers worked away from their own team areas with one particular other group. The teachers designed inputs based on the needs of the particular group of children and their own special strengths. The initiative was simple, short, and successful. Resources were used flexibly and efficiently. Planning time was kept to a minimum. The spin-offs from this successful co-operation were increased motivation, experience and expertise for everyone involved.

Modular approaches, which are specific to purpose, tend to encourage specialist input within, or from outside, the school and such input is made on a positive rather than a 'troubleshooting' basis, which greatly increases its value. Liaison work with *other schools* is facilitated, and curriculum areas can be developed through modular planning. An extended example has been given of such a project organised between secondary and junior schools.

Where communication among teachers is concerned there would seem to be the need for one specific person or group to take the responsibility for co-ordination. Teachers' centres; advisers; outside agencies such as the Fulmer Research Institute; secondary schools with their larger, more flexible resources, can all help primary schools here. Self-help groups are developing where primary schools or primary/secondary schools get together with each other. These are popular but tend to lose impetus quite quickly unless carefully planned.

Modular approaches lead to an interactive teaching style. Positive feedback and evaluation of the teaching taking place is sought from the learner. This dialogue is as suitable between a *teacher and a young child* as it is between adults in learning situations, where it is more commonly found. Not all desired outcomes can be discussed but teachers can gain immeasurably from communicating clearly to the pupils their purposes and the context of their actions.

This is a major 'user friendly' feature of modular approaches. Another is that where goals are clearly defined the learner can be offered a greater choice of pathways. In these and other ways modular approaches fit the primary school ideal of the promotion of learning situations tailor-made to individual needs.

4   Motivation is increased

Success is motivating and modular initiatives, because of their simplicity, represent definite and often successful achievements. Modular approaches are easily communicated, so that all those closely involved can understand, and support the particular plans. This can increase commitment and the chance of success. It is generally true that interactivity increases but coherency is maintained because each interaction is kept simple, and carefully contained in an overall framework.

The following example bears out these general comments. It is an account of the first of three sessions on handwriting, where the teacher had used a modular design structure coupled with a result-getting approach.

The children in a class of third and fourth year juniors were told by the teacher that her objective was to help them improve their handwriting, and they would spend three sessions on this. However handwriting was so personal to them that they would need to decide the best way to go about this. Initial groans died down and in the ensuing conversation the children decided that good handwriting should be readable, fast and pleasant to look at, in that order. They considered 'What?' before they considered 'How?' because they had been specifically taught to look for objectives and use analysis, and some of them spotted that this was a time to use the strategy. They also said that different tasks required different handwriting, and their scripts were quite different from each others' and from the teacher's.

They looked at and talked about each others' writing with a view to spotting problematic features, and finding their own unique solutions. Reminders that it might be spacing, relative letter sizes, letter shapes, or slopes, recalled previous handwriting lessons where skills teaching had rightly been very specific. They practised a little and queries on the best way to practise began to arise which became the starting point for another session.

To complete the session the class and teacher reviewed what they had been doing and what they had achieved. Feelings were very positive all round. The children had been contributing actively the whole time and decided on ways forward for themselves. The teacher was receiving constant feedback on what they were thinking and feeling. They were helped to produce their own ideas and work on their own script. The interest and application in the room was obvious. It was a very purposeful session. One boy who said he would write a story to practise his handwriting was told by his friend that he had changed his objective. It would be difficult to do both together so perhaps he should decide which he wanted to do.

Here, the process of learning involved brainstorming, analysis, synthesis, hypothesis, planning and reviewing. In *Practical Curriculum* the Schools Council comments that the children and their teachers 'are more likely to enjoy school, and stay on their toes, if their days and weeks are varied by skilful choice of mode. Sometimes the mode or process of learning has its own lessons, more potent than the formal subject matter of the lesson'.[1]

Understanding, commitment, individual work patterns and multiple interactions, all very much to the purpose, are evident in this example of a modular approach.

Two more sessions, using the same approach, completed this particular modular input on handwriting. In the belief that consolidation is necessary, specific work on handwriting was left for several weeks, then a new module on speed writing introduced.

5 Modules encourage the development of thinking skills

Most people gain from giving more careful thought to the results they would like to get. It is necessary for teachers in the formalistic teaching situation to decide what they want and how they are going to set about achieving it before they can begin to take meaningful actions.

---

[1] Schools Council *The Practical Curriculum* (Schools Council Working Paper 70) Methuen, 1981.

A simple, result-getting strategy is to decide what result you want, consider all the possible courses of action you could take to get it, choose the most suitable, plan it, do it, and evaluate it. Children also can be taught, and be helped to practise using such strategies.

Purposeful thinking like this lies at the heart of modular approaches. As in the example above, teachers and pupils can practise the approaches together. The teacher's modular design of three sessions, with the purpose of helping children to improve their handwriting, led to the implementation of a process-based, result getting approach.

Problem-solving skills are closely related to the thinking skills used in getting results. In a problem-solving situation you cannot go ahead because you have encountered an obstacle of some kind which requires consideration. Professor Keith Jackson, in *The Art of Solving Problems,*[2] suggests that P = O + O, that is, a problem consists of an *objective* (as in result-getting) plus an *obstacle*. Once the obstacle is identified a result getting situation exists.

Modular, result-getting, and problem-solving approaches are connected in that they use methodical, purposeful strategies, with built in feedback and evaluation. However, these approaches are broad structures which leave that freedom for flair, initiative and enterprise which is essential for creative thought. Inspirational ideas should be allowed to flow freely and some may be helped to fruition by planning skills.

6   Modules help curriculum development

New material or approaches can easily be slotted into existing classroom situations by using a modular structure. The input may be from an outside agency wishing to trial something, from a specialist teacher, or from the classroom teacher.

For example, a teacher may wish to introduce a group reading scheme where a small group of children read together and discuss a particular book. The nature of the event will dictate the design that is used. The design would involve choosing between a 'dripfeed' approach of one session a week, or an intensive course of one session or more a day; continuing for three, five, or x sessions before evaluating; involving the whole class or only some of them, and so on. Steady practice does not come naturally to most children, and concentration spans vary considerably, so different modules which contain different emphases are suitable in a set of modules designed as part of the language programme.

---

[2] Jackson, K F *The Art of Solving Problems* (Bulmershe-Comino Problem-solving Project, Bulmershe College of Higher Education, Woodlands Avenue, Reading, Berks) 1975 (compact edition 1983) p. 43.

A structured commercial reading scheme may be used as well as a 'real' books approach, and the inputs be designed to be either concurrent or consecutive. The design of other modules in the language programme would affect this particular group reading module. For example, a class might read a full length novel together as quickly as possible, then spend a few weeks on group work with non-fiction material. Each module would receive its own evaluation. The set of initiatives could be checked at a suitable point for balance, proportion, and coverage of the essential input defined on the school's statement of language policy. The teacher's ability to respond sensitively and immediately to each child is not hampered by this overall scheme. Curriculum development is also helped because modules of work can be described easily and discussed.

3 Problems of planning

Terry Brown

'None climbs so high as he who
knows not whither he is going.'
Oliver Cromwell (1647)

King Edward VI is a 13–18 high school formed in 1977 from the amalgamation of two selected single-sex schools. Since 1978 the intake has been all-ability and the catchment area includes urban areas of Stafford Town, with a mixture of council and private housing, and the rural area to the south west of Stafford, which contributes about 30% of the intake. School roll has fallen steadily from around 1100 (250 in the sixth form) to the present 880 (160 in the sixth form). A current LEA proposal for reorganisation is with the DES and this will change the school to 11–18 in 1988.

Dr Brown joined the school as Headteacher in September 1982, against the background of an LEA inspection which indicated the need for a number of management and policy changes. At the time it was also clear that not only did the staff generally feel the need for change, there were also many teachers who felt intensely frustrated by their lack of opportunity to make progress. During 1982–83 the following changes were made, with staff support:

- *introduction of staff consultation and decision-making processes;*
- *rationalisation of year and house systems – to a year-based structure;*
- *a review of pastoral practices and the implementation of agreed changes;*
- *introduction of a Life Skills programme for all years;*
- *removal of the continuous lunchtime;*
- *introduction of a fourth/fifth year curriculum based on a 40 period week and bringing in the notion of a broad, balanced curriculum based on a 'constrained core', 'compulsory core' and limited 'free options' approach (see Figure 3.1, p. 45).*

At this point the discussions and planning began, that were eventually to lead to the introduction of a modular framework in September 1986 and commit the school to a four year development programme.

There are three aspects in the background to the development at King Edward VI that have contributed to the overall aims of introducing a modular curriculum. These are:

- staff discussions in King Edward VI that began in earnest in the spring of 1984;
- a collaboration between myself and two other local headteachers that began during 1984 and still continues;
- the establishment (in January 1986) of the Stafford Education Industry Project (SEIP) in which the curriculum development, well underway in the schools, was incorporated and given a sharper focus towards working with industry. This was largely LEA inspired and a response to ideas put by the three headteachers.

Shared views

Following internal discussions and discussions at headteacher level, both in the context of the Staffordshire TVEI pilot scheme, a number of shared views emerged.

It was agreed that there was a need to take a wide view of the term 'vocational'. It should certainly include learning experiences concerned with industry and commerce but it also needs to encompass experiences based on the community and to include opportunities for young people to develop awareness of themselves and others. In this context 'vocational' comes to mean 'preparation for life'; the inherent danger in the emphasis on science, technology and technical studies, of creating a utilitarian curriculum, is avoided by emphasising the role of the creative and expressive arts and programmes concerned with personal and social development.

Those involved acknowledged that the initiative was really about generating a whole curriculum shift – both in content and methodology – and that this should, from the outset, involve all youngsters in a year group and not just selected cohorts. This curriculum shift concerned, at least in part, the need for greater collaboration and partnership with industry.

There was a shared belief that the traditional structure of schools in years 4 and 5, based on two-year courses leading to a final examination, had the following implications:

- it imposed severe constraints on development, in terms of finding timetable space;
- students were committed to two-year courses with little possibility of being able to make course changes as circumstances alter;
- this two-year commitment led, in many cases, to poor motivation and low achievement;
- this pattern also led to the development of an academically-based curriculum for all, where failure was significant and practical, experiential learning largely non-existent.

Modular approaches to the curriculum, it was felt, had the potential to solve many of these stated problems. Finally, it was hoped that the introduction of GCSE, with associated grade-related criteria and emphasis on measuring achievement rather than failure, would enable such developments as modular courses to be accredited at national level.

Aims of going modular

The main purposes for going modular are set out below:

1   to effect a *whole* curriculum shift to TVE style learning for *all* students
2   to encourage change in teacher style in methodology towards *practical and experiential* learning
3   to increase student motivation by:
   i   allowing students to *renegotiate* a significant proportion of their curriculum
   ii setting students *short term realisable goals*
   iii generating a more *relevant* curriculum
4   to *collaborate* with *industry* in the preparation and delivery of material
5   to develop a *community-based* curriculum and the possibility of *education for life*
6   to preserve *breadth and balance*, introduce *new areas* and protect the *expressive arts*
7   to link modules to accreditation based on *continuous assessment*
8   to mitigate the effects of *falling roles* on the curriculum

In terms of accreditation at GCSE (aim 7 above) all arrangements have been made by the school directly with the Midlands Examining Group.

On the basis of these shared beliefs, planning and implementation of the modular scheme got underway. The key stages are summarised in Figure 3.1, and I would like here to draw attention to some general

Figure 3.1 Key stages in policy planning and implementation

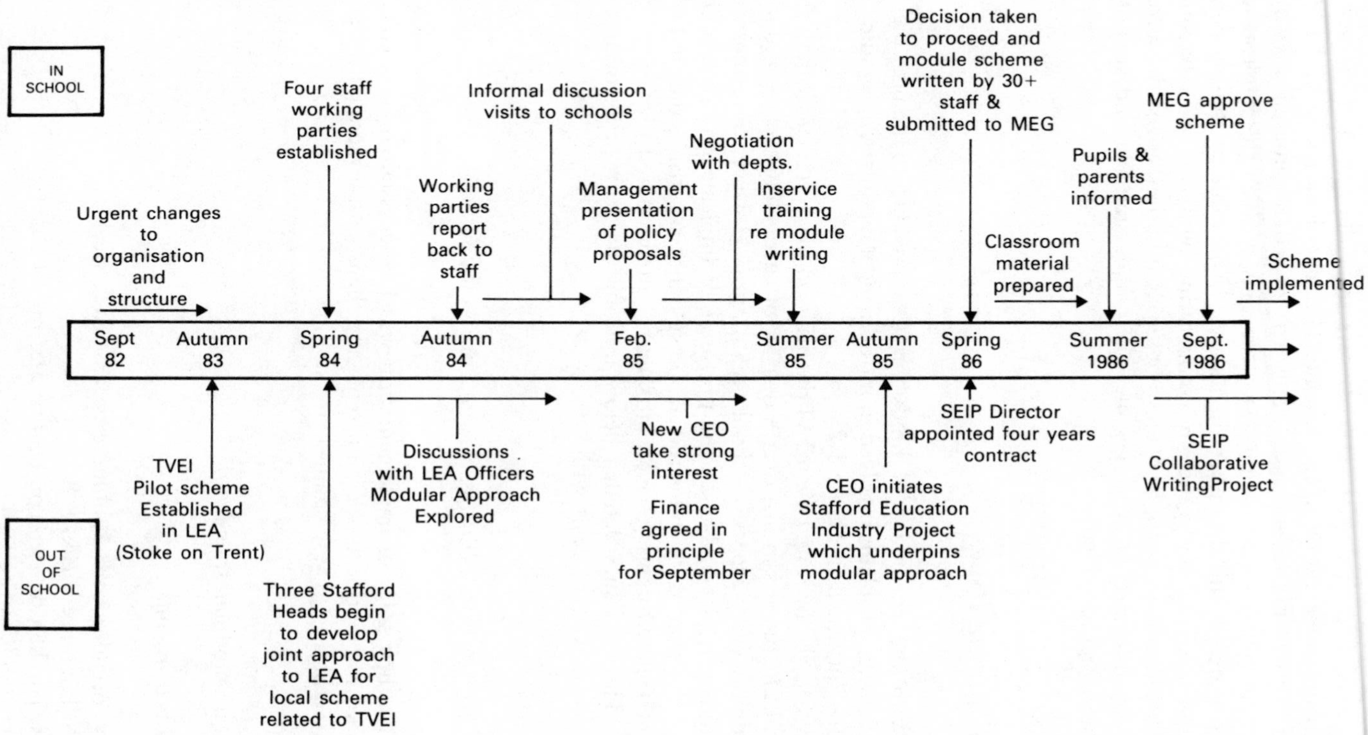

points. It took two and a half years from the first staff discussion to the implementation of the scheme. The school started from the base of a 'non-TVEI' school and, while determined to proceed anyway, the complementary discussions with the LEA enabled the implementation to proceed quickly rather than slowly. The value of sharing concerns and anxieties, and generally co-operating with two other like-minded Headteachers cannot be overestimated. In addition, governors were kept fully informed at all stages and their understanding and support has been highly valued.

Planning issues

With the advantage of hindsight it is possible to itemise the main planning problems involved in introducing a modular curriculum. These are illustrated in Figure 3.2.

Clearly for King Edward VI the decision to effect a curriculum change for *all* students in just over a quarter of curriculum time had to involve almost every aspect of school organisation. However, priorities can be, and were, set and given the pressures of implementing such a change in the context of industrial action it is not surprising that not all the interrelated items received satisfactory attention and planning.

The six issues detailed below indicate the main problem areas and how they were dealt with.

Curriculum change: Stage one – 1986

The first stage of implementation was based, essentially, on collapsing two free option blocks and replacing them with a modular framework (see below). These changes are summarised in Figure 3.3.

The modular framework

Each module

- occupies four 50-minute periods each week
- lasts nine weeks
- is taken on two consecutive afternoons
- stands on its own
- can be combined with others for GCSE

Figure 3.2

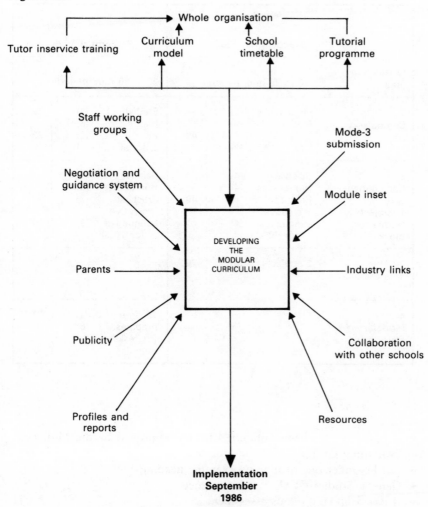

Each student

- takes two modules in each nine-week block
- takes fourteen modules during the fourth/fifth year
- has a free choice of 12
- will take two Life Skills modules
- can renegotiate choice at regular intervals
- can choose from around 60 modules
- is assessed during the nine-week modules

Figure 3.3   Summary of curriculum changes, 1986.

Curriculum area	September 1985 40 × 35 min periods			September 1986 30 × 50 min periods		
1 Compulsory core	English Maths PE Life skills	(5) (5) (4) (2)	% 40	English Maths PE Tutorial	(4) (3) (2) (1)	% 33

2 Constrained core 1 subject from each block	Science
	Humanities
	Practical/
	  creative
	Languages
	(for 70%)
		(4)
		(4)
		(4)
		
		(4)
			
			40
				Science
				Humanities
				Practical/
				  creative
				Languages
				(for 70%)
					(3)
					(3)
					(3)
					
					(3)
						
						40

3 Free options	2 subjects —	(8)	20			
4 Modular framework	—			12 'free' modules 2 Lifeskills modules	(8)	27

GCSE certification

- is based on a scheme submitted to and approved by the Midlands Examining Group
- can be under one of nine programme headings
- General Studies GCSE can be awarded
- is based on continuous assessment

Timetable

- fourth and fifth year are timetabled together in modular time

Figure 3.4 outlines current modular programmes.

Figure 3.4 Current modular programmes

Programme title	Module No.	Module title
Countryside in action (GCSE)	1 2 3 4 5	The wealth of the countryside Our changing countryside The countryside – a practical approach Wildlife in the countryside Man's effect on the countryside
Science and technology (GCSE)	1 2 3 4 5	Electronics – 1 Computer – 1 Electronics – 2 Engineering design Control technology
Information systems (GCSE)	1 2 3 4 5 6	Electronics – 1 Computer – 1 Information retrieval Information processing Computer – 2 Computer control
Physical education (GCSE)		Physical education Modules 1–5
History (GCSE)	1 2 3 4 5 6 7	Modern dictator Modern Britain The search for power History around us Learning from country houses Conflict Elizabethan England
Community in action (GCSE)	1 2 3 4 5 6 7	Community – 1 Community – 2 Community – 3 First aid Family care – 1 Family care – 2 Health and welfare
Expressive arts (GCSE)	1 2 3 4 5 6 7	Photography Art & Design for the theatre Drama – 1 Drama – 2 Dance Music 1 Music 2

Figure 3.4   Cont.

Programme title	Module No.	Module title
Drama (GCSE)		Drama 3–5
Music (GCSE)		Music 3–5
Keyboarding (RSA)		Keyboarding 1 and 2
Geology Business enterprise Catering Textiles		**Non-accredited modules** Geology 1 Business enterprise – 1 Catering for the family & entertaining Catering for the family and small businesses Dressmaking Soft furnishings, toys and crafts Pottery 1 Art 1

Planning the curriculum framework and timetable model

As the notion of a modular framework began to develop among the management group, we started to identify what it was we wanted the timetable to do. I felt that this was an important stage in planning because many a theoretical development has floundered through not identifying the specific organisational objectives that will enable theory to be translated into practice. Before approaching staff I also wanted to be able to demonstrate exactly how we could achieve the curriculum change and to provide the means for departments to examine the implications for them.

Given the aims stated earlier (p. 44) we wanted the initial timetable framework to meet the following objectives:

1   It should aim to provide a total curriculum structure that had a balance between the new modular courses and the traditional two year courses based on the compulsory and constrained core approach. This would initially limit the amount of material to be prepared and, it was hoped, seem to be within the capacity of the staff to respond. Retaining traditional elements would ease the anticipated problems of approaching parents and gaining their

support. The approach would also enable the school to retain breadth and balance across the main areas of experience whilst widening opportunities in the modular area; and provide a sound base for further developments.

2   In order to meet the need of accreditation within the modular area, the framework needed to provide for courses of around 30 hours which would be taken over 8–12 weeks.

3   To encourage the change in teacher style the teaching blocks in modular time needed to be longer than normal, ie longer than the standard 70-minute double period;

4   If student negotiation was to be significant the total allocation of time to modular work needed to be sufficient to provide for at least two programmes to be followed, ie 10 modules;

5   The framework should include the introduction of a tutorial period within which the processes of student negotiation could be placed.

6   It should allow for the retention of some life skills taken by specialist teams in years 4 and 5.

7   It should provide the facility for certain subject combinations to be retained as the modular curriculum developed. For example, the school has a very strong science tradition with a number of students taking three sciences to 'O' level and this facility would be needed as the department began to develop a double certificated modular science programme (it is hoped that this will be available in 1988).

Framework and timetabling decisions

A number of models were examined and eventually a 30 period week (six periods × 50 min a day) seemed to offer the best solution. Within the 30 periods the core and constrained core would occupy 22 periods. Subjects taken over the fourth and fifth years would be allocated three periods (10 mins more than four × 35 mins). The modular allocation of eight periods (27% of overall time) could house two module courses taken in double periods on consecutive afternoons – 1 hour 40 mins representing a significant increase in length of teaching time.

Nine-week module courses seemed ideal in that this would allow for flexibility over the year. This would enable the system to make adjustments for bad weather closure, occasional days etc without shortening any of the nine-week courses. The nine-week allocation would mean a total of 36 periods for each module, representing 30 hours teaching time. Students would be able to take 14 modules, two of which would be compulsory life skills modules.

The timetable would be organised on the basis of consistent half-year blocking between maths–English; language–humanities; and science–practical. This arrangement would allow existing subject combinations to continue as the modular framework developed. For example, three sciences could be taken by taking one in the core science block, one when the rest of the half year was taking a practical/creative subject and one in the modules. Those students taking three sciences would have to take at least two practical/creative modules to ensure balance. This kind of arrangement is for the short term only.

It was decided to timetable fourth and fifth years together for modular work. This was partly because it was difficult, on the proposed timetable, to insert eight separate module blocks and also, in a positive sense, because combining the year groups would increase the potential range and flexibility of courses. Given this arrangement, staff needed to be prepared for the one-year problem of the fifth year completing four-year courses in the time allocated for modular work (ie two 50-minute periods on two consecutive afternoons).

Interrelationships with the total organisation

The notion of combining compulsory core, constrained core (both based on two-year courses) and modular framework with a tutorial programme in which guidance, counselling and formative profiling could occur, is illustrated in Figure 3.5.

Curriculum change: Stage two – more material

One of the main problems was that implementation in September 1986 would involve three main constraints:

1　The fifth year would still be completing the courses begun in the fourth year and therefore would not be involved in the modules although timetabled at that time. This would inevitably restrict fourth year module choice in the first year but would be a one-year problem only.

2　A number of subjects would be taught in the modular time that were, in fact, still Mode 1 courses. These would be organised in five units and students would take a fifth year June examination. While students could opt out of such courses at the nine-week negotiation stage, it would be difficult for other students to opt into units that did not stand on their own.

Figure 3.5 *Inter-relationship between core and modular framework*

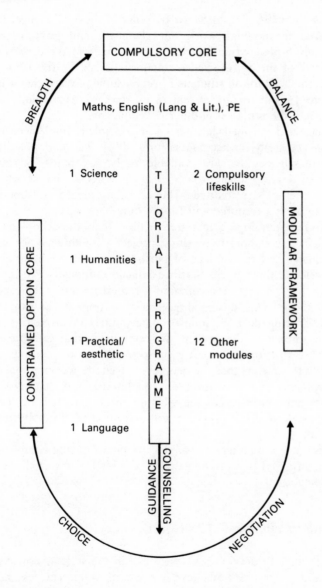

COMPULSORY CORE

BREADTH

BALANCE

Maths, English (Lang & Lit.), PE

1 Science

2 Compulsory lifeskills

TUTORIAL PROGRAMME

1 Humanities

MODULAR FRAMEWORK

CONSTRAINED OPTION CORE

1 Practical/ aesthetic

12 Other modules

1 Language

GUIDANCE COUNSELLING

CHOICE

NEGOTIATION

3   It was clear that even though some 60 modules were available we needed to expand the areas covered, through developing more material.

One of the main areas affected by point 2 above is science. Biology is involved in modular work but chemistry and physics are not. Accordingly a planned approach has been made to the department in the context of the 5–16 Science statement issued by the DES (which indicates the need for all students to retain some physics, chemistry and biology to 16 and for no student to exceed 20% curriculum time on science), and the school's modular developments.

The science department has agreed in principle to implement a Mode 3, double certificate science course for 1988. It will, undoubtedly, take account of schemes that are available (eg NEA Modular Science) but is likely to develop an approach through MEG as that is where the school's scheme is accredited. The LEA has agreed to support the venture by giving resource and supply time backing.

In terms of developing material in new areas the school has been involved in a collaborative writing project with three other schools, local industry and the College of Further Education. This project has been developed through the Stafford Education Industry Project and is based on five writing sets containing representation from each area detailed above. This means direct collaboration at the point when material is being devised; industry is genuinely involved rather than being an adjunct to the process. It seems likely that the project will attract MSC funding because it is based on an 'Action learning' model. Essentially this means that the people involved are working together to solve problems that they meet on equal terms and that measurable objectives have been set to see whether the programme achieves the stated aims. A model of how this writing project works is illustrated in Figure 3.6.

At this stage a number of modules are near to being completed and the areas involved will provide exactly the kind of material needed to strengthen the modular scheme.

Curriculum change – 1988 onwards

There are already development pressures in the system. For example, history and geography both have Mode 3 modular schemes and both are prominent in the humanities constrained core. Why, therefore, should they operate one scheme in the modules and a different one in the core? Likewise for biology. In fact these departments have decided

Figure 3.6 Collaborative writing project

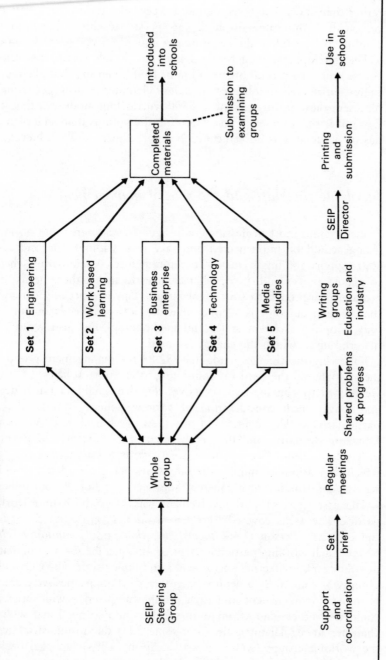

to move their modular courses into the core by operating over 12 weeks rather than nine. The three period a week allocation means that they can achieve the same 30 hour, 36 period teaching time and will comfortably complete the requisite five modules over years 4 and 5.

The development of a Mode 3 modular double certificated science course will need careful organisation in 1988 to ensure that all students follow an agreed number of modules. Planning is now occurring to represent these features in the 1988/89 curriculum model. At this stage I do not wish to pre-empt discussion but the point is that such planning has to occur now if implementation is to be successfully achieved.

Involving the staff and the role of management

I am sure that most professional colleagues would agree that no major change could be implemented and take root without real and active staff support and involvement. Therefore before contemplating whether to make changes and, if so, what changes to make, there needs to be a planned approach to staff involvement. This is especially true when the eventual outcome is a policy that depends completely on staff not only adopting different styles and methodology but also writing the material upon which the change is based.

Following the changes made in 1982/83 the management group and the staff shared the need for continuing to examine policies. I felt that we needed to aim for two objectives. First, to enable a much deeper and longer term consideration of various policies to take place – particularly in the context of the new Technical and Vocational Education Initiative and the involvement of five Staffordshire schools in a pilot scheme. Second, to move towards a long-term strategy in which the various seemingly separate issues being considered would be seen as contributing to a coherent approach to whole school policy.

The first stage of staff involvement was to establish four working parties. The areas covered were *Curriculum, Profiles and Records of Achievement, Personal and social education* and *Community school policy*. Each working party had eight or nine members – a combination of volunteers, invited members, senior and junior staff. The *Curriculum* group was chaired by a deputy, the other working parties were chaired by middle management and each group was given a wide brief and could visit other schools, invite in speakers and so on. I met with the chairmen at regular intervals. After some delay due to industrial action the working groups (which started in Spring 1984) reported back to the staff in the Autumn of 1984. In their reports the working parties between them raised many issues, stated problems, explored options and, in some areas, made recommendations.

One of the big planning problems is when and how to make decisions. In the context of the working party reports it might have been possible to implement bits here and bits there, but in reality the scale and interrelationship of the issues raised merited a much more in-depth response.

At this stage the management group did not have any predetermined policy response – rather ideas that need further exploration. Accordingly a period of visiting schools departments that seemed to be offering different approaches to the curriculum, was started. Again this involved staff, enabling them (and the Head and Deputies) to explore practice elsewhere and start the process of setting the working party conclusions against the ideas and practices occurring in other institutions. During this period (late Autumn 1984/Spring 1985) we all became more aware of the development of modular work, primarily in the TVEI schools we visited.

The Head and Deputies began to evolve an overall policy response which involved the introduction of a modular curriculum and to plan exactly how this should be communicated to staff. This phase, in hindsight, reveals much about the planning problems associated with decisions. Over half the staff had been involved in the working parties; in addition the staff, as a whole, had discussed the conclusions and considerable consensus had emerged. However, the range and interrelationships of the issues were very complex and could not be resolved by simply 'tinkering' with the organisation. There was also a question of timing – a radical management response too early could be seen as 'autocratic', while delaying too long could cause intense frustration amongst those who have devoted time and energy to working parties.

To some extent the problem of 'when' was answered by the proposed industrial action, although half-way through the Spring Term 1985 seemed about right anyway. I was prepared to operate on the basic assumption that staff agreement with much of the working parties' conclusions represented a decision by the staff and, further, that the function of senior management was to translate these decisions into the context of overall policy for the school – to give the school overall direction. In planning terms the problems were: to maintain the involvement of staff; to encourage staff 'ownership' through incorporat- ing as much as possible of the working parties' conclusions; and to make the whole proposal a practical proposition.

The build up and presentation were carefully planned and included a period where modular organisations were discussed by the management group, informally, with various individuals and departments and a formal, verbal presentation to staff of a policy statement, backed by a document which tried to:

- link carefully the various outcomes of the working groups with the proposed new structure;
- establish a philosophical base for introducing modular work, detail how the organisation would work – complete with timetable model and period distributions for departments, and offer all individuals and departments the opportunity to discuss reactions and negotiate where necessary;
- establish an 18-month period for preparation before implementation – targeted for September 1986.

I have to say that the principles underlying the main proposal were not challenged. I am sure that this was partly because the proposal was presented as a policy statement (albeit based on a staff consensus) and partly because it actually made sense. As events have turned out, with over 30 teachers having co-operated to produce a large submission to MEG, I do believe that the 'logical imperative' of the modular approach was the main factor.

Once the decision was taken and the 18 months preparation time underway I had to overcome the problems that none of the staff had ever written modular material, and that there was very little material available to use or adopt. At that stage, also, there were no formal guidelines from the Midlands Examining Group. It was essential too, to retain staff ownership of the development and the writing of our own material would not only serve that end but also involve teachers in a major staff development programme.

There is certainly a danger of 're-inventing the wheel' but I would still argue, strongly, that successful implementation of such a scheme demands real staff commitment and involvement and this can only be obtained through responsibility for the material. However I also believe that a point can be reached where staff who have gone through that process then become good judges of what material will work for them and what will not. Accordingly I am now encouraging staff to look at modules that have been approved by MEG and explore whether we can use them. There are real planning problems here for schools now starting – deciding on the balance between home-grown and already approved material could be crucial in the eventual outcome of whatever scheme is introduced.

In planning the preparation of our modular scheme I managed to share some SCDC finance with two other schools and, with an LEA 'top-up', we organised a module-writing workshop. Each school sent ten teachers – staff who were committed, likely to deliver the goods and with potential for communicating skills to others. From that base over 30 teachers from King Edward VI worked together to write a submission consisting of nearly 60 modules and leading to GCSE certification in ten subject headings.

I have referred above to the staff development aspects of implementation. There is a problem to be faced in a proposal that sets out to change the teaching and learning situation towards learning by doing and experiencing. Again in planning terms it underpins the philosophy proposed for students to learn if staff find that *they* have learned by following such a methodology. So at one level staff have implemented a modular curriculum; at another level the processes underlying that implementation, for example learning how to write modules by writing them, learning how to collaborate with colleagues by producing material together, etc – reinforce the philosophical base. Literally, staff have been 'learning' by 'doing'.

In conclusion, I would underline the following points. Involving staff in policy change leads to 'ownership' and a better chance of success, and must, therefore, be consciously planned. In planning change there is a distinction to be made between the taking of decisions and managing the implications of these decisions. The former involves all the staff and the latter is primarily a function of management. Change can be perceived as being piecemeal without the separate parts contributing to a coherent whole. It is important therefore to plan on a whole-school basis and try to communicate this to all involved. If changing methodology is involved then using the 'new' methods to implement the scheme will underpin the change required.

Student negotiation and guidance

Regular negotiation of curriculum throughout the fourth and fifth years, involving some 450 students, threatened to give the timetabler just a few anxious moments! During 1986/87 there would be only one year to deal with but the system will need to encompass two year groups in 1988/89.

The main problems envisaged were:

1 How to manage the variable demand for modules. Some were bound to prove more popular than others and the times when they were put on might need to be phased over the year.
2 Related to demand would be the question of what to do with staff

who might find no takers in any nine-week block. A number of staff could take modules from more than one programme (eg the biologists had participated in the preparation of modules from three programmes) and for some staff variable free time would be built in; that is, when teaching in the modular time the teaching load would be higher than average, when not, then lower than average.

3   How to involve students, staff (teachers and tutors) and parents in the negotiation process with sufficient time for all parties to be involved and for counselling to take place. Would it be possible for tutors to manage to counsel and deal with others in the group? How much support would be needed?

4   For at least the first two years (as more material was developed) there would be subjects taught in the modular time that were not operating through a Mode 3 submission. Students would be prepared under Mode 1 arrangements and this would have certain implications. The subjects themselves would need to be planned for teaching over five of the seven nine-week blocks and in the timetable formed of the modular time. This could begin to limit the choices offered to youngsters. For example in the third block, Chemistry Module 3 would be part of the Mode 1 course and would not be designed as a stand-alone unit. It would therefore be difficult, if not impossible, for any student who had not taken Modules 1 and 2, to then take No 3. Students could, however, opt out of taking, for example, Chemistry 3, even though they had already taken Modules 1 and 2.

5   The formative aspects of profiling and regular student negotiation have obvious strong links, and this would need to be considered as the school develops its profiling.

The procedure for negotiation and guidance was based on the following elements: The tutor group, form tutors and tutorial period would be the basis for guidance and choice, and there would be further staff support through the year heads, head of careers and deputies. A careers programme in tutorial time would introduce the curriculum framework, parents would be informed and students asked to complete an option form with the following information:

- an indication of any programmes that they might like to follow;
- an indication of any specific individual modules that they would like to take;
- the four modules they would like to take over the first two module sessions;
- choices in the constrained options.

Each student's prospective total programme would be examined, initially by the tutor, for overall balance and further discussions would take place as necessary with students and parents. Five weeks into the first nine-week block, students would be issued with *Modular News* – a broadsheet that would emphasise various points, give further information etc.

Individually, pupils would be reminded of the two modules they had chosen for the second nine-week block and asked to confirm or change their choice and to select two modules for block 3. Tutors and support staff would have to look closely only at those students changing modules. The same process would again be followed five weeks into the second nine-week block. Regular in-service training would be needed for tutors. The pastoral organisation was already based on tutors remaining with their groups, and all student programmes and choices would be recorded on computer, so that tutors could have easy access to information about their tutor groups.

Planning for parents

It is one thing to develop a curriculum structure that you believe in; it is quite another to convince parents that departing from traditional approaches is in the educational interests of their children. When the curriculum structure is modular there is a further problem – before going on to convince parents, how does one explain the scheme? This thought had exercised the minds of the management group for some time, based simply on the difficulties we experienced in explaining the scheme to professional colleagues. This is one area where I can claim that we gave the problems a lot of thought, planned our approach and, within the limited objectives set, succeeded.

In organising the parents' evening, I was aware of a number of issues. First, I could not conceive how I could explain the scheme through a 'set piece' approach, even if I wanted to. No matter how many informative OHPs I could devise, no matter how simple I tried to make the necessary points and explanations, all I could envisage was rows of faces – all with a distinctly glazed look in the eyes!

Second, in terms of objectives, I wanted parents to become aware of problems within the curriculum, to understand the essence of our approach in solving these problems and to be prepared to give us support as the system began. Clearly after that the views of students and whether the process of accreditation worked as we said it would, would determine the long-term attitude of parents.

Finally, one of the main aims of the scheme was to shift teacher style and methodology – surely, then, we should set out to involve parents actively and use the methods with parents that we felt should be used with students.

On the basis of the above thoughts, the evening was planned as follows. Groups of chairs were set out in the hall (eight to ten in a group), 220 parents attended, and each was given a sheet listing:

- all the subjects taught in the third year
- new subjects that are offered in the fourth year
- the subjects or areas that the Secretary of State thinks all youngsters should experience

(The sheet contained 27 subjects.)

All parents were asked to underline the eight subjects they would themselves like to follow *or* that they thought their youngsters would like to follow. This was tackled enthusiastically and with a great deal of sharing and discussion. After five–ten minutes I intervened and asked a number of general questions, eg *How many have left out English? Maths? Science?* I asked six–eight parents, at random, what combinations of subjects they had chosen.

At this stage it was easy to make the following points: first, that there was no way the school could organise and timetable for the wide range of combinations indicated, even if we wanted to. Second, should we try anyway? Surely the case for experiencing certain areas is overwhelming. In this school all students will take English, mathematics, a science, humanities, practical/creative subject and a language.

An OHP setting out the 'constrained blocks' was then shown and parents were told that in addition to English and mathematics they could take one subject from each block. *Given the original eight subjects, what problems does this situation raise?* The problems raised by parents were very similar to those raised by youngsters: *How do I take a second/third science? . . . a second language? . . . keep subjects I like? Take more than one subject in a particular block? Have experience of technology, computing, industry?* and so on.

At this point I could introduce the idea of a third element to the curriculum that would, in a brief outline description, be seen to meet many of the stated problems. The notion of short courses linked to GCSE accreditation could be established with a group of people who now understood some of the problems that the traditional curriculum was creating. The formal input at this point lasted around 10–15 minutes.

Feedback during the evening and subsequently would indicate that we largely succeeded in our aims. For the staff it was one of the best parents' evenings we have ever held; of the parents, many stated that they enjoyed being involved and participating – hardly a parent could avoid taking part. The range of questions, level of discussion and the lack of tension were all positive outcomes. While staff taking the meeting needed to be confident and positive, the real winner was the methodology.

Resource problems

There is little point in pretending that changing the curriculum will not cost money. From the outset, I and two other Headteachers had started the process of persuading the LEA that it would be a very good idea to have a kind of TVEI project, funded by the LEA, in the Stafford area. It has to be admitted that, in the early stages, we were making this move without having anything definite in our schools to propose. However, as the policy direction hardened we could begin to identify needs. We were not looking for, nor did we expect to be able to obtain, funding on the level that MSC was supplying for the pilot TVEI schemes.

It was equally true as the policy idea developed that we were determined to press on irrespective of gaining any extra support. Outside help would, in effect, speed up the implementation of agreed policy. Therefore the problems of financial planning were tackled in four ways:

1 Reallocation of existing funds

Within school, the capitation allowance was restructured, so that provision was made to finance module development. Clearly this meant that departmental allocations were lowered but, obviously, extra money was available for those departments, or individuals, who were prepared to become involved in the modules. I seem to remember that as a management group we overdid the amount we retained and had a very interesting heads of department meeting. However the principle was established and in spite of obtaining other funding I have continued to organise capitation in this way.

Other sums that I had access to (in Staffordshire we have an annual Furniture, Apparatus and Equipment allowance for more costly items) were also diverted to support new developments. A particular instance was in computing where, I believe, the LEA showed that it was prepared to listen to funding arguments based on proposed curriculum development. In this case I allocated the whole of my annual FAE allowance to Staffordshire Computing Centre and they more than matched the figure in providing a fully equipped electronic office and a distributed network around the school in addition to the standard computer resource area. This kind of resource meant that our aim of involving all youngsters in this area of the curriculum, albeit for one or more 9-week courses, could be a practical possibility.

2   LEA support

I made a direct request to the LEA for support. By this stage (Summer 1985) I could identify the problems:

- heavy demand on typing and reprographics to produce the GCSE submission and classroom material;
- allocation of supply teaching time so that staff could be released for writing;
- provision of appropriate, additional equipment and resources to meet the new demands created by some modules;
- other areas, like transport, which were not so easy to identify.

The LEA responded positively by allocating to each of the three schools around £9/10 000 per year for a four-year period, starting in September 1985.

3   MSC support

An approach to MSC for support, particularly in the context of the now functioning (from January 1986) Stafford Education and Industry Project. Currently this has not proved successful although a more recent bid to support a collaborative Writing Project (see p. 55) looks as if it will gain support.

In the general context of MSC I am hoping that Staffordshire TVEI Extension bid will provide further support.

4   Appeals to industry

We have made appeals to industry for help. This need not be directly financial but could be through using premises, supply of apparatus and so on. I have been encouraged by the support we have obtained in this way.

Summary

At the time when the policy statement was made to staff – in February 1985 – I stated that it would be the task of management to find the resources to support the material the staff would be writing. Some can come from internal adjustments and this then helps to persuade others to support. Certainly, with Staffordshire, if the curriculum case can be made then support is there in a variety of ways. Above all it takes a long time to persuade people to 'cough up' and the value of persistence should not be underestimated.

More change?

I have no doubt that making the move to a modular framework has generated the need to consider a vast array of other issues. It is interesting that this need to consider further developments in other areas of policy is being raised by staff simply because the modular curriculum is forcing us all to face these issues. Good examples are:

1 *Parents' evenings, internal exams and reports* – currently the system is based around examinations being taken, reports being written and parents being seen; but what do we do now when not only do we have continuous assessment in the modular area, but also in the Humanities core and English (which has opted for the continuously assessed language and literature GCSE)?
2 *16–19 education,* continuing the philosophy now being established for 14–16 year olds.
3 *Evaluating pupil experience* – how do we know that we are succeeding in our aims?

The overall effects are summarised in Figure 3.7.

General reflections

The school has begun to implement a modular curriculum and will continue to develop this over the next few years. In describing why, how and what is being developed a number of practical planning problems have been outlined. Some general lessons have also been learned and I would like to refer to the following.

Sharing responsibility

Making explicit moves to change teacher style towards a more active and participative approach means that students become more responsible for their learning. Such a change in style also needs to permeate the way in which staff are managed. If staff are given real involvement and can take real responsibility they themselves can develop and learn. Through this process, 'ownership' of change is established and while

Figure 3.7   Self generating model for change

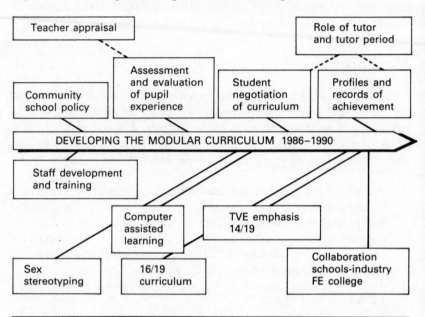

this does not guarantee success, success is very difficult to achieve without it.

I prefer to use the term 'sharing' responsibility rather than 'delegating' or 'devolving' responsibility. This theme recurred throughout the lengthy period of development and implementation, during which:

- staff have been involved in policy discussions – their views have helped to formulate eventual policy, and will continue to do so;
- I have been totally reliant on staff to produce the material upon which the whole scheme depends;
- I have relied upon staff at all levels to take responsibility for developing specific responses to identified needs;
- management responsibility has been primarily in the area of articulating long-term aims, maintaining a consistent direction, ensuring overall coherence and obtaining funding and general resources.

It seems to me that the risks in such a strategy are small and the potential rewards great. I have to say that the hard work and commitment of the staff are impressive and that individuals, freed to develop their subject and interest areas in the way they want, have shown vision, imagination and great skills. It is a tribute to over 30 teachers plus others who gave valuable support that they have written a Mode 3 Submission containing 60 modules, presented it and had it approved by MEG.

Failure

It would be dishonest to imply that throughout this period all has gone well. Throughout, accommodation has had to be made for those areas that, for one reason or another, are out of sympathy with the main policy thrust. This is perhaps a planning problem that needs to be faced – it is most unlikely that a 100% staff commitment for any policy could ever be attained; attained, that is, from the point of view of real commitment as opposed to neutral acquiescence. Obviously, reasons for lack of commitment vary from individual to individual but certain subject areas do have basic problems in coming to terms with a modular approach. This is particularly so for languages and I have great sympathy with their position. Unlike other departments which are not directly involved, but have been able to make contributions to cross-curricular modules (eg Maths and English), it is difficult for the Languages Department to formulate a positive contribution. I believe there is a way forward and, in time, I hope that a policy will develop – the point is that there will be failure and, on reflection, I am not sure that enough was done to give or find the help needed.

Creating climate and sharing learning

There has to be a climate for change – if it does not exist it has to be created. This climate has obviously to embrace the staff but must also extend to key areas like the Local Education Authority and governors. The supporting role of governors has been vital in establishing local credibility. This support has been derived from keeping governors well informed and discussing the issues and implications regularly throughout the period of development. Various individuals and departments in the LEA have played a crucial role in affecting the pace, extent and, in one important sense (the Stafford Education and Industry Project), the direction of development.

Essentially, for all involved it has been a shared learning and development experience; for staff in reaching a deeper understanding of the process of learning and their role in that process through developing material; for management (at all levels) in learning about managing through the process of doing it; for the LEA representatives most closely associated with the school in being able to develop their curriculum thinking through the process of supporting and influencing developments; and for industry and education representatives in learning more about each other through the process of working together towards agreed objectives.

As for modules ...

Without doubt the main reason why a modular curriculum has been implemented is because it makes sense. It makes sense because it deals with the inherent limitations and inflexibilities that are contained in the kind of structure based on eight or nine subjects followed for two years and concluded by a formal exam. At the same time there is a tremendous potential for dealing with the wide range of issues previously detailed.

However the emphasis, at this stage, must be on 'potential'. Equally, there are potential drawbacks and great care will be needed if modules are not to become a bandwagon, supposedly transporting us all to paradise. This school has taken this route for reasons which have been described, we are proceeding carefully – in a limited way to start with – and will develop at a pace which will keep everybody's feet firmly on the ground. At this stage I cannot see that we will want, or consider it desirable, to extend much beyond 55–60% modular.

4 Starting from scratch

Glinys Weller and James Williams

West Swindon is an area of massive expansion. It is a new development of housing and industrial units started in 1977. The population of West Swindon is growing rapidly, and eventually it will form its own community of 30 000 people. The industry is mixed, consisting of some manufacturing industry and other commercial activities; many people also commute to other towns, including London – only a short motorway journey away. Housing is also mixed, with expensive, privately-owned houses, cheaper 'starter' homes, and property owned by the local council for rent.

Schooling in West Swindon has followed the traditional pattern, starting with small local primary schools, taking children from five to ten years. These have been built as the area expanded, and at present there are six local primaries, with a further two planned for the future. At secondary level (11–16 years) local children have been bussed out of the area to a number of secondary schools in other parts of Swindon. The normal policy in an expanding area such as West Swindon is to provide secondary schools when the population is large enough to support them.

Greendown is thus part of the normal response to such expansion. Opened in 1986, the school is designed to provide secondary education for all abilities of students in the age range 11–16 years. The first intake of students consisted of 150 11 year olds, and the school will continue to accept students of this age group each year – maximum capacity being attained in 1991. By that time there will be a total of 900 students housed in new buildings constructed over the first five year development of the school. The initial intake of 150 is smaller than the design size, which is 180 students per year. It is anticipated that the first intake at the design size will occur in September 1988.

The buildings are to be built in two phases. Phase one, designed to provide accommodation for the first three year groups, was completed ready for occupation in July 1986. Phase two will be ready for occupation by September 1990. It is possible that a third phase may then be built. This would allow the school to increase to 1200 secondary places and provide for an expansion in the annual intake to 240 students per year group.

Phase one is mainly classroom accommodation, but includes a gym, youth and community suite, drama studio and temporary provision for sciences and design subjects. Phase two includes a further gym and a specialist block for science and design subjects. Phase three, if completed, will consist of sports hall, further classroom accommodation and an additional exterior all-weather floodlit playing surface. Within the existing buildings, provision has been made for a radio room, a television studio, a resources centre and appropriate dining and social facilities. The school has a computer network, with machines in each teaching area.

In view of the national educational debate, the experience at other schools of new methods, and as a response to a new national examination system which appears to be changing the priorities, it was decided from the outset at Greendown to question traditional organisational patterns and existing teaching methods. To do this one key question was asked and will continue to be asked: What are we expecting our students to have acquired at the end of the five year period of compulsory secondary education? The answer to this question should determine the pedagogy and the organisation of the school.

Broad aims

In reviewing debates over the past five–ten years about the future educational requirements of the nation, it is possible to produce a set of broad aims:

1   The system must respond in such a way as to produce appropriate attitudes in the students. They must become more flexible to change; be prepared to learn and relearn different skills throughout their lives; be capable of a highly developed sense of personal initiative; acquire the ability to work constructively in a team or on their own as required; be able to apply strategies to problem solving; build on their own personal confidence and be more aware of the needs and function of the society in which they live. In short, this is defining what we now call the 'process' curriculum.

2   Our students must develop certain basic skills – in numeracy, in communication and literacy, in the new technologies, in understanding society, its structure and function.

3 It should develop a high sense of moral awareness in the student. Our students should become caring, concerned individuals, aware of the traditional differences between right and wrong, and willing and able to become tolerant, thinking, individuals in a true multi-racial society. They need to acquire political knowledge, social skills and an understanding of the problems facing the world and its peoples and economies.

4 The school systems must be capable of responding to the needs of individual students rather than using the 'assembly line' method of education prevalent in our schools to date.

5 Students should be capable of applying skills and knowledge in a variety of different situations.

From the above list, the obvious priority must lie in the pedagogy of the approach and it is in this area that the school concentrates its efforts. Thus all organisational aspects of the school are directed to improving the pedagogy and hence the overall quality of the educational process.

Focus on pedagogy

At Greendown our pedagogy is designed with several specific aims in mind:

- to recognise the student as having an individual need and therefore requiring a far more personal style of education;
- to present a range of approaches and levels of material to the student so that each student achieves to their full potential
- to encourage the student to take gradually increasing responsibility for their own learning. The curriculum must therefore involve negotiation between student and teacher and imply a high level of counselling skills from the teacher.
- to include experiential methods, problem solving, group work, individual work, discussion work, and when appropriate, didactic methods of learning;
- to encourage the student to communicate accurately in a wide range of ways, through the spoken and written word and through graphics, and to enable the student to acquire a knowledge of the power and use of the media;
- to ensure that students become aware of what, and why, they are learning – they must become able to apply ideas and develop personal initiative.

Our curriculum, therefore, provides a fairly radical approach to secondary education. The foundation staff have been provided with an opportunity to reassess the content and approach of most of our teaching. The total experience of the students is considered to come within the remit of each of one of three curriculum schools. These schools have the following titles:

Personal development – consisting of the creative arts, special needs, PE, social and personal education.
Humanities and communications – consisting of foreign languages, humanities, English, media studies.
Physical and environmental studies – consisting of sciences, mathematics, design, technology and computers.

The three areas can be loosely defined as experience concerning the development of the individual, experience concerning the relationships between people, and experience concerning the physical world. These areas are not mutually exclusive and clearly have considerable overlap.

Each of the three teams is led by a member of the management team. These team leaders are called School Directors. Each subject specialist within the school at middle management level is known as a 'coordinator', the term 'Head of department' being deemed inappropriate. Each school has produced a curriculum which integrates the subjects in that school. Thus the traditional 'subjects' of secondary education have been removed.

The school day

Traditionally, schools have been organised into a day which normally commences at around 9.00 am, has various registration and assembly periods, breaks for recreation and meals and lessons, and which then finishes at 4.00 pm. This pattern, and perhaps the obsession with school bells, is a direct result of the old factory-type organisation of our schools.

Although the pattern of Greendown would be considered to be quite radical in approach, it nevertheless is certainly not the first school to break with tradition. Many factors were considered in determining the pattern of the day to be adopted. In view of the need to develop the radical type of curriculum being proposed, it was essential that curriculum planning time was included within the teachers' normal working day. (In practice the staff all work considerably longer than this minimum time). Experience in other schools where the day has been changed indicates that learning efficiency is increased if lessons are compressed into the earlier part of the day. Breaks for rest and relaxation are essential if learning efficiency is to be maintained. These breaks require careful control and students must have good social facilities in a controlled environment.

Since the curriculum is divided into three curriculum schools, each of these requires a large block of time which can be used in a manner suiting the particular learning experience. Thus large groups of students are taught by a team of staff able to organise the teaching sessions in any appropriate manner.

The pattern of the day is shown in Figure 4.1.

Figure 4.1   The school day

8.15 am	The buildings are opened. Students should not arrive before 8.15am.
8.40am	Start of school – a registration/assembly session followed by the first teaching unit.
10.15am – 10.30 am	A short break. Canteen facilities are available during this time.
10.30am – 11.55am	The second teaching unit.
11.55am – 12.35pm	A longer break. Full canteen facilities will be available during this time. Snacks or full meals can be purchased and facilities provided for students who bring their own food.
12.35pm – 1.55pm	The third teaching unit.
1.55pm – 2.10pm	Tutor period.
2.10pm	The core time ends and many students will leave the premises at this time.
2.10pm – 3.30pm	The final session, known as enrichment.

All students are required to attend at least one of the enrichment activities, and the majority attend two. The school does not use bells, and movement around the buildings is minimised through the grouping of the classrooms into the curriculum schools. Each of the curriculum schools is given a block of time during the day and it is up to the director, in consultation with his/her colleagues, to determine how this time should be spent. So far a system has evolved which results in either team teaching or in staff taking pupils for long periods of time. As a result of this most students in the school are taught by just three or four staff, rather than the usual much higher number. A further consequence is that staff are not only teaching their subject specialisms, but other subjects within their curriculum team. Support is provided by the team and the fully integrated nature of the curriculum.

All students have to do one enrichment consisting of recreational/ sport activities. In addition, they must also choose one further enrichment activity and may do up to a further three activities. On one afternoon per week the school closes at 14.10 to allow for staff planning and curriculum development.

One major advantage of the system, which has a direct effect on the parents, is that at the end of the module (ie during the last week before a holiday), the enrichment programme is cancelled and the parents visit the school to discuss the progress of their child. Thus parents are able to receive reports on progress, including staff interviews, once every six weeks. This contrasts with the normal pattern of once per year in the majority of UK schools.

The modular system

The management of the curriculum involves the creation of work modules, usually lasting half a term. At the beginning of each of the six weeks of work (called a module) the pupils set themselves a series of what are called 'Work targets'. This is usually completed in conjunction with an interview/discussion with either the pupil's tutor or subject teacher. The students are set work targets, which may be renegotiated during the course of the module. At the end of the six week module the pupil reviews the work target with their particular teacher. That teacher then submits a profile to the pupil's tutor, it being designed to assess certain skills and processes/concepts. Each of these assessments and the three school assessments are passed to the pupil's tutor every six weeks. They are then collated, and parents contacted. The parents are made aware of the situation, and may take this opportunity to discuss and add to the child's profile, in conjunction with the tutor. This allows a fairly rapid resolution of any specific problems that may arise.

Categories of module

The modules at Greendown may be classified under four distinct headings.

1   Modules may be *integrated* across a number of different subjects. A module in 'energy' could cover the same aspects of the national criteria in science, technology and possibly maths. Such a module would require careful analysis to determine exactly what aspects of the national criteria are being covered.

2   Modules may be *single subject*, for example, a module covering a particular aspect of English literature.

3   Modules could be *'continuous'* – where a progression can be clearly shown between different modules of work. For example, a single subject module in mathematics could involve statistical work which relies on some previous statistical experience.

4   Models could be *discrete* – a particular area is studied, where previous experience is not necessary. An example could involve basic typing skills.

Any module could involve a combination of 1 or 2 with 3 or 4. This scheme may be related to the types of module defined in the various SEG discussion papers. Although these descriptors may be adequate for some purposes, they do not take into account the difficulties caused by the integrated type of module, where one learning experience can be seen to be part of the criteria in a range of subjects.

Subject integration

The integration of subject areas has proved problematic. The main difficulty is the lack of published material designed to cater for the type of course we want to offer. This means that much of the material has to be written and we have found that it eats into the time we would like to spend on discussing/organising classroom techniques, approaches and management. Some subject areas blend very well with others and a promising level of success has been experienced in some areas, eg English and humanities. The school is looking at how foreign languages might integrate with the English/humanities course and also how it might be brought into other curriculum schools. The following is an account of a joint French/humanities session written from the consumer's point of view. In humanities pupils were studying the way in which the community can help handicapped people.

2.2.87
Today we had to guide someone around the drama studio. We had to give them instructions and guide them around the drama studio blindfolded and around the obsticle that had been set out. But the

instructions we gave them had to be in French. I thuoght that it would be quite hard to speak Frênch all the time but I got used to it and found it quite easy after sometime. When I was blindfolded I was a bit worried because I might bump into someone or something. If I was blinded for life I would think that it was very very hard to carry on living. I think that I am very lucky not to have anything wrong with me. Blindness is a sad thing because you cannot see the world changing like when the flowers come out and it snows or when it's Summer. You can not see children playing and enjoying themselves.

2.2.87
We were in the drama studio and an obsticle course had been set up. We were in pairs and I was with Claire. We had to lead a blindfolded person around the obsticle course in French. I think I can remember how to say turn right, turn left, go straight on. What made it more difficult was the amount of people also in it. Claire was blindfolded first then me. I knew I could trust Claire and it was fun to be directed around. But sometimes I felt I wanted to look so I would not be permantly blind. I would always need someone with me if I was blind. You also have to trust people to guide you properly. Being blind is like having your life cut in half and you are only allowed to keep half of it. You lose the other half. The half with sight and sight is proberly the most important sense. Because if you lose your sight you can't watch anything, ride anything e.g. bike, drive a car etc. You cannot see your friends or family or animals. So I would never, never like to be blind. You would never have to transform your life and practically start from the beginning again.

The creative arts have successfully devised an integrated approach and an example of a module planning document is attached. The main area of concern has been the integration of PE. To date practical difficulties have been the main stumbling block, in that we only have one gymnasium and one person qualified to teach gymnastics. Since we have identified elements of gymnastics as important aspects of the first year curriculum we have operated a system which has involved each tutor group going off at a specified time each week for a gymnastics input. The actual gymnastics work has been geared to the module content and has tied in very closely with the work undertaken in the rest of the arts. We have succeeded therefore in coordinating these areas but have not yet found a way of integrating. We have stopped short of forcing the issue and choosing ideas and activities because they fit into an integrated approach. Clearly we do not want to integrate for the sake of it.

The potential weakness of the three school division has been overcome to some extent by the commonality of approach to planning facilitated by module proforma (see p. 80). In addition the schools make conscious efforts to point out links to pupils and to use areas of overlap in a positive way. Through directors the schools keep in touch with each other's plans. Attempts are made to coordinate work where appropriate. For Module 6 the schools of physical and environmental studies and personal development will both tackle 'environment'. The work of both schools will focus on the local park but a different emphasis and approach will be used by each school. In the second year a fully integrated joint module is planned. It will involve the formation of new teams made up of representatives from each school division. The focus will be China and planning is in the early stages.

Initial planning

The importance of planning in any scheme such as Greendown's cannot be overestimated and, being an entirely new school, this began some time before we opened.

The appointment of the Head at the new school was the first step in developing the new structure. The Head had made a clear statement of his own personal philosophy and the employing authority had a good understanding of the implications of this. Consequently, the Officers of the Authority have been willing to give full support to the initiative at Greendown – the first prerequisite for any new development. The staff have also been appointed with the philosophy clearly stated – they have been subject to a rigorous selection procedure and have very specific job briefs. Clearly this has given the school a considerable advantage.

After the appointment of the Head, the Deputies were then selected. This was done on the basis of a national advertisement and over 400 requests for further information were received. The information supplied was very specific, and detailed clearly the differences between Greendown and other, 'traditional' schools. One result of this was that only a total of 150 applications were then received, although these were generally of a very high standard. The need for the creation of a detailed job brief was thus justified and applicants were required to address specific issues in completing the applications as well as the more general and usual educational areas.

The major difference between the posts at Greendown and similar posts at other schools, lies in the requirement for the management structure to reflect the emphasis being placed on pedagogy. In many secondary schools, the senior staff are more concerned with administration than pedagogy. Thus for example, most schools with two deputies will have one working on curriculum organisation and management and one on so-called pastoral management. The wider view of curriculum taken at Greendown results in the elimination of these separated tasks and both deputies are specifically directed to take full control of a whole area of student learning experience. They are required to develop an integrated curriculum, and to lead a team of subject specialist staff covering a range of traditional subject areas.

Following the appointment of the deputies, a third member of the team was then appointed to cover the remaining curriculum areas. Thus the school management team consists of four people, Head, two Deputies and a Senior Teacher. The team differs from the usual practice in that each member has a specific responsibility for the development of a whole area of student learning experience – this is not an administrative role, but one totally devoted to developing pedagogy in the direction of the philosophy previously indicated.

The remaining members of the teaching staff, a further eight subject specialists, were then appointed. Few restrictions were placed by the Authority on these appointments except that the school was required to look first at local teachers. The area outside West Swindon is subject to falling rolls and teachers are being shed from other schools. In the event, some appointments were made locally, although these were all made because those concerned seemed suited to the task rather than due to any local pressure. Finally, national advertisements were placed to find the remaining four members of staff after the local 'trawl' had been completed. Again, as for the Deputies, all teaching staff were given clear information about the nature of the posts and all were subject to a rigorous selection procedure.

In making fairly fundamental changes to the traditional school structure, and in selecting the special type of teacher required for the posts, the importance has been demonstrated of the need for clear and precise planning and detailed job specifications. The selection procedure has also been changed to include not only the traditional letter of application, which requires response to specific and general questions, but also the techniques of interview. These included the use of team interviews where a candidate was questioned about specific, prearranged areas by just two interviewers. At the completion of up to five such interviews the interviewing teams would then meet to determine the selection of the appropriate candidate. This system has resulted in the creation of a very close-knit team of staff who all share a common philosophy. It is intended that all subsequent appointments will be made in this way.

The next major problem was the realisation that the location of the staff around the UK was going to prove difficult. If real curriculum innovation was going to take place much of the material would have to be trusted to either the telecom or postal services. This would obviously introduce an unacceptable time delay. It was therefore decided that there was a crucial need for the staff to actually meet and weld into effective teams which could tackle the problem of curriculum development. Three conferences were arranged, and two of these were of a residential nature. These proved to be highly effective and we believe that as a consequence of both the residential experiences and the selection procedure the teams quickly formed and started producing ideas.

Planning in teams

Planning is fundamental to the development of the Greendown curriculum. One of the obstructions to team planning in schools with a traditional structure is the lack of opportunity within the school day for meetings. Even if meetings are held during 'free' time, there is usually no guarantee that staff will be willing or able to turn up on a regular basis. At Greendown the latter part of every Monday afternoon is devoted to curriculum planning.

Meetings begin when pupils leave the premises at 2.10 pm. The school day officially ends at 3.30 pm, although in practice, planning meetings often go on beyond this. The meetings are organised in school divisions and the agenda is very definitely confined to curriculum matters. The second Monday of each module is a 'thinktank': all staff excluding the senior management team meet to discuss curriculum issues. Simultaneously the three school directors meet to discuss inter-school curricular collaboration. We have, so far, resisted the temptation to introduce matters of a more general nature into Monday meetings. To accommodate this the following pattern of meetings has been agreed:

- Every fourth Thursday a *form tutors' meeting* takes place during assembly time. This is chaired by a member of the senior management team.
- A *full staff meeting* takes place on the second Wednesday of each module. Since this is held after 3.30 pm attendance is voluntary.
- A *learning group* meets after school every Thursday, primarily for *in house INSET*. Attendance is voluntary.
- In addition to the above there is a *full staff briefing* on several mornings each week. These are purely for information. The SMT meet briefly every morning and attend a diary meeting each week.

The modular proforma

The planning of modules takes place in curriculum schools. Inevitably the schools vary to some extent in the exact methods employed and this is not discouraged. The schools do, however, use a common planning proforma (see Figure 4.2). The planning proforma indicates the detail of the planning process and it can be seen that the *skills, knowledge* and *concepts* of the *content* area selected for the module must be stated. In addition, *specific learning outcomes* are listed in the first column and it is to these that assessment is linked. They form the basis of a *profile of achievement* which is compiled for each pupil during the course of the module and summarised at the end to make an assessment which can be passed to form tutors and parents. The planning proforma was introduced by the Headmaster, who also determined the grouping of the subjects into curriculum schools. Initially schools found the planning proforma difficult to use and often it seemed to put a straitjacket on thinking. With the passage of time, however, it has proved an effective tool for focusing attention on processes rather than content and has encouraged us to be more rigorous than we might have been in cutting out 'clutter'. Thus the content of a module is determined in the light of skills and processes rather than vice versa.

Figure 4.2 Planning proforma.

Specific learning objective(s)	Teaching strategies	Teaching materials	Competencies		Concepts	Assessment techniques	
			Skills	Knowledge			

Planning within the schools

In this way teams of between three and four staff started to map out experiences that they felt important to the pupils as individuals. Processes, concepts and skills were felt to be far more relevant than the traditional content-laden syllabuses that the majority of the staff had been used to in the past; obviously the time for change was ripe. Having mapped the areas of importance from each of our specialist points of view the next thing was to look for the areas of overlap between these individual disciplines and ascertain the points where integration could be achieved. The school of personal development began by listing some very broad aims which would be appropriate to pupils in the first three years of secondary education. This list was used as a starting point for planning courses in the creative arts and PE and led to the formation of a list of general objectives for year one. The next stage was to plan a very loose set of titles for the six modules in year one and to ensure that each general objective could be represented under one or more of the module titles. It was quickly realised that some of the objectives would need to be 'revisited' and would have to be built in to more than one module. Others, only touched upon in year one, would be explored in greater detail in future years.

These broad areas were then laid out under a general topic heading and module planning sheets issued to the teams so that the real planning of the modules could proceed. The head of the school had had previous experience of these module sheets while head of a TVEI school, and assured the staff that this was the best way to proceed. Despite the head's assurances, many doubts passed through the minds of staff members about these sheets as few of them had had experience of being so precise in their module work planning.

Two different methods of using the module sheets ensued. Some staff preferred to find the curriculum material available on the general topic area and then refine it so that it fitted the format of the sheets. Others chose to start with a totally blank page, write the module sheet and then resource it after the team knew exactly what they wanted.

The real difference between this type of planning and what had gone before was the move towards identifying skills and processes rather than the traditional knowledge-based approach. The danger we felt was that the curriculum pendulum seemed to be shifting very heavily in the direction of skills and processes with an inference that knowledge was no longer really needed. Although this is an extreme position it was felt that at Greendown certain experiences were essential for the full development of the pupil. Skills and processes without a context would really be meaningless. Another problem with starting with a completely blank page was that many of the exciting and valuable initiatives that have gone on before might become neglected, with teachers sitting around spending many hours 'reinventing the wheel'. They would then produce their own material which would have to go through the usual trial and refinement stage, when very often they might find that this had all been done for them, if only they looked for and extracted what they wanted from other courses, material then only being written to fulfil a perceived need.

All too often it was felt that new initiatives fall on stony ground because the course material is well written but the teaching methods simply are not up to scratch. Either staff are required to have eyes in the backs of their heads, to observe several different activities taking place in the classroom – or they are forced to teach to the middle ability range, losing either end of the ability spectrum. How was Greendown going to cope with this?

A modular approach was chosen in the belief that:

- children respond well when they have a real part to play in the system;
- negotiation with a student about work targets improves motivation;
- short-term goals improve motivation;
- integration improves the pupil's ability to form a sensible, 'whole approach' to their education;
- initially pupils would find the first course at Greendown an extension of their primary practice, which would help them settle in.

Teamwork

An interesting spin-off from the team approach to modular planning at Greendown is the supportive nature of staff interaction. Because teachers do not work in isolation, responsibility for what goes on in the classroom is shared. Cooperative planning, joint preparation of materials and discussion of issues associated with aspects of the curriculum are everyday features of the modular planning and they encourage team ownership. Spontaneous discussion of how the session went follows naturally. There is an openness which leads to an awareness of the needs of colleagues and mutual support is fostered. This sense of belonging is heightened by team teaching with its associated need for the development of strong personal relationships and cooperation between staff working together in the same room with a large group of pupils.

The emphasis on detailed planning does not imply that personal styles and approaches are not developed and used by teachers at Greendown. It does mean that staff share the same objectives for each module but all are free to choose their own techniques and strategies for meeting the agreed objectives.

The team approach also encourages accountability. At the planning stage, the workload for the mosule is often shared between team members. People who are disorganised or late with their contribution let down the whole team, as the piece of work is for general team consumption. It is one thing to share a rather scrappy worksheet with 4z, quite another to present it to colleagues as a teaching resource.

As the school grows, the curriculum teams will become too large for this process to occur without some form of framework. We have in mind the creation of small teams of staff based on curriculum schools. We anticipate they will be three or four in number and be of mixed status, eg a Scale 4, two Scale 2s and a Scale 1. They would form a cohesive group for the purpose of mutual support.

Assessment

For the purpose of the above planning, the school has developed an analysis system which defines the learning experience of the students. As has been seen, each module has *general objectives* – these can be defined in the form of a title, although usually the general objectives are more detailed than this. The general objectives are then expanded to give a set of *specific learning objectives* – these are further analysed to give a list of *concepts, skills* and *knowledge* appropriate to the module. The specific objectives then lead directly to a set of *assessment objectives* and the methods by which the assessment is to be carried out. Links with the *national criteria* are then established.

This system, far more detailed than the conventional syllabus, will allow the board to ensure that the standards are maintained and the national criteria attained. It will also allow those modules which are integrated to be clearly seen to cover a number of traditional areas – this will allow some form of accumulated accreditation towards single subjects.

Figures 4.3 and 4.4 are examples of the analysis system as applied to modules covering a range of areas. This material does not cover a full module, but is a learning objective within a module.

The application of this system in the schools

The work of each curriculum school occupies about eight hours per week. Students will therefore be taking a large common core with a number of electives. Each element of the learning experience is represented by a module and it is hoped that these would be available for assessment from year three onwards. The school wishes to start the system in September 1988. Initially, relatively few modules would be available for accreditation, increasing in range as the students approach

Figure 4.3

SPECIFIC UNIT CODE 2 'MATERIAL SYNTHESIS'

Specific Learning Objective(s)	Teaching strategies	Teaching materials	Competencies		Concepts	Assessment techniques	Links	Enrichment
			Skills	Knowledge				
Personal criteria for art and design and equivalent performing and expressive arts criteria	To facilitate development of one or more of these alternatives. i) sketches/ photographs/ video into 2D/3D artistic form. ii) tapes/video/ sketches, etc. into improvisation/ scripted work into performance. iii) appreciation and performance or improvisation based on appropriate music. iv) appropriate dance styles and techniques into performance	Students' own starting points: reports, tapes, sketches, photos, video, etc. Range of art materials. Theatre Arts facilities, inc. staging/ lighting/make-up, etc. Audio/video equipment. Keyboards/ percussion.	Sketching selecting material use of line, colour, pattern, texture, form. Negotiation with peers role play improvisation polishing performance. Listening to & analysing appropriate music composing and/ or performing Analysing appropriate dance methods arranging performing	Some local social history geography Application of appropriate techniques (see skills). Properties of art materials.	Gaps between students' experience and that of old people. Selection and synthesis of appropriate material into performance or expressive medium. Change in historical perspective.	Profiling Assessment of course work*. Assessment of performance/ exhibition (controlled test)* * against assessment objectives linked into grade descriptions. Students would select mediums for working and would be assessed in the process of preparing for and presenting their work.	Written accounts could be assessed as GCSE English, GCSE Humanities work. Music/Dance work as part submissions for GCSE.	GCSE Music GCSE Dance

Figure 4.4

SPECIFIC UNIT CODE								
Specific learning objective(s)	Teaching Strategies	Teaching Materials	Competencies		Concepts	Assessment Techniques	Links	National Criteria
			Skills	Knowledge				
Current flow is the result of a difference in voltage.	Experiment, Demonstration, Problem solving.	Circuit apparatus Ammeters Power packs	Setting up a circuit. Read and interpret circuit diagrams. Reading scales.	Circuit symbols. Correct connection procedure.	Potential difference & current flow.	Open problem solving/ proven ability in circuit design. Selection & use of a pattern from data. + 10.6 10.7 10.8 10.9 10.10		12

the end of compulsory education. It is essential that the modules in year five have the possibility of accreditation with the Joint Board to ensure a smooth transition between pre- and post-16 education.

Modules would need to be designed at different levels. For example, a module could include work appropriate to foundation (level 1), or intermediate (level 2), or higher (level 3). It is hoped that many students will satisfy the Board that they have reached foundation level in mathematics in their third year.

Each module is analysed according to the scheme previously outlined. This analysis is very similar to the system proposed by the Board in their own discussion document. The analysis is a statement of the learning experiences which the student will undergo. Each of these experiences may be associated with two variables:

1   The experience is a specific learning objective which may be directly related to an objective within the national criteria.
2   The learning objective will be at a specific level which will relate to GCSE grades.

In many subject areas, eg mathematics, the analysis of content can be precisely determined. In contrast, the analysis of English is far more difficult. The obvious method for marking and assessing such modules would appear to be the use of course credits – with each contributing a number of credits towards the final total. Where a module is seen to be part of a single subject, it could be given a number of credits appropriate to the attainment level. These credits would then be accumulated with those from other modules to give an overall total resulting in a GCSE grade.

Each module would be associated with a matrix, which would identify the learning objectives and the levels, together with an appropriate credit count. A module which covered several traditional subject areas could be analysed in the same way, although it would be a more complex task. Each learning objective would be 'marked' and a module total mark could then be equivalent to a number of course credits. This would allow interchange of learning objectives between subjects. For example, a series of essays could be marked to give so many credits towards one subject and a different number towards another. Hence it should be possible to provide credits towards single subject GCSE qualifications, transferable across subject boundaries. For example when a student produces some form of written work in science, it could be credited towards another subject. It may eventually prove possible to eliminate certain subjects entirely with the traditional content being taught via other subjects. An example of this is the lower level of mathematics. A study of the humanities could involve the presentation and interpretation of statistical data – and this could be credited towards both mathematics and a humanity.

To achieve any of the higher level grades, the course of study undertaken should clearly cover the equivalent content of a set of single subject modules. The concept of criterion referencing should allow a student to take, for example three science modules, which would accumulate to give a total of an intermediate level grade. Additional modules could then be taken to give the higher level if required. Where a module does not fit readily into a subject category, an independent assessment will be made.

The final certificate would need to include a module matrix. Each module would have a title and have an overall classification at either foundation, intermediate or higher level. Appropriate modules would then be accumulated to give GCSE single subject grade.

In total it is anticiapted that a student could take up to 50 modules in the course of the final three years of secondary schooling. Not all of these would need to be named on the certificate – particularly those concerned with the common core subjects of maths, English, science etc. The final certificate could, therefore, include grades for single subjects, together with a list of additional module titles and the appropriate level of attainment.

Pupils with special needs

At Greendown we consider that all pupils are special and all have special needs. Flexibility and differentiation are built into each module so that the individual needs of pupils can be met. Pupils with learning difficulties and also those with adjustment difficulties find the short term objectives of modules easier to come to terms with than many traditional courses which must seem to stretch unendingly into the mists of time. Since each module is a separate, self-contained package a sense of 'starting again' is evident at the beginning of each module, rather like the start of a new school year.

It has been argued that modularised curriculum lacks coherence. However this assumes that the coherence of linear courses is of direct benefit to pupils. It is arguable that much of this coherence is lost on many pupils with behaviour or learning difficulties. In fact, the modular design of lower school courses is spiral and therefore has a coherence which stems from the repetition of key concepts in several modules. This creates opportunities for pupils to consolidate and extend their learning. This is very much a feature of process curriculum and the idea does not lend itself easily to a content-based syllabus. (One of the key concepts of the first year humanities course is: 'What makes man human?' This is approached from various angles in several modules via a range of content . . .)

It is envisaged that a special educational needs specialist will be attached to each year group. They will act in an advisory capacity, working alongside subject staff, creating resources and materials for modules and will provide support in lessons via team-teaching. At present pupils with learning difficulties receive special help within their own classrooms. They are not withdrawn to work on separate materials. Instead they are given study packs which supplement the modules. These break down the curriculum objectives into steps suitable in size to meet the needs of the individuals with special educational needs.

Pupils work on study packs in collaboration with either the subject teacher or the special needs 'support' teacher. However the support teacher is responsible for checking and updating packs on a regular basis. In addition, particular learning needs can be met via special modules put on during enrichment sessions.

The future?

Having outlined the present situation at Greendown, the next question is where do we go from here?

The answer . . . first, our system lends itself very much to the TVEI scheme, the method of presentation and analysis of the modules seem very compatible. We have therefore applied for the Wiltshire phase 2 TVEI plan and hope to become one of the centres for the initiative in Wiltshire. The second, and the most important, of the future initiatives is to establish where the Greendown scheme fits within the GCSE scheme. The feelings of the staff were that to have a negotiated, skill/process-based curriculum that encouraged the students to take responsibility for their own learning and then to place them in the present 'sausage machine' system of examinations seemed slightly incongruous. This is not to belittle the examinations that a school offers, but it does question the way in which the examinations on offer often predetermine the path to be taken by an individual pupil.

There is obviously a need to direct a pupil towards a broad and balanced education but there is also a need to allow some individual freedoms. We feel that these need not necessarily be irreconcilable alternatives. As far as we are aware the uniqueness of the Greendown system allows a predetermined balanced core curriculum, while still

Figure 4.5

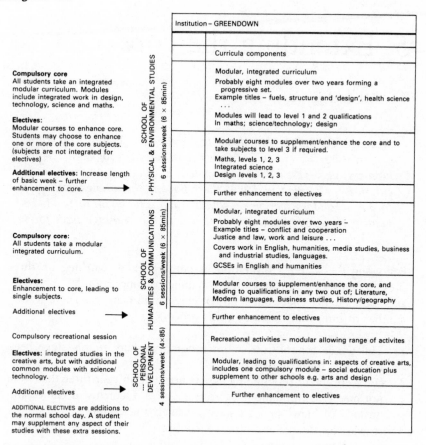

allowing the enrichment to offer support for the pupil's particular choice.

A practical example might help to illustrate this: in the core time a pupil might cover the essentials of an integrated science course, while in enrichment time (the pupil's choice to stay on in school and do extra work) the pupil might follow a course leading to certification in electronics. Perhaps a more *avant garde* suggestion might be that if the pupil attended the enrichment session in the evening, he/she could be offered 'time off in lieu', possible as Greendown functions as a community school open from 8.30 in the morning until 10.30 at night. All in the future? Perhaps not, we have already met with the Southern Examination Group and some of our proposals are listed in Figure 4.5.

5 Extending the core

Michael Jones

Wantage School is based in the town of Wantage in rural Oxfordshire. The town is the centre of world recognised science industry and research with related business and commercial enterprises. Formed in 1984, the school is the amalgamation of former secondary schools of Wantage and is based on three 11–16 Halls each of 600 students together with the Wantage sixth form of 250.

Following the school's formation in January 1984, working on three sites, September 1986 presented a number of opportunities to review and subsequently enact our mode of curriculum delivery. There were a number of important factors in this process.

1 The whole school curriculum programme had at this stage been built into the first two years.
2 We were intent on building experiences within year three that were not merely continuations of years 1 and 2. Elements of choice and 'tasters' of 'new' subjects were considered essential.
3 It was considered essential to continue to build the curriculum around core experience.

At the same time we were gaining in experience from the introduction of trial materials in our piloting of OCEA (Oxfordshire Certificate of Educational Achievement). The pertinent learning experience was being produced by the concept of graded tests – and the enormous impact of designed short-term learning goals. This impact was felt forcibly by both teachers and children. Developing CPVE course structures at sixth form level was providing similar learning experiences. It seemed opportune, therefore, to plan the introduction of some elements of modular course structure – which for a number of us had been a long-

A tribute. In writing this brief account I am conscious of the dedication, inspiration and sheer hard work by my colleagues that makes possible the developments the school has undertaken. This article is a tribute to them.

cherished plan – as a way of changing the way in which the curriculum is delivered.

Curriculum coherence

To ensure curriculum coherence across the age range we have set out to establish:

- real links with partner primary schools (a term's secondment for four colleagues gave great impetus to this relationship);
- Years 1 and 2 as foundation years with a curriculum of:

English (6)	PE (4)
Maths (6)	Science (6)
Humanities (10)	Languages (6)
Art and craft (6)	Tutorial (2)

  by no means radical but allowing for cross-school and cross-curriculum development. The only difference in year 2 is the introduction of a second foreign language;
- Year 3 – the post-foundation year – to be a preparation for the last phase of statutory education;
- Years 4 and 5 to be the bridge to leaving or for further education but as far as practicable to be the commencement of a four year 14–18 continuum – predicting national movement towards a combined education and training policy.

Extending and adding to the core

Using our own knowledge of local demand, coupled with HMI documents and related missives, defining the core became relatively simple. Assuming 'balance, breadth and differentiation' it covers 60% of time and has in partnership English, Maths, Languages, Science, Art and Craft, P.E. For us, this allows the imposition of the added managing criteria of all core being Hall-based.

We were anxious to begin a move away from the conventional option system, because of its deferential effect, and to establish ways of extending or adding to the core. Thus the concept of modules of study was introduced. For us a module is a unit of work, taking up about three hours per week and lasting for around ten weeks. Hence the total time commitment per module is around 27 hours.

In simple terms, therefore, if 40% of a student's time is spent on extensions and completely devoted to modular courses, a total of sixteen modules could be covered in years 3, 4 and 5.

As well as using modules as an extension to the core we began to look at ways of introducing additions to the core — free-standing modules. Such areas of study could be either *service modules* — eg statistics for science or — *interest modules* — eg a life-saving course.

Assessment

As modular structures were being planned, along came GCSE which, initially at least, seemed to be at odds with the developments within OCEA and modular courses *in toto*. However, with experience of modular courses at post-16 level and with favourable signals from the examining bodies, GCSE soon turned into a boost for modular courses and not a death knell. Experiences in other parts of the country were also encouraging and colleagues began to adopt a quite remarkably inventive approach to curriculum design. In Oxfordshire we received the added bonus of the formation of the County's Credit Bank — an embryonic plan to share in the building and accreditation of modular courses.

All courses, therefore, could lead to GCSE qualification and, with formal accreditation of each module, a pattern of course structure began to emerge. Students could therefore study a series of end-on modules ending with formal GCSE qualification, in a conventional sense, as well as selecting an occasional 'addition' module which could be accredited either through RSA and related examinations or count as '1/5 of a GCSE'. Or they might accumulate a number of free-standing modules each with part GCSE accreditation. In practice we assume that most students would take combinations of these different course approaches.

The offer in detail

Following planning and consultation, a curriculum offer was presented to third years for September 1986 (see Figure 5.1).

English (seven hours per fortnight)

Of the seven hours, five hours are taught in class groups and two hours devoted to interest and specific skills choices for a range of modules such as *An introduction to Shakespeare, Media studies* and *Journalism*.

Figure 5.1

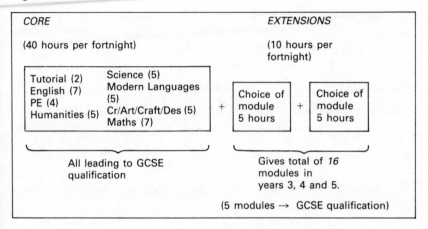

Creative/Art/Craft/Design/Technology (five hours per fortnight)

This whole area of study is modular within the core and offers elements of all subjects available at GCSE. Students may choose a different area each term or stay with the same area throughout. The caution to this freedom of choice is the necessity to put together the right combination of modules to gain GCSE certification in a specific subject area. To study more in this area a student is expected to take extra modules in extension time.

Humanities (five hours per fortnight)

This area is modular within the core, containing elements of History, Geography and RE. With appropriate choice, a GCSE qualification is possible in either of the individual subjects or for GCSE Humanities. Appropriate choice within extensions can lead to additional qualification.

Modern Languages (five hours per fortnight)

All students are expected to study either French or German. For two language qualification it is necessary to take French within the core and German from extension studies.

Physical Education (four hours per fortnight)

Core PE is intended as a foundation experience for later life. For GCSE PE, extension studies must be undertaken.

Science (five hours per fortnight)

For most students, core studies lead to GCSE Science. Using appropriate extension modules it is possible to pursue study in one, two or three sciences of Physics, Chemistry and Biology.

Mathematics (seven hours per fortnight)

Initially, no modular elements are being introduced for Mathematics.

Extending or adding to the core

The detailed offer of extension modules made in September 1986 is shown in Figure 5.2.

The tutorial

The critically important counselling for course choice is centred upon the tutor and there is a one-hour tutorial per week. The programme also continues the work of earlier years by focusing on personal and social development. The main themes are social skills, study skills, health education, careers and community. It aims to support academic programmes and to provide the main link between home and school.

Development planning

When launching new schemes of working it is of obvious importance to preserve good practice and not make that practice impossible by imposing new structures. As a consequence we set the introduction of the core and extension programme as a trial for the third years during 1986/87, with evaluation targeted mid-year to assess progress and potential continuance and development. In so doing we made certain that a reversal to more conventional two year courses would be possible at the commencement of year four, without jeopardising the progress of that particular cohort. By all evaluation measures, much has in fact been gained and little, if anything, lost.

Implications for timetabling

An indisputable fact of experience is that conventional courses and modular courses do not make conventional timetabling partners. With a module length of ten weeks (approximately one term) teacher availability becomes a controlling factor. Without going into technical detail, one way through to a solution for us has been to have the cohort either on core time or extension time. All of the extension time has assumed modular structures. An interesting development has been that many subject areas have adopted a modular approach to core studies . . .!

Evaluation so far

At the time of writing, a considerable amount of evaluation has been possible and we are already beginning to amend practice in the light of experience. In summary, the evaluation tells us that:

1 Children respond very positively to shorter-term learning goals, especially where subject material and learning outcomes are carefully specified.
2 Parents have remarked on the increased motivation and involvement of their children in learning.
3 Teachers are very concerned over time constraints imposed by a 27-hour duration module. However, where content considerations have given way, however limited, to focus on process, concern has been relieved.
4 Teachers have detected a positive enhancement in classroom relationships where they have entered dialogue with students over learning goals.
5 Formal assessment every ten weeks imposes considerable burdens on teachers. We need to establish a way of staggering such assessment.
6 At third year level children are probably not yet ready for full GCSE-style assessment. Some perform at levels way beyond what we expected but the majority display a lack of maturity, especially in written work.
7 All end-of-module assessments contain an element of students' self-assessment. This experience has had by far the most impact on student–teacher relationships and has been welcomed by parents.
8 Teachers' fears about lack of contact continuity still exist although not with such force as previously.

Figure 5.2

FIRST TERM

ICKNIELD HALL

A	B
Science: introductory chemistry	Science: introductory physics
Further science: Food chains etc.	Information technology (Awareness)
Science: Car engines	History (1)
Geography (1)	Keyboard skills
Keyboard skills	German (1)
Design: technology	Music in greater depth (1)

KING ALFRED'S HALL

A	B
Science: introductory biology	Science: introductory chemistry
Further science: wave motion	Information technology (Awareness)
Science: photography	PE (Racquets)
Geography (1)	Latin
Art/Ceramics: option extra (1)	Textiles (garment construction)
Design: technology	Music in greater depth (1)

SEGSBURY HALL

A	B
Science: introductory physics	Science: introductory biology
Further science: periodic table	Information technology (Awareness)
Science: Growing things	Geography (1)
History (1)	Art and Design: option extra (2)
Child development (intro)	Textiles (garment construction)
Design: technology	PE (Health related fitness)

SECOND TERM

A	B
Science: introductory physics	Science: introductory biology
Further science: periodic table	Information technology (Applications 1)
Science: growing things	Geography (1)
History (1)	Keyboard skills
Keyboard skills	German (2)
Design: technology	Music in greater depth (2)

A	B
Science: introductory chemistry	Science: introductory physics
Further science: food chains etc.	Information technology (History/Social)
Science: car engines	PE (Health related fitness)
History (1)	Latin
Art/SD Option extra (7)	Textiles (Toymaking)
Design: technology	Music in greater depth (1)

A	B
Science: introductory biology	Science: introductory chemistry
Further science: wave motion	Information Technology (Technical 1)
Science: Photography	Art/Design: Option extra (8)
Geography (1)	History (1)
Child development (intro)	Textiles (Toymaking)
Design: technology	PE (sports)

THIRD TERM

A	B
Science: introductory biology	Science: introductory chemistry
Further science: wave motion	Information Technology (Programme 1)
Science: Photography	Keyboard skills
Geography (2)	German (3)
Design: Technology	Music in greater depth (3)
Keyboard skills	History (2)

A	B
Science: introductory physics	Science: introductory biology
Further science: periodic table	Information technology (Application 1)
Science: Growing things	PE (GCSE)
Geography (2)	Latin
Design: technology	Music in greater depth (2)
Art:SD/Ceramics	Textiles: clothing/accessories for children

A	B
Science: introductory chemistry	Science: introductory physics
Further science Food chains	Information technology (Technical 1)
Science: Car engines	Art/Design: option extra (9)
History (2)	Geography (2)
Child development (intro)	PE (GCSE)
Design: technology	Textiles: clothing/accessories for children

9 Introducing modular course structures into one year only produces considerable complexity for timetabling. However, when such structures are worked through to fifth year, the complexities will be removed.

10 Student or teacher absence has caused concern over 'catching up'. We have to devise programmes of study to overcome this problem. However it is interesting that no-one raised this issue in conventional courses!

The next steps

Our experience during the year has led us to two firm conclusions. First, that modular courses *improve motivation* for all children. Second, that the constraints of a two year course leading to terminal external examination can be removed by this different style of curriculum delivery. The concept of courses consisting of *learning 'building blocks'* becomes a reality.

The implications of these conclusions are focused principally upon the need for high quality tutorial guidance and on the need for block timetabling. The latter means a great simplifying of timetabling and greater organisational responsibility being placed upon heads of department. In consequence our curriculum offer is developing beyond the initial trial phase into the pattern shown in Figure 5.3.

The move to block timetabling provides more freedom (and teacher responsibility) over group size, setting, grouping and team teaching. Simultaneously, we allow a greater responsiveness to change; the development of different teaching strategies; changes of emphasis; simpler timetabling; a more effective staff distribution.

Another point that needs adding, and emphasising, is that whereas modular structures are not a compulsory development requirement for subject areas, blocking has enabled the development to occur.

We are working closely with the Oxfordshire Credit Bank for the formal accreditation at GCSE for modules. For 1987/88 we expect such accreditation in Arts and Crafts plus Humanities. Our current development plans anticipate the possibility of 4th year modular accreditation in Science to be in place for 1988/89. Currently, no further development is anticipated within the school although community education in the area is likely to adopt modular accreditation through the Credit Bank for a number of its courses. The link between school and community education structures then takes on a very different and exciting prospect.

Figure 5.3

Year 3   1987/88 .

	MATHS/PE	SC/DES/TECH	HUMS/C. ARTS	ENG/LANG
T U T O R I A L	*Plus* ITKS	Sciences Design Home EC Textiles	Humanities Mus/Art/Dr/ Cer *Plus Second Language*	

2p   12p   12p   12p   12p

$\underbrace{\qquad\qquad\text{MODULAR}\qquad\qquad}$

Year 4   1987/88

	MATHS/PE		ENG/LANG		SC/DES/TECH	HUM/C. ARTS
T U T O R I A L	Maths/PE	M E	Eng	Lang + *BS* + *IT*	Sciences design home etc. textiles *Plus PE*	Humanities Music/Art/Cer *Plus 2nd language* BS, IT

2p   ←—— 18p ——→   6p   12p   12p

TIMETABLED ACROSS WANTAGE SCHOOL

Into the future

To presume that one day we will be 'totally modular' is a nonsense and in no way the intention of anyone. A continuum of study in many subject areas will always be the most positive learning experience for many children. What our development has opened up is the prospect for:

- the powerful motivating force of short term learning goals for teachers and students;
- a more flexible course structure;
- curriculum design and delivery becoming the responsibility of teams of teachers;
- the opportunity for access to some courses being available to a cross age group, eg sixth forms and fourth forms working together on a music module. Why not adults too?
- the building of a course matrix covering the 14–18 age range;
- building community education courses that reflect, add to and reinforce the course matrix within the school.

Above all else there is a very real sense among colleagues that we are releasing energies of course design and motivation that were not present hitherto. We are equally conscious that to effect any change we really are still only on the very first steps of development. But we feel that a dynamic is being set up within the school. From that, all of our students stand to gain.

6 Negotiated pathways

Susan and Bruce Pyart

Ysgol Emrys ap Iwan, Abergele, is an 11–18 coeducational comprehensive school established in 1967 as a result of the merger of the local grammar and secondary modern schools. The number of students totals 1150 with a sixth form of about 150.

The catchment area of the school is approximately 60 square miles extending along the North Wales coast from Rhyl to Colwyn Bay. Students from the Welsh-speaking, rural hinterland also attend Emrys ap Iwan and members of staff are bilingual. Thus the school population comes from quite a cultural mix with a wide range of educational expectations.

Abergele is a small holiday resort which is a centre for caravan holidays. Tourism leads to many seasonal jobs but unemployment exceeds 20% at times. In recent years many people have retired from the North West of England to the Abergele area. This has led to a growth in services for elderly people, creating some employment. The major manufacturing companies in the area are Pilkingtons and Hotpoint with smaller companies supporting local tourism and agriculture.

Gareth Newman was Headteacher of Emrys ap Iwan from 1980 until 1985 and it was under his direction that the modular curriculum was introduced and established. Bruce Pyart has been Headteacher since 1985. Susan Pyart has been the internal TVEI evaluator for Clwyd since January 1986.

Throughout the 1970s Ysgol Emrys ap Iwan had retained many of the characteristics of the former grammar school and was failing to meet the needs of the majority of students. This was made manifest by the high non-attendance rates and feelings of disaffection within the classroom. It was felt strongly that students needed to become fully involved in the life of the school and that, to quote Bernstein, 'If the culture of the teacher is to become part of the consciousness of the child, then the culture of the child must first be in the consciousness of the teacher.'[1]

The need for change

By 1982, it was felt by the Headteacher, Gareth Newman, that radical changes should be made to the school's curriculum, pedagogy and assessment. The school's management team were attracted to the idea of a modular form of delivery that could be suited to the needs of all the 14+ students. It was decided to introduce the new curriculum incorporating modified content, emphasis on student process, new teaching processes, student negotiation of pathways and assessment based on 'fitness for purpose'. The Technical and Vocational Educational Initiative, under the aegis of the Manpower Services Commission, was the vehicle by which this radical change could be made. The Clwyd TVEI pilot project focus was high-tech and allowed exciting changes to be made to the curriculum, but this was not enough; students needed to gain experience in taking responsibility, not only within the classroom, but in determining their path through the school.

The model introduced was that of a system of 40-hour modules leading to GCE or CSE accreditation. The emphasis was to be on choice and change. New courses were written specifically for this mode of delivery and some established courses were converted to this form. This was a major departure from established curriculum delivery which caused consternation, panic and relief for different participants. In the first year of its operation (1983–84) 70% of the pupils were involved. In the following year all the fourth and fifth year pupils followed a modular curriculum for between 30% to 70% of the week and have continued to do so. The demand for the new courses has necessitated the spread of the modular curriculum into the rest of the option groupings. Indeed, for the students of Emrys ap Iwan the modular curriculum is now the norm, rather than two-year courses.

Figure 6.1 shows the structure of the week for fourth and fifth form students.

Figure 6.2 shows the structure of the curriculum as it is presented in the form which parents and students receive at the end of the third year.

---

[1] Quoted in Adelman and Walker 'Open space – open classroom' in Harris, A, Law, M and Prescott, W (eds) *Curriculum Innovation* Croom Helm, London, 1975, p 167.

Figure 6.1

	Monday	Tuesday	Wednesday	Thursday	Friday
am	Core	Core	Core	Core	Core
pm	Module	Module	Core	Module	Module
	1	1		2	2

The need for negotiation

Education in Britain is compulsory for young people between the ages of five to sixteen. Moreover schools are obliged to prepare their students to meet life in a rapidly changing world. At 16 young people can marry, take up full-time employment and become fully involved in many aspects of society. This needs preparation, not only in terms of acquiring knowledge and skills but also in exercising control and taking responsibility for their lives. Traditionally, before the age of 16, students have had a very limited choice in schools, in the form of restricted options. Often 'academic' or 'low-achieving' students have been further constrained or overtly sex-stereotyped courses have been set against each other, further increasing this effect.

In Emrys ap Iwan the approach has been to devolve responsibility to the students and, thereby, to democratise the school. Democracy has been welcomed but, as we all know, it has its costs. It is 'easier' to run heavily restricted options; teachers know that their group will remain substantially the same for two years and can concentrate on course content rather than on the day-to-day progress and involvement of each student, knowing that these students are evaluating the experience in the light of impending choice a few weeks away.

The major influence of negotiation has been in providing for the careful monitoring which a 'floating' fourth and fifth year population requires. Computer recording of modular groups and student course profiles has been particularly helpful. 'Information is power' in this case: power to implement, power to innovate and cater for change.

Devolution of responsibility has involved enormous changes to the academic and pastoral ethos of the school. Equal value has been attributed to the needs, desires, interests and achievements of *all* the students. This has enhanced the 'academic' atmosphere of the school, but that was not the only aim. All along it was realised that the modular curriculum would only be a remedial measure for a few students. Nine years of schooling where perhaps success was infrequent had meant

Figure 6.2

CORE STUDIES

ENGLISH		COMMUNICATIONS
Language Literature	AND	French or German or Welsh or Business Systems or Computing

MATHEMATICS

SCIENCE		TECHNOLOGY
		Control Technology or
Biological Science or	AND	Craft Design Technology or
General Science or		Media Systems or Food &
Physical Science		Home Technology or Biological
		Science

HUMAN STUDIES   .
Economics or Geography or History or Commerce

RELIGIOUS EDUCATION

ADDITIONAL STUDIES

Art	Interview Techniques
Biological Science	Introductory Computing
Calculus	Leisure
Child Care & Home Management*	Looking After Yourself
Community Relations	Mass Media
Computers in Business	Motor Vehicle Studies*
Computer Control	Music
Computer Graphics	Personal Grooming & First Aid*
Computer Programming	Photography
Drama	Practical Office Skills
Electronics	Psychology
Electronic Music	Robotics
Experience of Work	Technical Graphic Art
Food Preparation for Catering*	Tourism
French	TV Production
Home Gardening	Typewriting
Home Maintenance	Welsh
Information Systems	WordProcessing

* Taught in the Fifth year at Llandrillo Technical College

PLUS other modules as required

that even the inclusion of Rhyl Fair in the curriculum would lead to only limited response. The whole process of change in Ysgol Emrys Ap Iwan has highlighted the need for a continuing sympathetic and successful world for the students. This is the reasoning behind close links with primary schools and moves towards improving experiences in the first three years at Emrys ap Iwan.

Conditions for successful negotiation

It is felt strongly within Emrys ap Iwan that, for the process of negotiation to succeed, several constraints have to be fulfilled. This is not a new situation but, because student decisions are made more often in the modular curriculum, we are confronted by reality to a greater extent. It is considered essential to have a sound pre-active situation; this is reflected in terms of both the situation within the school, and the roles of parents and students.

The first step in making a decision is to acquire all the relevant information. Not only do vocational and educational opportunities have to be explained to the students and parents but also the complex arrangement of modules and pathways. Many of the GCSE courses operating in Emrys ap Iwan are Modes 3 written specifically as modular courses in new areas of experience such as *Media*. Modules can be combined in different patterns – some are at different levels and others are parallel. Several courses require projects to be presented which may or may not be completed within a timetabled project module.

Thus the situation is a complex one and students must be provided with all the information on which to base their decisions. It has been found that they have a good understanding of the pathways and combinations as well as their long-term implications.

Teachers within the school also need this information in order to liaise with the module coordinator and to guide uncertain students. Every teacher is considered to have a pastoral and careers responsibility.

Students need practice in considering and analysing alternative futures, in making decisions, and in communicating their feelings and perceptions to others. It has been found that students have some difficulties in establishing priorities for themselves after years of accepting a teacher-dominated situation. Careers lessons and pastoral periods are used as a time in which students can express their views and respond to those of others.

Teachers within Clwyd also have good support in the field of personal and social education (PSE). Since 1976 Clwyd has supported a programme of PSE which has resulted in training for many teachers in guidance and counselling. PSE has been given a high profile which has been enhanced by the enthusiasm of a caring staff.

The basis for negotiation

It was felt that the process of negotiation should be founded as far as possible on an agreed basis, as follows.

1   Individual students vary according to their abilities, motivation and attitudes. The cultures and home environment of students are as different as their histories of interaction with the education system. Thus individual differences are to be recognised and appropriate responses to be made.
2   Each module is to be made up of a body of knowledge and associated student processes. The levels of difficulty and the relative mix of knowledge and processes are different for each module. This must be understood by staff and explained to students. Parallel and progressive modules of the same course vary quite markedly in the demands they make, so teachers are encouraged to explain the issues to students.
3   Many modules are based on relatively new subject areas so there has been a need to update careers guidance in these areas. The bald issue of unemployment has made this a highly pertinent consideration.
4   The modular system has allowed a greater breadth in the curriculum but constraints do exist. Modules are designed for approximately 18 students and major change from this damages the learning experiences for all the students. Thus availability of modules does remain a problem – for example, word processing has proved so popular that many students have to wait until the fifth year to find an available time.
5   Initiative and decision-making skills must be practised if they are to reach their optimum strength; teachers must provide the means for this to occur at a valid level.

Two strands in the process

Negotiation at Emrys ap Iwan is designed to be a two-strand participation of students, parents, coordinator and teachers (Figure 6.3). Negotiation operates via formal and informal methods. *Formal* negotiation involves

Figure 6.3

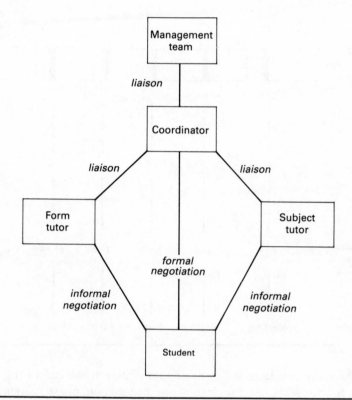

planned counselling sessions at which plans for future progress are finalised. *Informal* negotiation decribes a programme of on-going guidance within the teaching/learning situation.

Formal negotiation

Formal negotiation with the coordinator for modular courses takes place at intervals corresponding to the need for selection of modules (Figure 6.4). The negotiation occurs a few weeks before the end of a module so that groups can be formulated and problems resolved. This negotiation is considered formal in that the agreement reached between the coordinator and student will lead to an implementation recognised within the school as a whole.

Figure 6.4   Time plan of formal negotiation process

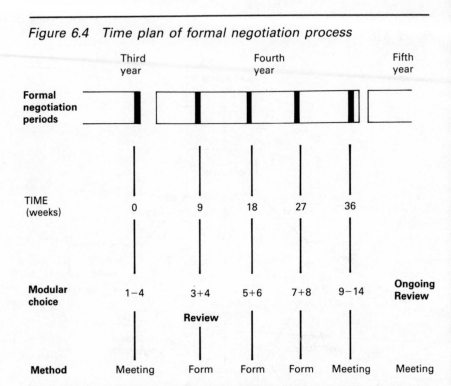

	Third year		Fourth year			Fifth year
Formal negotiation periods						
TIME (weeks)	0	9	18	27	36	
Modular choice	1–4	3+4	5+6	7+8	9–14	**Ongoing Review**
		Review				
Method	Meeting	Form	Form	Form	Meeting	Meeting

There are two large scale negotiation phases at the end of the third and fourth years. At the first major negotiation phase, parents are invited into school to discuss courses and careers guidance with their children and the course coordinators. This follows a parents' evening at which subject tutors give a resumé of the students' achievements and discuss educational and vocational opportunities. Students initially select 4 modules, two of which they will pursue as modules 1 and 2. (The coordinator uses this principle of two from four to accommodate fifth-year selections.) Enquiry is made by a proforma to parents and students, checking whether the choice of modules 3 and 4 has been changed, near to the time of completion of modules 1 and 2. Similarly modules 5+6 and modules 7+8 are chosen by form. The coordinator checks carefully the implications of choices but, due to the thorough counselling, students are very responsible in their choices. Subject and form tutors provide informal counselling throughout the two years.

Before the end of the summer term in the fourth year, parents and students are invited to an interview with the coordinator to discuss the final six course modules. This is an important session in which students must resolve their modules into viable accreditation outcomes. To some extent this is the end of the formal negotiation process because constraints within the school demand that groups are formed and arrangements made for the year so that accreditation can materialise. However, in some cases changes are made in the fifth year by request of students and parents.

The coordinator undertakes most of the formal negotiation process. She is assisted by other staff but the level of understanding of students and parents is such that most attend meetings with a clear idea of their selection, thereby reducing her workload.

The format of this negotiation involves either

- the student and parent meeting the coordinator using the subject teachers' recommendations;

or

- the student and parent completing a form which the coordinator checks.

The process of the meeting is shown in Figures 6.5 and 6.6.

The plan of the meeting suggests a rather dry diagnostic session but this is far from the truth. The coordinator's experience and interpersonal skills lead to a valuable counselling session which has been praised by parents and students. The coordinator's enemy is time, so, to overcome this, information on module and courses is structured and put on computer. This allows the implications of decisions to be seen immediately, giving more time for discussion. As might be expected the majority of students are clear about their choices and 'contracts' are drawn up promptly. Students who are uncertain about their futures have more problems and are given more opportunity for guidance. Most students are encouraged to take a few courses which do not lead to accreditation as this is felt to be a more balanced approach, particularly as up to 11 GCSE courses could be attempted under the core/modular system. Thus a little flexibility is introduced when courses such as Leisure and Psychology are introduced into the framework.

The process of *formal negotiation* demands particular skills of the coordinator:

- good interpersonal skills;
- time for liaison, guidance and administration;
- computer skills;
- administrative skills;
- skills in educational and vocational guidance.*

---

* For further information regarding the processes of negotiation see Appendices 1–5 (pp 116–21).

Figure 6.5   The formal negotiation process

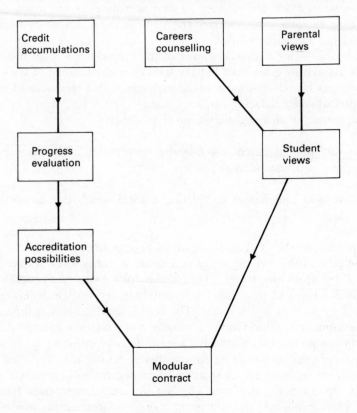

Informal negotiation

Informal negotiation takes place with two main groups of teachers – *form tutors* and *subject tutors* (Figure 6.7).

Form tutors, as part of their pastoral role, take a keen interest in the progress of their students and liaise with other staff over problems such as absence through illness. The form tutor often acts as a back-up to the module coordinator by providing a greater knowledge of the student and more time for informal counselling. Form tutors have been found to be the best people to liaise with parents, coordinator and subject tutors over problems such as absence. Sometimes pupils repeat a module or complete remedial work at home; the form tutor arranges this and monitors the views of all the parties.

Figure 6.6

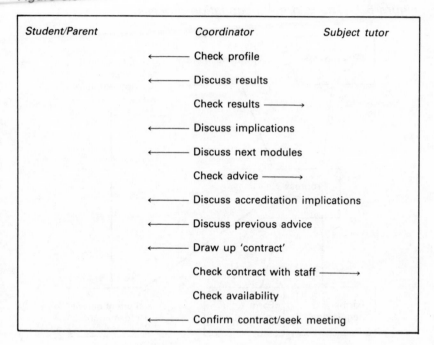

It has been found beneficial for students to discuss their modular choices with the form tutor before a more formal interview with the coordinator. This saves time, while giving the tutor a greater insight into the views of the student. Similarly, within the tutor group setting, pupils are given opportunities to discuss with other students their experiences of different courses.

The skills informal negotiation demands of the *form tutor* include:
• good interpersonal skills;
• time for liaison, guidance and administration;
• knowledge of the modular system;
• skills in educational and vocational guidance.

Subject tutors are clearly the experts in analysing the progress of their students within a field of study, but it is considered vital in Emrys ap Iwan that the student is involved in his or her own self-assessment. Assessments are recorded on various types of profiles with the student present (Figure 6.8). Students are given the opportunity to query this assessment and certainly benefit from an intimate knowledge of standards expected. They are made fully aware of their progress at all stages of

Figure 6.7 The informal negotiation process

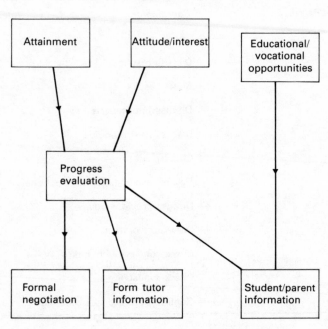

a module, and of their tutor's interpretation of their attitude and personal qualities. Student responsibility for their own learning is at the heart of this approach. They rapidly become aware of the fact that they are responsible for the pace and quality of their öwn work.

The coordinator is then informed of the views of the subject tutors regarding the suitability of different pathways for each student. This acts as a valuable guide for pathways involving modules of increasing difficulty. The coordinator checks the negotiated choices with the subject tutors to ensure that no problems arise.

There is an element of the subject tutor/student interaction which might be termed formal in that profiles – as records of assessment – are completed. Though these are the property of the student they can provide parents and employers with valuable information.

Informal negotiation demands of the *subject tutor*:

- good interpersonal skills;
- good knowledge of the attainment and attitude of each student;
- a changed pedagogy allowing student responsibility;

Figure 6.8 Student's assessment profile

Name .... Module no: ....

Form .... Date: ....

ELECTRONICS INTRODUCTORY

	Basic Level			High Level
RECALL AND COMPREHENSION OF COMPONENTS	Can recognise and name most common electronic components	Understands the behaviour resistors as current limiters, capacitors as charge stores. ICS and transistors.	Understands the action of some simple IC's a transistor as a switch	Can recall circuit diagrams and can introduce new systems by combining circuit elements
MANIPULATIVE SKILLS	Can build simple circuits from diagrams on proto board	Can build simple circuits on matrix board using soldering	Can assemble circuits on PCB	Can construct complicated circuits on 'Vero board'
INTERPRETIVE SKILLS	Can use a logic probe to identify 'I' and 'O' digital circuits	Can use a test meter to check voltages	Can use an oscilloscope to display square waves	Can use oscilloscope and a function generator to measure the air of an op. amp
ANALYSIS AND COMPUTATION	Can express numbers in binary form	Can use resistor colour code to calculate resistor value	Can calculate gain of op. amp from experimental results	Can infer relationships for gain of op. amp from experimental results
PERCEPTIVE SKILLS	Can follow a pictorial diagram in order to make a system	Can construct circuits from layout diagrams for PCB	Can realise circuits directly from circuit diagrams	Can realise systems needing only block diagrams
DEDUCTIVE SKILLS	Can make simple routine checks on non working systems	Can check for simple assembly/mechanical faults in system	Can infer faults in components from system behaviour	Can use test requirement to check a non working system, suggest solutions and implement cure
PROBLEM SOLVING	Can implement a suggested solution to a problem	Can select the better of two suggested solutions	Can suggest a possible solution to a problem	Can suggest several possible solutions and select the best and implement it
SYNTHESIS SKILLS	Can suggest components needed to complete a system	Can modify simple systems by changing input/output devices	Can combine circuit building blocks to meet a . specification	Can combine and modify circuits to meet a design specification
CIRCUIT ANALYSIS	Can recognise the action of components in a simple system	Can understand a simple system and explain its action	Can explain the action of components within a complicated circuit	Can understand the action of complicated circuits and their interaction
APPLICATIONS	Can appreciate the performance of a system within the classroom	Can appreciate a practical application of a simple system	Can appreciate a commercial application of a system	Can appreciate a range of practical commercial applications of several systems

Ysgol Emrys ap Iwan, Abergele   Total score out of 40 ☐

- time for liaison, guidance and administration;
- knowledge of the modular system;
- skills in educational and vocational guidance.

The implications of negotiation

For management

The modular innovation has raised many management issues. It was essential for the preactive conditions for this increase in student responsibiity to be sound. Priorities were: structured liaison between participants; on-going communication to all staff, students and parents; and encouragement for the development of student/tutor interaction.

Staff interpersonal skills were good in the school as a whole but the practice of negotiation has meant that a new warmth and understanding has developed between students and staff.

Negotiation of student pathways has caused surprisingly few problems, however, the members of the management team are aware of the goodwill of the staff which contributes so greatly to the success of the negotiation. Of course, an authoritarian management approach would be inapplicable in an environment in which students are given more responsibility. Thus a genuinely democratic atmosphere needs to exist at all levels.

For staff

The staff within Ysgol Emrys ap Iwan have responded positively to demands for a major change in role. They have become increasingly involved in the process of counselling and handing over responsibility for decision-making to the students. The teaching process has been altered to provide for a student-centred approach so that students have been able to practise making important learning decisions as well as those involved in negotation of modules. The process of negotiation appears to grow as students and teachers enjoy its benefits.

It is felt that handing over responsibility for modular choices has enhanced the motivation of students and thus increased the enjoyment of teaching. The teachers are closer to the 'culture' of the student and thus gain in understanding.

For students

The students are generally more involved in their education since the introduction of the modular curriculum. Their opinions and needs have been given a new status – allowing control and, therefore, responsibility to be adopted for their learning. They are gaining expertise in making important decisions and learning to live with their errors. Some students feel more committed to their modular courses than their core subjects and this is reflected in their attitude. The short-term goal of the module appears more tangible to some students, a fact which has implications for pedagogy in all subject areas.

For parents and community

Parents are well aware of the increased maturity of their children and welcome opportunities to meet staff in the process of negotiation.

Parents have found the modular system more confusing than the previous option system; it has therefore been found necessary to provide a very thorough analysis of the system for parents to keep at home in the form of a booklet *Decisions 14+*.

The Welsh Joint Education Committee has been responsible for the accreditation of modular courses which now include unit accreditation. They have responded to the needs of negotation by allowing a five year period in which students can gain sufficient credits for a GCSE qualification.

Local employers have recognised the maturity of the students leaving Emrys ap Iwan. The young people are motivated and experienced in being held responsible for their own actions. The Clwyd Record of Achievement given to each student is a means of providing employers with this information.

The way forward

The staff at Ysgol Emrys ap Iwan are of the opinion that it would be unwise to extend the modular curriculum downwards, into the first three years of the school. We feel that there is a body of knowledge and processes which each person needs to master before adult life. However, the processes of negotiation and decision-making should not be lost in these years but should based on the learning outcomes and learning processes within the teaching groups.

It is felt that negotiation – formal and informal – is a part of the way of life of the school. The ethos has changed; students are making their own decisions. They have started to negotiate their future.

Bibliography

Bernstein, B in *Education for Democracy* Rubenstein and Stoneman, 1970, Penguin.

Hargreaves, D H *Interpersonal Relations and Education*, 1972, Routledge and Kegan Paul.

Tomlinson, P *Understanding Teaching. Interactive Educational Psychology*. 1981, McGraw-Hill.

Appendices

Appendix 1   Letter to parents at end of fifth year

CLWYD COUNTY COUNCIL.

Tel: Abergele (0745)822287

Cyf./Ref.

Prifathro/Headmaster
Bruce Pyart, B.Ed.,M.Ed.,B.Phil.

CYNGOR SIR CLWYD

YSGOL EMRYS AP IWAN
ABERGELE
CLWYD
LL22 7HE

8 April 1986

Dear Parent/Guardian

Your son/daughter will shortly have completed his/her
third pair of additional study units. It is now time
to choose the last two of the current school year.

A list of additional study units to be offered in
the next session (beginning Tuesday 6 May) is attached.
I would be grateful if after discussion with your
son/daughter the completed form could be returned
by Friday 11 April. Should you encounter any difficulties
Mrs Smith will be available to give advice.

Before the end of the summer term all Form 4 pupils
will be interviewed in order to prepare their courses
for Form 5. Each pupil will be made aware of which
courses lead to qualifications and will be advised
on planning accordingly. Parents are encouraged to
attend these interviews and further details will be
sent out in early June.

Yours sincerely

B Pyart
Headmaster

Appendix 2 Proforma for selection of modules 5 and 6

ADDITIONAL STUDY UNITS
FORM 4   MODULES 5 & 6

TICK TWO BOXES IN COLUMN 'A' and TWO BOXES IN COLUMN 'B'

COLUMN 'A' Monday/Tuesday		COLUMN 'B' Thursday/Friday	
COMPUTING 2		ADDITIONAL MATHS	
ELECTRONICS 2		ART 2 (once only)	
HISTORY 2		COMPUTING 2	
INFORMATION SYSTEMS		ELECTRONICS 2	
Language for Business JAPANESE		ELECTRONIC MUSIC 2	
& Tourism			
LEISURE		FOOD TECHNOLOGY 1	
MINI COMPANY		HOME MAINTENANCE	
PARENT CRAFT		INFORMATION SYSTEMS	
PSYCHOLOGY		INTERVIEW TECHNIQUES	
TECHNICAL GRAPHIC ART		MINI COMPANY	
TYPEWRITING1		PE 2 (once only)	
TYPEWRITING2		PHOTOGRAPHY	
WELSH2 (once only)		PRACTICAL OFFICE SKILLS	
WORD PROCESSING		TELEVISION PRODUCTION	
		WORD PROCESSING	

NAME ....   FORM ....

ANSWER THE FOLLOWING QUESTIONS *BEFORE* YOU
COMPLETE YOUR CHOICES.

You must NOT choose

INFORMATION SYSTEMS
TYPEWRITING1
WORD PROCESSING

Do you take
BUSINESS SYSTEMS?   ⬆ YES   ⇨ NO   ANSWER NEXT QUESTION

You must NOT choose

PHOTOGRAPHY
TV PRODUCTION
SOUND BROADCASTING

Do you take
MEDIA SYSTEMS?   ⬆ YES   ⇨ NO   ANSWER NEXT QUESTION

You must NOT choose

FOOD TECHNOLOGY 1
HOME MAINTENANCE

Do you take
FOOD & HOME
TECHNOLOGY?   ⬆ YES   ⇨ NO   TICK MODULE CHOICES

Student's signature ....   Date ....

To be returned by Wednesday 21st January 1987.

Appendix 3   *Proforma for selection of modules 9–14*

FIFTH FORM INTERVIEWS   June 1986

Name of pupil ....   Form .... Date ....
                                                          Interviewer ....

GEC COMBINED SYLLABUS EXAMINATIONS

BUSINESS SYSTEMS   ☐   CITY & GUILDS   ☐
COMPUTING & COMMUNICATIONS   ☐
MEDIA SYSTEMS   ☐

Monday/Tuesday	Thursday/Friday
BOOK-KEEPING	ARCHAEOLOGY 3
COMPUTING 1	ART 2
COMPUTING 3	COMMUNITY RELATIONS
DRAMA 3	COMPUTING 1
ELECTRONICS 1	COMPUTING 3
EXTRA PHYSICAL SCIENCE 1	ELECTRONICS
FOOD TECHNOLOGY 1	ELECTRONICS 3
INTERVIEW TECHNIQUES	ELECTRONIC MUSIC
INFORMATION SYSTEMS	ENGINEERING
LANGUAGE FOR BUSINESS & TOURISM (Russian)	FRENCH 3
LEISURE	HOME GARDENING (Horticulture)
MINI COMPANY	HOME MAINTENANCE
MUSIC 3	INFORMATION SYSTEMS
PHOTOGRAPHY	LEISURE
PSYCHOLOGY	MINI COMPANY

Appendix 3   Cont.

SOUND BROADCASTING	PHOTOGRAPHY
TECHNICAL GRAPHIC ART	PRACTICAL OFFICE SKILLS
TELEVISION PRODUCTION	STATISTICS
TYPEWRITING 1	TELEVISION PRODUCTION
TYPEWRITING 2	TEXTILES
WELSH 3	TYPEWRITING 1
WORD PROCESSING	TYPEWRITING 2
EXPERIENCE OF WORK	WORD PROCESSING
CHILD CARE & (Tech)	EXPERIENCE OF WORK
HOME TECHNOLOGY (Tech)	FOOD PREPARATION FOR CATERING (Tech)
PERSONAL GROOMING & FIRST AID T/F	MOTOR VEHICLE STUDIES (Tech)

MODS for November	Level 4 Mods from Feb 87		*Forecast of final 6 Mods (order not important)*
ART 3	ARCHAEOLOGY 4	MUSIC 4	1
CALCULUS	COMPUTING 4	WELSH 4	2
PARENT CRAFT	DRAMA 4	JAPANESE	3
SPANISH	ELECTRONICS 4		4
TYPEWRITING 3	FRENCH 4	Extra Physical Science 2	5 6

Appendix 4 Computer print-out of core courses

FORM 5E CORE STUDIES Sept 1985 – July 1987

REF NUMBER NAME	ENG	COMMUNICATIONS				MATHS	SCIENCE	TECHNOLOGY								BIOL SCI	STUDIES
	ENG SET	LANG	BUSINESS SYSTEMS IMF	POS	CST TY	MATHS SET	SCIENCE SET	T	MEDIA SYSTEMS PHO	TGA	TVP	FOOD & HOME TECHNOLOGY HG	HM	LAY		BIOL SCI	HUMAN STUDIES SET
5E601 DAVIES Tracy Tina	M	FR				3	PSC-P									BSC	HI-B
5E602 EDEN Nicola Jayne	M		1	2	3	2	PSC-P					2	3	1			GG-B
5E603 EVANS Linda Mary	Y	FR				2	PSC-P					3	1	2			GG-A
5E604 GYVES Annette	E	GE				1	PSC-P									BSC	EC
5E605 HANNAM Ruth Alison	S	W				4	BSC		3	1	2						HI-C
5E606 JILGE Denise Helen	R	GE				2	PSC-J	T								BSC	GG-B
5E607 JONES Beverley Ann	M	FR				5	GSC		3	1	2						HI-C
5E608 JONES Pamela Susan	M	GE				1	PSC-P									BSC	EC

Appendix 5 Computer print-out of modular courses

FORM 5E

ADDITIONAL STUDY UNITS

Sept 1986

REF NUMBER	NAME	1	2	3	4	5	6	7	8	9	10	11	12	13	14	MODE 3 BSy	16+ MSy	CCn	C & G
5E601	DAVIES Tracy Tina	TY1	GST1	INT	INF	TY2	WP	EL1	POS	BKG	CRS	INF	TY3			YES			
5E602	EDEN Nicola Jayne	AR1	PSY	DR1	BSC1	LE	ARC	AR2	ARC2	CC	ARC3	BKG	AR3			YES	YES		365
5E603	EVANS Linda Mary	CST1	INF	TY1	POS	MCO	WP	TY2	CRS	FT1	FP	FT1	TY3			YES			YES
5E604	GYVES Annette	INF	POS	TY1	RO	AR1	MCO	TY2	LE	XPSI	AR2	WP	TY3			YES			
5E605	HANNAM Ruth Alison	MU1	PSY	DR1	EMU	MU2	PSY	TY1	EMU	MU3	TY2	CC	CRS				YES		
5E606	JILGE Denise Helen	MU1	TY1	WP	POS	TY2	TEX	INF	PHO	FT1	FP	BKG	TY3			YES			YES
5E607	JONES Beverley Ann	MU1	TY1	DR1	POS	CST1	PSY	DR2	MCO	DR3	CRS	CC	EXP				YES		YES
5E608	JONES Pamela Susan	INF	TY1	FR1	WP	AR1	TY2	FR2	LE	XPS1	FR3	BKG	AR23			YES			YES

7 Modular developments and the pastoral curriculum

Edward Goodhew

The term 'pastoral curriculum' was first used by Michael Marland in 1980 in his chapter in *Perspectives on Pastoral Care* to describe 'those items ... which are essential for the personal growth of individuals, for their learning growth, and are not there mainly because it is part of the logic of a subject.'[1] The concept thus expressed was that of a curriculum aspect to pastoral care, an aspect which had been increasingly evident, both in writings about and the practice of pastoral care.

Background

Blackburn[2] has shown how the development of pastoral systems during the past 40 years has been much influenced by the growth of the comprehensive school. In the early 1950s the size of the new schools (up to around 2000 pupils) posed three major problems:

1   It was easy for the individual to become 'lost' in such a large school, as distinct from the smaller, with its more intimate atmosphere, so pastoral staff and tutors were given responsibility to ensure that every child was known by someone who was concerned with his or her welfare. One way of providing this contact was by dividing the school into 'Houses'. The new systems suffered, however, from the fact that these 'Houses' were up to four times larger than those in the public schools, from which the system had been copied, and that the tutor's role was often not adequately defined. Certainly,

[1] Marland, M 'The pastoral curriculum' in Best, Ribbins and Jarvis *Perspectives on Pastoral Care* Heinemann, 1980, p 156.
[2] Blackburn, K *Head of House, Head of Year* Heinemann, 1982, pp 3–7

the tutor was not given any curriculum role, being largely expected to mark the register and to respond to individual concerns as they arose. In-service training for this role was conspicuously lacking.

2   Larger schools meant increasing amounts of administration. Much of this was conveniently passed through the form tutor as he or she was the only person who could be guaranteed to see a particular group regularly. Administration thus became an important part of pastoral care.

3   Larger schools also presented potential discipline problems. Best, Ribbins and Jarvis[3] have suggested, for example, that pastoral care may be 'a consciously evolved device for managing a potentially explosive situation'. As a consequence of the increasing size of schools, mixed ability teaching, ROSLA, option schemes, the proliferation of examinations, and the fact that recaltricant pupils were now a feature of most schools and classes, not just the 'D' stream in the secondary modern, it was important that efficient administration and discipline should go together. The 'House master' and, later, Year Head, often took on a 'trouble-shooting' role, being seen as a disciplinary figure whose job was as much to 'back up' other staff as it was to concern him- or herself with pupil welfare.

These three concerns were perfectly legitimate but the effort to respond to them placed a great burden on the pastoral systems in schools, unrelated to welfare as such. Certainly, curriculum was not considered the concern of pastoral staff, except in so far as they may have been needed to explain the timetable to parents and pupils.

The raising of the school leaving age in 1973, and the consequent development of elaborate option schemes, meant that a much greater emphasis was put on educational and vocational guidance, to ensure that children chose their subjects carefully. Careers departments were created, with the emphasis largely on individual guidance, although programmes of careers education were developed. In some, but not all, schools, pastoral staff were involved in this development. Along with this there was a growing interest in giving support to the increasing numbers of pupils who were identified as experiencing problems which were affecting progress at school. Counselling courses were set up to train staff to take on the role of school counsellor; the one-to-one counselling role of pastoral staff and the tutor became the predominant model.

Few of these developments involved any curriculum input, although developments in careers education increasingly focused

---

[3] *Ibid*, pp 11–12.

curriculum attention on 'self-awareness' and decision-making skills. It was Hamblin (1978) who attached a considerable curriculum responsibility to pastoral staff with his concept of 'critical incidents'.[4] Hamblin aimed to 'isolate points at which pupils are likely to affiliate with the school or dissociate from it' and to 'provide both the skills and perceptions which allow pupils to deal with these incidents constructively'. These 'critical incidents' he identified as being:

- *Entry into the comprehensive school* Curriculum content would include material on adjusting to new teaching situations, homework and study skills, coping with the expansion of social relationships, use of the pastoral care system itself etc.
- *The third year* Curriculum content would include group activities dealing with reasons for choice, cost of choices, nature of subjects, parental involvement etc.
- *The fifth year* Content would centre largely around study skills, effective revision strategies, methods for coping with anxiety and negative feelings. The curriculum would also concern itself with helping pupils to make decisions at 16 plus.
- *Entry into the sixth form* This would involve an induction programme, understanding new demands, study skills, group guidance sessions and, later, preparation for careers and higher education.

These 'critical incidents' were to form the basis for a properly planned curriculum, related to the development of the individual and to the possibilities for learning provided by the school organisation itself. The curricular and pastoral were thus to be integrated, with pastoral staff taking particular responsibility for organising the curriculum area related to these 'critical incidents'. This is the most recent stage identified by Blackburn, that of pastoral care 'contributing to pupils' learning experiences'.

Hamblin's scheme was for a *syllabus*, to be the concern of the pastoral staff and taught mainly, by implication, in tutorial time. The *Active Tutorial Work* books[5] and Leslie Button's *Group Tutoring for The Form Tutor*[6] were also based on this idea. Marland's pastoral *curriculum* was meant to be a broader concept in that he proposed that it would appear across the whole curriculum.

---

[4] Hamblin, D *The teacher and pastoral care*, Blackwell, 1978, p 19.
[5] Baldwin, J and Wells, H *Active Tutorial Work* (1–5) Oxford, Blackwell 1979.
[6] Button, L *Group Tutoring for the Form Teacher* (1,2) London, Hodder and Stoughton, 1981/2.

Marland argues that it is impossible to focus on individual help and guidance without considering the curriculum content that lies behind it. He proposes that every school should create a pastoral curriculum to establish the concepts, attitudes, facts and skills which are necessary to the individual; the individual client would then bring these to the counselling session. There would never be sufficient time for all pupils in a school to have all the necessary guidance given individually. Unless we have an agreed background curriculum, he argues, we are dependent on children having crises before we can offer them any help, by which time it might be too late. This means that to rely too heavily on pastoral care given individually is actually a let-down for the majority of children. The crisis-response model of pastoral care leaves the majority to their own devices. For Marland, a school must find ways of preparing for the expected needs, following up the discovered needs, and providing the necessary basis for the personal seeking of advice. As he puts it, 'The art of the pastoral system is to help all individuals without always giving individual help'.

This pastoral curriculum would be taught not simply by tutors, but also by subject teachers and specialist departments, such as Careers. The idea is to move from a crisis-centred approach to a more anticipatory and educational approach. Marland suggested that the content of this pastoral curriculum might usefully be gathered under three headings:

1 **Personal** eg

- the self: temperament, personality, needs;
- how to assess, understand and cope with physical and emotional well-being;
- the individual in relation to family, neighbours, friends;
- getting on with others – interpersonal skills;
- rights and obligations, decision-making;
- recreation and leisure, hobbies, etc.

2 **Educational** eg

- the school as an organisation, study skills, subject choice, the examination system, other educational agencies, newspapers, magazines, broadcasts, museums;
- the sharing of educational experience in the tutor group;
- helping pupils use feedback.

3 **Vocational** ie careers education, which is often organised around the themes of self-awareness; opportunity awareness; decision-making; transition learning.

These suggestions were in no way meant to be exhaustive; it would be up to the staff in each school to consider what the programme might contain.

Chris Watkins[7] suggests that the areas of the pastoral curriculum might usefully be considered under the following headings:

- bodily self
- sexual self
- social self
- vocational self
- moral/political self
- self as learner
- organisational self

The first five could relate to Health Education, Sex Education, Social Education, Careers Education, Moral Education and Political Education. The latter two relate to how the individual organises himself/herself for study and life generally.

Watkins also suggests seven possible 'locations' for the pastoral curriculum:

1 Tutorial programmes
2 Specialist guidance lessons
3 Subject lessons
4 Extra-timetable activities
5 Residential experience; work experience
6 Para-curriculum/hidden curriculum/informal curriculum of class-room and school life
7 Links to the community

To these could be added the use of assembly time.

Process

It could be argued that much of this says little that is new; most of it has featured in social education programmes in the past, particularly those for the 'less able'. There are, however, important differences:

- it is for *all* pupils;
- there is substantial involvement of pastoral staff in the planning and

---

[7] Watkins, C 'Does Pastoral Care Equal Personal and Social Education?' in *Pastoral Care in Education*, Vol 3, No 3 pp 179–83.

implementation of the programme;
- even so, it appears in all areas of school life;
- it makes explicit, and therefore amenable to monitoring, what was often implicit and unplanned;
- the concentration on the development of skills and attitudes as well as the learning of facts has implications for teaching method. Skills have to be practised if they are to be acquired and retained; the teaching strategies used, therefore, need to include a considerable amount of activity-based learning in order to allow these skills to be developed. The *process* becomes an important part of the pastoral curriculum. As Watkins puts it: 'Educational programmes which aim to promote self-knowledge and skills and to offer personal guidance must be activity-based, person centred, engaging social and familial processes, cumulative and continuous'.[8]

An important point is that this pastoral curriculum needs to be carefully co-ordinated in any curriculum organisation. With numerous 'locations' possible, numerous teacher teams involved, and a curriculum which needs to extend across all pupils in all years, there is great potential for omission and repetition. This co-ordination and monitoring becomes all the more important if the notion of some degree of negotiated curriculum with pupils, a feature of most modular schemes, is accepted.

Modular developments

Work of this kind can be greatly facilitated by the use of modules, and here a variety of alternatives are at a school's disposal.

Modular specialist courses

Schools have increasingly adopted Personal and Social Education as a planned course in the fourth and fifth years and these courses have often been planned on a modular basis. In one school, for example, seven-week modules have been developed on *The family, Study skills, Computer literacy, Design, First aid, Health education, Politics, Local government* and *Equal opportunities*. Lesson length is a single 35-minute period and it is doubled up with a lesson of careers education, organised in modules on *self-assessment, using the careers library, decision-making, applications and interviews, personal finance, leisure,*

---

[8] Watkins, *op cit* p 182.

industrial relations and *taxation and benefits*. The course also includes *JIIG-CAL*, the computer-assisted learning program designed to help youngsters to consider a variety of careers. Each double period, therefore, has an element of 'specialist' careers education, plus a cross-curricular social education topic; both are usually, but not always, taught by the same teacher.

This scheme has certain advantages. As each module is clearly defined and prepared, each one can be evaluated at the end, and the same module can be taught by the same teacher each half term. However, the scheme can be somewhat complicated in that, for example, it is not always convenient or desirable to switch to 'careers' after a period of social education. It is also possible that such a 'rag bag' can lack coherence; on the other hand it does ensure that topics considered desirable are covered. One problem, however, is that, as with linear subjects, there are parts of the course which ought to appear at certain times in a child's development. It makes little sense, for example, for self-assessment to turn up for one group at the end of the fourth year, or for 'application procedures' to come after pupils have already applied for, and often obtained, jobs. Similarly with *JIIG-CAL*, it is desirable that all pupils should do this at about the same time. The modular design can here be seen to be in conflict with the developmental nature of careers education, which attempts to help pupils in their vocational development.

Clearly the modular scheme taught as a specialist subject has to take account of the developmental nature of personal and social growth. It can do this by having a core of modules done at particular times, with the others organised around them. Around this core, modules can be developed which, if adequately staffed, allow for choice and therefore negotiation. In the course outlined above, for example, an introductory module on self-assessment, done by all at the same time, can be followed by a choice of other modules, returning to *JIIG-CAL* for all, followed by other modules, and so on. The uniting theme is the teaching methodology, as activity-based teaching approaches are used to develop personal and social skills.

If carefully structured, this modular approach can allow for consider-able flexibility and the use of individual teachers' expertise, while taking into account the developmental needs of the pupils. It can thus be a very effective and efficient way of delivering this type of course.

Tutorial courses

Tutorial courses are often organised in modules which may encompass subjects such as *Friendship, Bullying, Homework, Leisure, Health education* etc. These modules may be developed by individual teachers, usually for all tutors in the year group to use. It is less usual for such programmes to be organised so that pupils can opt into them, but there is potential for modules to be developed in this way. Most schools have teams of tutors and some non-tutors attached; these can be organised so that different tutors and attached non-tutors offer a selection of modules for the pupils to opt for. It will then be possible for a variety of modules to be developed and 'banked', leaving the flexibility for tutors to teach a number of different modules if desired, or to concentrate on one or two, repeating these with different groups in the year.

If the latter course is chosen, with tutors concentrating on teaching and repeating one or two modules, there needs to be a reasonable amount of time allowed for both the tutorial lessons and for the other functions which a tutor performs, otherwise it could be argued that the tutor will not get to know tutees well enough. On the other hand there is potential for the tutee to be known well by one member of staff, who keeps an overview, and fairly well by other tutors in the year group. If staff move up with their tutor groups this can help lead to a cohesive Year/House group based on mutual support. Again, modules that are deemed to be necessary at particular times can be written in as the core, and this will ensure that each tutor does at least some work with his or her tutor group. This kind of administrative arrangement can also help to ensure that staff, and indeed management, give tutorial work due status. In the ordinary tutor lesson, pressure of administrative work can often take precedence over tutorial work, to the detriment of the course. A well structured modular tutorial work programme will, however, give it greater status and ensure that it does not give way to what may seem more pressing day-to-day problems.

Some examples of possible content for such schemes are given in Appendices 3 and 4 in Keith Blackburn's *Head of House, Head of Year;*[9] the examples given are the tutorial programmes of Bishop Douglass School, the Priory School, and Quintin Kynaston School. Each scheme is set out in a way that makes modular development possible. The Priory School, for example, organises its second year programme into eight topics:

1 School home
2 School life
3 Getting organised
4 Helping hand
5 Playing safe
6 Spare time
7 The body in question
8 Conflict.

---

[9] Blackburn, *op cit* pp 175–205.

Quintin Kynaston specifically sets out to ensure that topics are returned to at a later date, by organising their programme on a spiral basis, revisiting topics previously discussed. It is important that any modular structure should allow for this process.

These examples indicate that a well planned and structured tutorial programme can benefit from being organised on a modular basis, linking in with what happens elsewhere in the curriculum. It also allows for an element of pupil negotiation in the exact part of their curriculum where the process of negotiation is expected to be part of the learning. Started early in the school, it allows pupils to exercise real choice – but at a time when making the wrong choice is not so disastrous as it would be later. It thus helps to give pupils the kind of real experiences the pastoral curriculum is designed to offer.

'Experience' courses

Such courses lend themselves well to modular approches, since they are often already limited to a certain length of time at a particular time of year. A school may, for example, send all its fourth year out on work experience for two weeks in the middle of July. However, the module will involve more than the experience and may, in fact, be split into parts. At Langleywood School, in Berkshire, for example, where all fourth year pupils are sent out in the first week of July, preparation is done in April/May (job search, letters of application, interviews etc), based on the situations, and the period of work experience is followed up by a period of debriefing. Similarly, with community service and residential experience there will be preparation and debriefing, to ensure that the intended learning takes place.

It is probable, therefore, that such modules will be flexibly organised and spread over a period of time. It is equally possible' that the experience itself may be similarly spread – the community service module may, for example, take place every Wednesday. Within that, it should be possible to organise modules which allow for different experiences over that period of time. This is indeed the potential of the modular approach.

The pastoral curriculum and 'subject' lessons

The *Hargreaves Report*[10] suggested that Personal and Social Education must be part of the compulsory core in the fourth and fifth year of the secondary school and suggested a time allocation of $7\frac{1}{2}$% per week

---

[10]   Hargreaves, D *Improving Secondary Schools* ILEA, 1984.

for PSE and religious education. These PSE programmes would be devised to tackle what the report labels *Achievement aspects III and IV.*

Achievement aspect III includes 'the capacity to communicate with others in face to face relationships; the ability to co-operate with others in the interests of the group as well as the individual; initiative, self-reliance and the ability to work alone without close supervision; and the skills of leadership'. Public examinations tend to ignore this aspect, the report argues.

Achievement aspect IV 'involves motivation and commitment; the willingness to accept failure without destructive consequences; the readiness to persevere; the self-confidence to learn in spite of the difficulty of the task'. Such motivation is a pre-requisite to achievement but it can also be regarded as an achievement in its own right, the report says.

The writers of the report found much good practice in the ILEA schools they visited, but they pointed out three major problems:

1 Some aspects of this area are dealt with in some of the traditional subjects rather than as a distinct entity.
2 Some schools provide PSE as an alternative to academic courses leading to public examinations.
3 The relation between PSE in the formal curriculum and the use of tutorial time is often unclear.

All this can lead to severe fragmentation in various parts of the school timetable, lacking coherence for the pupil. The report recommends that there should be a course of study in PSE which is compulsory for all pupils in the fourth and fifth years, and which is carefully co-ordinated with the activities followed in tutor groups; that a senior member of staff should be given the responsibility for this co-ordination; that most departments should be involved in this compulsory course; and that PSE can be examined by the use of Mode 3 examinations, 'supported by appropriate methods of assessment and recording, perhaps by profiles or related methods'. This last recommendation was designed to ensure that the course was given 'due recognition' by pupils and parents, the feeling being that 'at all costs we must avoid the danger of creating courses of personal and social education which then suffer the fate of free-floating, inconsequential courses in "general studies"'. This PSE course is not to be conceived as a 'rag-bag of curricular loose-ends, but as a mechanism for making the total curriculum diet both more coherent as a whole, and more relevant to the individual pupil and the world in which he or she lives and will move after the age of 16'.

Allied to all of this the report suggested that there should be a greater emphasis on more active approaches to teaching and learning, with more social interaction, pupils collaborating over tasks in pairs or small groups, the teacher acting as a resource or consultant rather than solely as a purveyor of information.

The Hargreaves Report thus presents curriculum designers with considerable problems when it comes to the area of personal and social education. This area should be part of a balanced and coherent curriculum; it should involve all aspects of the curriculum, including tutorial work; it should be compulsory for all; and it should be capable of certification. In addition, it should be designed in a way that allows for the achievement of short-term goals, to aid motivation.

The suggested path to answering this problem was to design the fourth and fifth Year curriculum in half-term units, allowing the two-year course to be sub-divided into 11 or 12 interconnected units, each of which should be meaningful in itself and adapted to the time perspective of 14 year olds. Each unit would have clear course objectives and be open to a variety of assessment techniques. There would be more joint planning with pupils of methods and procedures of work. There would inevitably have to be more joint planning between departments and this would help (although the report does not mention this), to bring about a greater degree of co-ordination of the pastoral curriculum.

The *Hargreaves Report* does not advocate the development of the modular curriculum as such, but rather the development of short-term units which can be accredited for examination purposes. It does, however, prepare the ground for the potential development of a modular curriculum in which the pastoral curriculum is seen to be very much part and parcel of the public examination system, with assessment techniques being designed to demonstrate successes achieved (no-one should ever be allowed to 'fail' lifeskills!). Elements of what is learned through the pastoral curriculum will thus be included on a record of achievement which may also include records of examinations, graded tests and other experiences too.

Cross-curriculum activities

A general pattern adopted by some schools is to have a core of personal and social education, which may or may not be assessed, and the opportunity to extend that core in other areas of the curriculum. For example, at Peers School, Oxford, all pupils take the Community Studies programme in which two of the five sessions (in a 20 session week) have been used for a core course in PSE. The Oxford TVEI scheme involves all students taking modules for three TVEI courses – *Science and technology, Services to people, Business studies* – and what is called the *Integrating programme*. The *Integrating programme* includes counselling, guidance, careers advice and work experience, communications, information technology, problem solving and practical projects, as well as visits and residential-type experience – all aspects of the pastoral curriculum.

Another example is to be seen in the Humanities curriculum of Lipson School, Plymouth. The school has a core of personal and social education for all and this can be extended in the humanities by taking modules such as *Marriage and the family, Work and employment, Birth and childhood* etc. It could be argued that such topics could be done in the conventionally organised curriculum, but there is greater potential here for pupils to take modules which they would otherwise not take as part of a two year course.

In order to integrate the scheme each module is expected to cover specific *contextual* and *conceptual* areas.

Contextual levels

The relationship of each chosen topic to:

- the individual;
- the community and local environment;
- the whole country or comparative studies within the country (the national scale);
- the whole world or comparative studies between countries (the global or international scale).

Conceptual levels

The relationship of each chosen topic to:

- power and distribution – the political dimension;
- ideas and ideologies – the moral dimension;
- spatial interaction – the geographical dimension;
- continuity and change – the historical dimension.

In both contextual and conceptual levels, therefore, the scheme displays much of what it has been argued earlier would be part of the pastoral curriculum. Since all pupils also have to do at least one enquiry-based project which must entail personal initiative and enquiry skills, and teaching method tends to be activity based, it could be argued that this Humanities scheme makes a great contribution to the pastoral curriculum, whichever modules are chosen. It is of interest to note that the *Hargreaves Report* did not suggest that history and geography should be compulsory, except as part of the personal and social core. Humanities is thus regarded as part of the pastoral curriculum.

In addition, at Lipson School, the next module does not have to be chosen until near the end of the previous one. This involves guidance and counselling, the making of real decisions, and negotiation on a regular basis. Linked to an assessment system which ensures greater pupil participation, the potential for personal growth and development is great. The pastoral curriculum must involve methodology as well as content and a Humanities scheme such as this, involving certain integrating principles, can make a strong contribution to it.

Two schools in Berkshire, Langleywood School and Baylis Court School, have jointly developed a Mode 3 Business studies course. They have found that this has had a direct effect on their personal and social education programmes. Finding that they were having to teach basic lifeskills in their *Business studies* modules, they have modified and transferred these modules, in *Information technology* and *Information skills*, to the social education programme, lower down the school. In this case, the modular GCSE course can be taught in the 4th Year in the confidence that it is building on skills developed through the pastoral curriculum in previous years.

Greendown School, in Swindon, referred to elsewhere in this book (pp. 68–69), is another school which attempts to integrate its pastoral curriculum with the academic, making no distinction between the two. Organised into three curriculum 'schools', one of which is called *Personal development* (incorporating recreation, life and social skills) the emphasis is on the process rather than content of learning. The school is new, with only a first year intake, and is developing a modular curriculum which emphasises links between areas of knowledge, which encourages children to organise their own work, use their initiative and develop independence of mind, without the restraint of traditional timetable organisation. Again many of the aims of the pastoral curriculum are being met through the organised curriculum of the school.

To examine or not?

The *Hargreaves Report*'s suggestion that the personal and social education core should be examined will cause misgivings for many teachers. David Hargreaves himself has argued (1982) that 'all the sixteen plus public examinations must be abolished'. However, the report acknowledges that public examinations are here for the foreseeable future; the more immediate concern was the lack of motivation and underachievement of pupils in the ILEA schools. The examination path was, therefore, the pragmatic suggestion. As suggested earlier, much of the pastoral curriculum will be examinable anyway, as part of the separate subjects. It would appear unwise, however, to formally examine all the pastoral curriculum; to appear to have to validate all work through examination would deny the principles which much of the pastoral curriculum is designed to teach. However, every pupil is entitled to some kind of assessment of performance in *all* areas of school work. Although it may be wrong to formally examine parts of the pastoral curriculum, work in this area does need recognition, and records of achievement are designed to provide this. A modular pastoral curriculum can give an impetus to the profiling movement, therefore.

Conclusion

This chapter began with an analysis of how 'pastoral care' gradually began to take on a curriculum aspect, after much discussion about a pastoral/academic split. There developed the concept of a pastoral curriculum, designed to help all pupils rather than those with problems. This came from a greater realisation that personal and social education was the responsibility of *all* teachers and that there is much that schools can do to help young people in their personal development. It became clear that this pastoral curriculum had two important facets – content and process – and that it could be found in all parts of the curriculum of the school, including the so-called 'hidden' curriculum and 'extra-curricular' activities. Many schools set up tutorial work and social education programmes as their pastoral curricular, but these were often isolated from the rest of the curriculum work and of low status. The advent of the modular idea, however, gave the potential for the pastoral curriculum to be given due recognition and properly integrated into the rest of the curriculum.

If one of the advantages of the modular curriculum is that it allows the flexibility for 'new' subjects to be integrated into the curriculum then this advantage can help the introduction of the pastoral curriculum in schools. Modular structures, involving as they do the identification of aims and objectives, content, teaching and assessment methods, make the co-ordination of the pastoral curriculum relatively more manageable and recognisable in the ordinary subject curriculum. Schools which have developed modular curricula have managed to develop them along recognisably 'pastoral' lines in terms of content, concepts, and methodology, with the potential for co-ordination with tutorial work, specialist guidance lessons, work experience, and the rest.

Equally, as with any other developments involving the modular curriculum, the potential is also there for an uncoordinated mixture which ignores vital aspects of learning for young people in schools. Much of the pastoral curriculum should ideally be taught as part of the 'ordinary' curriculum of the school. The modular curriculum can play a key role in ensuring that this happens and that, with careful planning, the aim of a properly co-ordinated pastoral curriculum is achieved.

8 Industrial links

Sidney M. Slater

Park Hall School is a coeducational 11–18 Group 12 Comprehensive School with approximately 1450 pupils. It is the largest school in the Authority and is situated in the Northern part of the Metropolitan Borough of Solihull.

Our catchment area covers both Castle Bromwich, an old-established but expanding residential area, and Chelmsley Wood, a large residential area of corporation and private housing. The school badge is one of the oldest Coats of Arms in the country. It bears the Arms of the Arden family, descendants of Turchil of Warwick, Earl of Warwick before the Norman Conquest. We have permission from the present Head of the Arden Family to wear the badge on our blazers.

The school has an excellent reputation in the local area and is known nationally for curriculum development in terms of science, technology and industrial links, having recently been visited by the Minister of State for Education.

The school curriculum has been the subject of much research, discussion, debate and interest over the years. However, little has changed in terms of content or delivery until very recently. We are now in a period of change within the education service, one where we are witnessing new examinations/notions of achievement; a more coherent approach to staff development; new forms of accountability; developments in evaluation and appraisal; new teaching styles and strategies; and (particularly relevant to this paper), curriculum innovations, including links with industry through TVEI. We in the education service must, therefore, ensure a positive and coherent approach to these developments.

Some have suggested that this could be achieved through a national curriculum and it is, perhaps, interesting to note that prior to the 1870 Education Act, the state in the form of the Board of Education laid down a broad framework of what elementary schools should teach. In 1904 clear guidelines for the school curriculum were also laid down in the Regulations for Schools issued by the Board of Education:

'The course should provide for instruction in English Language and Literature, at least one other language than English, Geography, History, Mathematics, Science and drawing, with due provision for manual work and Physical Exercises and in girls' schools for housewifery. Not less than 4½ hours per week must be allocated in English, Geography and History; not less than 3½ hours per week to a language when only one is taken or less than 6 hours when two are taken; and not less than 7½ hours to Science and Mathematics of which at least 3 must be for Science. The instruction must be both theoretical and practical. When two languages other than English are taken, and Latin is not one of them the Board will require to be satisfied that the omission of Latin is for the advantage of the school.'[1]

This tradition of stating subjects continued until 1926 within elementary schools. The secondary school sector was still broadly prescriptive until the 1944 Education Act. Ownership of the school curriculum then moved to the local education authority, schools and teachers. This remains the case today, subject to the provisions within the 1986 Education Act enhancing the rights of Governors and parents and any future decisions enacted through Parliament.

Curriculum and the economy

It is perhaps appropriate at this stage to review, briefly, the factors which had led to some of those educational developments mentioned earlier.

> The period from the mid 1940s to the 1960s was not only marked by expansion in the economy and increased investment in education but it was also a period of change in educational thought ... at the micro level.[2]

What constituted good or satisfactory curriculum development at this stage in the history of education was 'tinkering' with the system that had remained the same for decades. This 'tinkering' with the system remained with us into the 1970s, along with the parallel development of a more questioning approach to the whole school curriculum by professional educationalists and others. Readers will be aware of the work of Hirst, Lawton, Phenix, Peters, Schwab and White[3] which

---

[1] Board of Education 'Regulations for Secondary Schools' (1904) in Schools Council Working Paper 53: *The whole curriculum 13–16* Evans/Methuen Educational, 1975.

[2] Slater, S. 'Aspects of secondary education: an in-depth survey of curriculum and grouping procedures' M.Ed thesis, Brunel University, 1981.

[3] Hirst, P H 'The Logic of the Curriculum' in *Journal of Curriculum Studies*, 1969, 1, pp 142–158; Hirst, P H 'The Curriculum and its Objectives – A defence of Piecemeal Planning' in *Studies in Education, The curriculum*, the Doris Lee Lectures, University of London Institute of Education.

encapsulates this movement on behalf of the academic school. However 'others' were also drawn into this questioning promoted by the Great Debate formally started in the now famous Ruskin College speech by the then Prime Minister, James Callaghan, who emphasised that the debate should '. . . not be confined to those professionally concerned with education'.[4]

This was followed by a plethora of documents on the school curriculum issued by the Department of Education and Science, The Schools Council, and HMI. These influential documents and discussion papers emphasised a more coherent whole-school approach to the curriculum, yoked together by areas of experience within the framework. They also emphasised a new role for education in terms of its interface with the economy and the need to develop a greater recognition within the service of the role of 'others', including governors, parents and employers.[5]

A number of projects and organisations were also launched during this stage to bridge the gap between education and industry, for example, the Schools Council Industry Project (now the School Curriculum and Industry Partnership – SCIP); Understanding British Industry (UBI) – a CBI initiative; Project Trident. These directed attention towards work experience for school pupils. The Department of Education and Science was responsible for the Education (Work Experience) Act of 1973 which opened up and, therefore, encouraged the possibility of work experience for school pupils.

In 1981 the DES and Her Majesty's Inspectors gave some direction and impetus to the advantages of links with industry in *Schools and Working Life*. However, probably the two most important government agencies developing this area, not just by encouragement and exhortation but by finance, were the Department of Trade and Industry (DTI) and, perhaps more importantly, the Manpower Services Commission (MSC). The former helped local education authorities with developments in science and technology, but was particularly influential in helping to fund the setting up of School Industry Liaison Officers. The latter

---

Lawton, D. *Social Change, Educational Theory and Curriculum Planning*, London, University of London Press, 1973.

Phenix, P H *Realms of Meaning* New York, McGraw Hill, 1964.

Peters, R A *Ethics and Education* London, Allen and Unwin, 1966.

Schwab, J J 'The Practical 3: Transition into Curriculum' in *School Review* 81, 1973, pp 501–22.

White, J *Towards a Compulsory Curriculum* Routledge and Kegan Paul, 1973.

[4] DES *Education in schools: a consultative document* CMND 6869, London, HMSO, 1977.

[5] DES and Welsh Office 'A view of the Curriculum', HMI *Matters for Discussion*, HMSO, 1979; DES *Quality in schools: evaluation and appraisal* HMSO, 1985; DES and Welsh Office *Better Schools*, HMSO 1985.

launched the now well-established Technical and Vocational Education Initiative (1983) at an annual cost of £25 million. Readers will be aware that the extension phase for TVEI has recently been announced. This will be a scheme broader in its emphasis and engaging the whole of the 14–18 cohort.

Linking with industry

These financial inducements to link industry and education are clearly welcome. The education service has everything to gain and nothing to lose from such an Industry/Education partnership. We need, as educationalists, to accept the view that 'others' – in particular, our partners from industry – can help us to determine the shape of the curriculum. This does not mean that we forego or surrender our professional expertise, rather, we add to it. If we are to ensure that our curriculum in the secondary school is broad based, relevant, interesting, motivating, demanding and open to all, we must 'grasp the nettle' for it will not sting. Dr I. Jamieson identifies clearly the goal of such a partnership.

> It is important to have a clear view of the goals of industry–education work. We need a symbiotic relationship between the local infrastructure of business organisations and local educational institutions. This means a constant flow of people between the two systems – managers, workers, teachers and students. There might even be a modest flow of resources as well. Each has specialist equipment and personnel which could be useful to the other. We must recognise that the business of education is a lifelong one that does not stop with the end of school or college. We need to revitalise our conception of schooling. Students can learn many things out of school in local industry, and those working in the local economic community can do a great deal to educate the young.[6]

The Park Hall school and industry partnership

The Metropolitan Borough of Solihull, in which Park Hall School is situated, became part of the second round scheme of TVEI in 1984.

> The Metropolitan Borough of Solihull is proposing to introduce the pilot project for TVEI in seven schools and five broad subject areas. The areas are: Food Technology, Manufacturing Technology, Caring Services, Commerce and Business Studies, Media Technology.

---

[6] Jamieson, I, 'Industry and education: where we are' in Jamieson and Blandford (eds) *Education and change: can you afford to ignore it?* CRAC, 1986.

The first two years will be entirely schools based, the second two will involve the Solihull Sixth Form College, Solihull College of Technology and a Sixth Form in an 11–18 School, as is appropriate, bearing in mind the qualifications being sought by the young people involved.[7]

Park Hall School was successful in its bid to the Authority to become one of the participating TVEI schools offering *Manufacturing Technology*. However, prior to the official start, much planning and development work was undertaken. The first step involved the setting up of a steering group to advise on the structure of the new programme of study. (Throughout my teaching career I have sought, where appropriate, the assistance of industrialists. Indeed, it was some 14 years ago that I first started the planning/implementation of a Post-16 Business Studies course involving work experience placements.) The membership of the TVEI steering group was then to be biased towards industry.

Manufacturing technology 14–16

The time commitment to this phase is two extended mornings a week, a total of eight hours. During this time three major areas of study are undertaken which are all examined at GCSE level. These are: Physics, Modular Technology, Applied micro electronics and computing. The cohort is approximately 30 pupils per year group.

The steering group proposed the view that Physics should be a core element in the programme. This was accepted, and Modular Technology was identified by the staff at the school as the next area of study. However, problems arose within the group because there were no appropriate courses available which would link or yoke together Physics and Modular Technology, and provide an overview of computing, information technology and micro electronics. This prompted the school to create such a course. The steering group acted as consultants at each stage, finally suggesting the addition of an extra module on the economics/financial implications of new technology. This was accepted and is now included in the Course.

The 14–16 phase also includes two weeks of work experience in each year, meticulously planned and integrated into the course. Two one-week residential experiences to develop team-building skills and to enhance personal and social development, are also an essential integral part of the course. Each pupil is profiled and counselled throughout the four years of the programme.

---

[7] Metropolitan Borough of Solihull Department of Education *Technical and Vocation Initiative Project Outline*, 1983.

The external examination results have been most encouraging and the first cohort has now passed onto the Post-16 programme. Added to this success has been the positive feedback from the pupils, the enhanced staying on rate and increased employment opportunities. It is also interesting to note that much of the work on the 14–16 phase has been disseminated into the school. In particular, we now profile all our 4th and 5th Year pupils (approximately 600), and offer Applied Micro Electronics and Computing (APEC) and Modular Technology as options on our mainstream curriculum.

Technology and Management Science 16–18. Park Hall School and Land Rover Ltd

Detailed planning for the Post-16 element of the programme began at the beginning of 1985 when we were only a few months into the initiative. Building on firm foundations, initial discussions began within

---

Figure 8.1   General aims of the course in technology and management science

General aims of the course in technology and management science

A   To enable the students to understand and explore our industrial and technologically based society.

B   To enable students to develop skills and awareness in particular areas of manufacturing industry and commerce.

C   To help develop a range of transferable skills which will equip students for work in our technological society.

D   To enable students to achieve specific qualifications and skills which will better equip them for work in manufacturing industry and related areas.

E   To enable students to understand the economic implications of technology in industry and society.

F   To enable students to have first-hand experience of training, work experience and problem solving in manufacturing industry. (Land Rover Ltd.)

G   To move students from dependent learning to independent learning.

H   To develop initiative, motivation and enterprise amongs the students.

I   To enable students to become accustomed to using their skills and knowledge to solve the real world problems they will meet at work.

J   To enable students to acquire a more direct appreciation of the practical application of the qualifications for which they are working.

K   To assist students in the transition from school to work and on to Higher Education.

---

the steering group but later focused down to an in-depth dialogue with the Land Rover Ltd representative, Mr T. Hanley, Manager of Enhanced Technology. This led to a strong partnership being developed between the school and the company. A small steering group was set up specifically to develop the course, it included myself, Mr Hanley and the Manufacturing Director. The group met regularly, mainly out of company hours – in the early evening, weekends, holiday periods and lunchtimes.

Our first task was to draw up the aims of the two-year programme, bearing in mind the course time constraints of one day per week (see Figure 8.1). These general aims helped to guide our discussions on the proposed contents of the programme. It was decided early on in the discussions that the course structure would be modular in nature. Each module would have its own title, aims and objectives, skills/concepts/attitudes, teaching and learning styles, assessment/profiling methods and financial requirements. However, all the modules were to be integrated into the overall programme of study. Our major problem was that we had initially identified a possible 30 modules of study. At this stage we called other staff into the discussions as and when it was seen as expendient and relevant. Focusing on the present seven Year 1 modules proved to be difficult but stimulating and worthwhile. It allowed the group initially to develop an in-depth educational philosophy and then to engage others at school and company level in the initiative.

The seven modules finally selected were:

Management	Finance
Materials	Computer Aided Engineering
Data Management	Modern Languages and Industry
Workshop Practice	

These were based on the Manufacturing Industry as a whole rather than on the automative industry in particular.

It become clear that the writing of the seven modules would need to be a joint exercise requiring expertise at the technical and educational level. However, it also began to become clear to the group that there would be advantages in Land Rover staff helping to teach parts of the modules under discussion. The question was raised and met with a limited but positive response.[8]

Having identified the modular framework for Year 1 of the course, we set about recruiting interested personnel. At school level this involved our senior teacher (curriculum), five heads of department and a second

---

[8] Slater, S M "Delivering the goods" Education and Industry: a partnership in action' in *School Organisation* 1987, Vol 7, No 1, p 37.

in charge of a department. Land Rover Ltd engaged the support of two directors, three managers, a supervisor and two senior training officers. The team was later extended to include one Head of Faculty and Scale 1 teacher and two supervisors from Land Rover Ltd. In support was my head of sixth form and our TVE school co-ordinator. Each module then had a school/industry representative, each with particular skills linked to the module to be developed, eg the 'Finance module' team involved the Finance Manager from Land Rover Ltd and the Head of our Economics Department; the 'Materials module' involved our Head of Chemistry and the Manager of Materials Development, the 'Management Module' our senior teacher with the Manufacturing Director.[8] At this stage a bid was made to the MSC for additional financial support for this unique industry/education partnership. Assistance and support was readily available from the Authority's Project Director, Miss M Schofield, and from the Director of Education. The bid was successful and some additional funds were contracted to the school. The funds were to be used to finance a very limited amount of teaching supply time to release module writers *but* more importantly, to run two Residential Weekend Conferences.

The first Conference was held at the British Leyland Training/ Conference Centre at Studley in October, 1985. It was opened by the Director of Education for the Metropolitan Borough of Solihull.

The aims were:

- to develop mutual understanding/working relationships between staff at Land Rover Ltd and Park Hall School;
- to develop a greater mutual understanding of Park Hall School's TVE Course in Manufacturing Technology at the 14–16 level, and its position within the National TVE Programme;
- to work towards the development of the proposed Post 16 jointly validated course in 'Industrial Skills'.

At the end of the Conference, delegates were able to define more clearly the roles/responsibilities of their opposite numbers in the planning group; understand the present TVE programme at Park Hall and its relationship to the national picture, and identify the aims and objectives and brief content outline for the seven areas of work.

This excellent task-orientated working weekend forged exceptionally good working relationships between school and company staff which still exist and prosper today. The teams of staff were given an agreed time plan/schedule for returns to the steering group. These curriculum returns included: the aims and objectives of each module, the schemes of work, assessment procedures, teaching styles and strategies, time commitment/requirements and finally financial requirements. Figure 8.2 illustrates an abridged example of such returns.

The second Residential Conference was held six months later in April, 1986. The general aim of the Conference was to review the development of the Year 1 programme, to determine, in detail, student assessment procedures, to agree and timetable constraints, and, finally, to discuss the development of the Year 2 programme.

The Manager of Organisation and Personnel Planning led our discussions on student assessment procedures. Valuable insight was gained into the assessment procedures used in industry, subsequently an overall course profile was agreed based on the company profile. The profile is an accumulation of the already-agreed individual modular assessment procedures. By the end of the second Conference it was clear that commitment to joint teaching within the modules was assured, subject to staff availability. At the end of June all staff had been issued with the detailed schemes of work for each module. An evening planning meeting was held at Sans Souci, the Authority's Teachers' Centre, just before the end of the Summer Term to finalise plans for the start of the course in September; to discuss induction procedures; and to review Year 2 planning progress.

Course structure – the partnership

The course is now fully underway and we have already passed our mid-year review. The high expectations from both industry and education have clearly materialised. The students have already gained a great deal from the Year 1 course. Indeed, they are assisting us with constant feedback for revised course planning for next year. The course is clearly flexible and open to change. The partnership between education and industry has now extended to include the students. It has become a genuinely negotiated curriculum (Figure 8.3).

The present Post-16 cohort is 25 students who are following, in addition to the TVEI course in Manufacturing Science and Technology, a range of advanced and non-advanced courses (Figure 8.4).

The Year 1 programme of seven compulsory modules has been jointly designed and is jointly taught and assessed (Figure 8.5).

The Year Two programme allows students to opt for areas of particular interest while maintaining the core elements of Manufacturing Technology and either Computer Aided Engineering or Workshop practice (Figure 8.6). Students who follow the programme are also involved in an integrated programme of work experience, industrial visits, work shadowing, residential team-building experiences and careers counselling.

Figure 8.2   Management skills module

Mr R. Dover, Managing Director
Mrs E. Tomkins, Senior Teacher

Aims

1   To enable students to develop and practise group based problem-solving skills in competitive environments.

2   To develop students' awareness and understanding of the driving forces in business and management.

3   To enable students to understand and practise management skills and to apply them in individual and group situations.

Objectives

1   At the end of the Module students should have a basic understanding of:
i) problem-solving skills
ii) the business environment
iii) marketing
iv) the duties of management

2   At the end of the Module students should be able effectively to utilize personal, presentation, group work and teambuilding skills at a basic level.

3   Where appropriate, students should be able to show leadership skills.

Overview

The Management Skills Module is activity based, supported by a theoretical framework.

Fundamental to the course are the following skills, to be revisited throughout the two years. They provide the links for the substantive elements of the course and we emphasise their essential role in successful management. These skills must be seen as part of a structured process.

1   Problem solving in groups
2   Working in teams
3   Communication skills
4   Participative skills

Throughout the course, each skill will be practised and refined in situations of increasing complexity; in particular,

i)   everyday situations
ii) in manufacturing industry
iii) in other industrial and business settings.

DUTIES OF MANAGEMENT

Content areas

1   Organisation

2   Setting objectives

3   Measurement of performance
4   Selecting and developing individuals
5   Communication
6   Motivation

Skill framework

Year 1		*Year 2*
Activity based group work	1	Extension of complexity of activities.
Analysis based on use of problem solving model.	2	Extension of analysis and review.
Identification and utilization of learning points.	3	Introduction and extension of theory.
Limited theoretical framework.	4	Use of situations further removed from students' experience.

MANAGEMENT – ASSESSMENT PLANS

1.1   **Record/Assessment Sheets**

Each session will be followed by the completion of a record sheet. The detailed format of each sheet will vary according to the activity involved, but will include spaces for:

i   description of the session/input/activity
ii   indication of main learning points
iii   self-evaluation   a of group activity
                         b of individual participation within group
iv   tutor comment

1.2   **Testing**

The following theoretical inputs are open to testing:

i   Functional areas of organisations   data response test
ii   Duties of management
iii   Written aspects of self presentation
                  a letter of thanks   by test
                  b letter for appointment   example
iv   'Personal' aspects of self presentation– by written or oral
                                                 response to a test
                                                 situation

1.3   **Group Evaluation**

Group activities will have success criteria. Each group/team will be assessed in relation to its criteria by the tutor *and* the group members. This assessment will be recorded on the record/assessment sheet and signed.

Individuals will be required to assess their personal contribution in conjunction with their tutors and, on occasion, their peers.

Figure 8.3

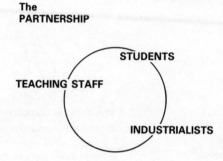

The
PARTNERSHIP

STUDENTS

TEACHING STAFF

INDUSTRIALISTS

Validation/accreditation

Students who successfully complete the programme will receive their course profile and a certificate endorsed by Park Hall and Land Rover Ltd. We are also negotiating with a number of other national companies who have shown considerable interest in and qualified agreement about endorsing our certificate.

Many visitors to the school have enquired why we do not write the course for GCE Advanced level accreditation. There are two main

Figure 8.4

GROUP 16–18

TECHNOLOGY
AND
MANAGEMENT
SCIENCE

GCE
ADVANCED
LEVEL STUDY

CPVE

BTEC

Figure 8.5

Course Structure

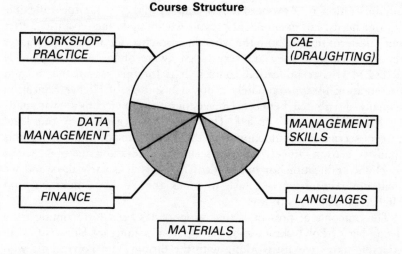

Figure 8.6

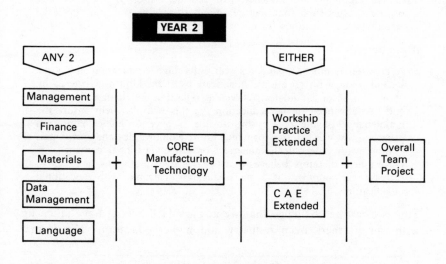

reasons, first, the course is taken by a range of students studying at advanced and non-advanced level, second, the present structure and administration of Advanced Level courses makes it far too inflexible for our needs. For example, at present we are updating/re-writing, after our mid-term review, both the workshop practice and modern languages modules. However, we are very much aware of the need to provide access to Higher Education courses. It is for this reason that a joint presentation to approximately a dozen Institutes of Higher Education (equally distributed between Universities and Polytechnics) was made by Mr T. Hanley and myself. The event was organised by our local careers service in conjunction with the TVEI Director and our Schools Industry Liaison Officer. We were seeking accreditation and open access to Higher Education for our students. Clearly it is early days and we shall not falter from our task to break the 'A' Level monopoly on Higher Education entrance.

The outcome at present is that support has been forthcoming from a number of Polytechnics and interest from a range of Universities. In concrete terms we are working with the Birmingham Polytechnic who are hoping to validate/accredit our course, for entry into Higher Education, with a Polytechnic Foundation Certificate for students who reach the appropriate standards. The submission to the Polytechnic is an attempt to enhance our links with higher education and, hopefully in partnership, to develop some of the issues raised in the government White Paper *Higher Education, Meeting the Challenge.*[9] This White Paper stresses the need

> ... to accommodate students with a wider range of academic and practical experience than before, many of whom will not have the traditional qualifications for entry. (2.15)

It continues,

> A growing number of students will enter higher education along the second route, with vocational qualifications of the kind now offered by about a sixth of candidates. As well as reflecting the changes in schools and non-advanced further education ... this will also help ensure the maintenance of the recent shift in the balance of higher education provision towards subjects for which future employer demand is strongest – those with a technical, numerical or other vocational content. The Government therefore believes that positive steps must now be taken to increase the number of higher education entrants with vocational qualifications. (2.18)

This is clearly a challenge that we at Park Hall School have taken up with our partners from industry and higher education. The formal

---

[9] DES *Higher Education, meeting the challenge*, HMSO, 1987.

course document presentation to the academic board was difficult for us for two reasons: first, we had no previous experience of writing a high level course submission and second, we had no experience of verbally presenting such a course document to the board. However, advice was forthcoming from both HMI and the Polytechnic. We worked on a sample course submission for a CNNA Degree. The contents page of our submission, shown in Figure 8.7 perhaps reflects the considerable efforts made by the staff and myself in compiling our weighty submission.

Since the formal meeting (a joint presentation by Park Hall School and Land Rover Ltd.) with the Academic Board to discuss our course document, much progress has been made. We shall be presenting our final re-drafted submission in October and are hoping for agreement on the award of the Polytechnic Foundation Certificate. This certificate would be retrospective in the sense that it will be used initially to accredit our 86/88 cohort.

Figure 8.7 Sample page of submission

CONTENTS
1 General information
2 Introduction
3 Course origins
4 Background
5 Philosophy
6 Admission requirements
7 Course organisation   Year 1
Course organisation   Year 2
8 Course progression
10 Current course team
11 Course aims
12 Module outlines
i   CAE
ii   Finance
iii   Materials
iv   Management
v   Workshop Practice
vi   Data Management
vii   Languages
viii   2nd Year Project
ix   Technology
13 Work experience/residential
14 Resources
15 Assessment

It is essential that others in the service develop processes to aid open access to Higher Education in the future if we are to encourage right and proper joint curriculum development with industry.

Areas of success – liquid not frozen assets

It is clearly necessary to release those frozen assets which exist in both the educational and industrial sectors of our economy. In terms of our Technology and Management Science Course we have all profited from the partnership. The school has clearly benefited from what can be thought of as ten part-time seconded industrialists. The close working relationship which has developed over the last two years has provided much professional development for the school staff. Teachers now have an increased awareness and understanding of manufacturing industry. Perhaps even more importantly, they are sensitive to the requirements of industry and of the continual need to review and update our school curriculum. Our stock of assets has increased in terms of modular curriculum developments, new teaching styles and strategies, new student assessment procedures and forms of accreditation, most important of all increased motivation and confidence.

Land Rover Limited has also benefited considerably through the partnership. Our industrial partners have developed a greater awareness and understanding of the needs of the education service. They have gained confidence in their abilities to change the face of the curriculum as a result of working with teachers. They are more aware of the aspirations, expectations and capabilities of young people. They have developed ideas about their own company training programmes while working with teachers, and have sought assistance where they felt it appropriate. There is also no better way to 'sharpen up' presentation skills than standing in front of a class of students. Increased motivation, professional development, and team-building skills are additional assets from the partnership. Some would comment that it is also good for Public Relations – indeed, it may well be, but that was a by-product, not the motivating factor.

Finally, let us turn our attention to the most important members of the partnership, without whom there would be no reason for its existence – the students. They have clearly and rightly gained the biggest share of the profits. A wide range of skills have been developed, and will continue to be developed throughout the duration of the course; independent learning skills, problem-solving skills, technological/transferable skills, teamwork skills, management skills, presentation skills and a wide range of hidden 'benefits'. The range of experiences offered to the students clearly enhances their awareness and understanding of the opportunities which exist for them in manufacturing industry. A recent survey by the CBI remarked that only 31.8% of students interviewed would, as a last resort, go into a career in the manufacturing industry. A sample survey of some of our students showed a figure of 69% who would readily consider a career in manufacturing industry. The wide range of experiences open to students has clearly enhanced their personal and social education. Our students are more confident about the kinds of careers they wish to follow after experiencing such a broad range of modules during the course. They are also much more aware of the interface between theory and practice as they can readily relate academic subjects to the world of work. Certification by a range of nationally recognised companies and from the Birmingham Polytechnic will also be useful additions to the students' curriculum vitae. Their only major complaint so far . . . 'not enough links with industry'. Need I say more.

The success of the partnership has led to many exciting developments. Some have already been mentioned, others are still in the pipeline, such as our consortium development with two other schools linked once again with Industry. We are breaking new ground, many were surprised to see the joint Land Rover Ltd and Park Hall School stand at the last British Association for the Advancement of Science Exhibition. A school at such a prestigious event for industry! Why not? It was undoubtedly one of the most popular stands during the Conference Week.

A *merger*

We need a merger to ensure the continued economic success of Great Britain. The merger must be between education and industry. Let us offer no excuses from either partner, the stakes are too high and there is no monopolies commission.

9 Modular accreditation

Henry Macintosh

Introduction

Before considering the issues involved in Modular Accreditation it is necessary to clarify what the two words mean. As applied to the curriculum, a *module* (the adjective is modular) simply means a unit of learning. The current interest in modules stems largely from concerns about the effective management of learning for the benefit of all students. One obvious possibility is to replace the one- or two-year courses which tend to dominate our secondary curriculum, largely because of public examinations, with smaller units. To these small units the name module has been attached.

It is important to appreciate that the length of a module is not something arbitrary or universal, but results from a careful analysis of the learning experiences or curricula one wishes to deliver and how one wishes to deliver them. It is also important to appreciate that learning units and assessment units are not necessarily similar in length. The extent to which they match must always depend upon course intentions and upon the points at which it seems most useful to appraise and discuss student performance collectively or individually in relation to these intentions. This could occur in the middle of a module, or require assessment which runs over several modules. The techniques used for assessment must, of course, ensure that appropriate evidence, upon which to base judgements about individuals and about the course as a whole, is available when needed.

As is so often the case with educational 'buzzwords', modules (which are also called units and credits) are nothing new although their use on any scale within the secondary curriculum in Britain has only occurred in the past five years. Further Education has, however, used modules for much longer, as has the Open University, and their use in North America, both in high schools and colleges (where they are more usually called semesters) has been extensive.

The second word *accreditation* describes the process whereby a body, possibly established specifically for the purpose, grants under agreed conditions its imprimatur to other bodies to undertake activities on its behalf. This imprimatur most commonly takes the form of a licence or a certificate. Within the secondary curriculum at the present time accreditation will primarily be concerned with the certification provided by public examinations such as the GCSE, CPVE, A/S or A Level or by bodies such as BTEC, CGLI and the RSA. It could, however, relate to the underwriting of individuals to undertake assessment on behalf of an agency without external monitoring, or to the underwriting of an institution's own certificate developed through profiling. One of the major issues over the next few years as far as accreditation is concerned is the extent to which locally initiated profiles will be able to secure and retain credibility with the public at large. This could occur either through the development of a national framework for Records of Achievement along the lines suggested in the DES *Interim Report* (November 1987), within which individual proposals will have to fit, or by institutional negotiation with agencies competent to issue certificates.

Modular accreditation

Modular accreditation is thus the process whereby a whole curriculum, or elements of a curriculum designed and operated as a series of units of varying lengths, secure external certification. In this process there are two major variables: first the modules and in particular the ways in which they are put together in order to provide coherent learning programmes. Second, the rules laid down by the accrediting agency for the issue of its certificate and in particular the methods used to describe performance. The distance between these two can be considerable. At the extremes one can have cross-curricula modular programmes which move horizontally through the exploration of themes, and activities seeking certification through examinations such as the GCSE which operate an essentially vertical subject-based grading scheme. The resolution of these differences is essential if the potential of modules is to be realised in practice and, in particular, if progression both in terms of individual learning and in terms of student movement between courses is to be successfully managed.

Curriculum management

At the heart of the problem are two issues: curriculum management and aggregation. As far as the first is concerned, it is particularly important that all courses of study for all students can demonstrate:

- clear connections between what has gone before and what is available in the future;
- a continuous relationship between process and content;
- the need and the opportunities for co-operation and interaction between individuals and, where appropriate, between subjects and between institutions.

It is equally important that assessment is seen as an integral part of whole course planning, built in from the outset and not bolted on as an afterthought. This must occur whatever the size or length of the course or the range and number of the learning units. Whole course planning requires three fundamental questions to be addressed:

1   What are the intended outcomes of the course?
2   What evidence will be needed/can be provided in order to establish that learning relevant to these outcomes has taken place?
3   What teaching/learning activities will need to be provided in order to produce that evidence?

The outcomes referred to in the first question will derive from different sources. Some, like the GCSE criteria, will be externally imposed. Others will result from negotiation and discussion between teachers and students. Effective feedback, particularly where short-term goals are involved, as would be the case with modules, is more likely to occur when outcomes are openly discussed and jointly developed. Currently the range of evidence regarded as appropriate for assessment purposes is extremely restricted. Writing tends to dominate at the expense of other forms of communication and the range of writing involved is itself extremely limited. It is important when extending the range of evidence to avoid over-assessment. The question as to what constitutes the minimum evidence upon which to base fair and sensible statements or judgements about individuals should always be asked.

The third question is the most problematic of the three. It assumes, as indeed do all three questions, an assessment-led view of the curriculum; a view which accords well with government policies. It is thus predicated upon the notion that if assessment is matched to outcomes then pedagogy will change to provide a three-way match. Unfortunately the evidence of projects like the Schools History Project (SHP), which have made a substantial investment in changing assessment, suggests that such changes are far from automatic and that changing pedagogy is an extremely slow process. It is possible that modules, with their stress upon short-term objectives and their capacity for feedback, may speed up this process. It is also possible that greater use of informal in-course assessment at the expense of formal end-of-course testing which modular curricula facilitate will help. We have no right, however, to assume that this will be the case, particularly when comparatively little is known as yet about the sequencing of children's learning within particular curriculum areas. Until this situation improves, a theoretical basis will be lacking for the development and delivery of a modular curriculum and hence practical assistance for the delivery of both coherence and quality through the use of modules will be at a premium.

Aggregation

Aggregation is essentially a process of reduction. In the context in which it is being discussed in this chapter, this will require performances which have taken place over a period of time and been demonstrated through a wide variety of learning experiences to be summarized in ways which accord with the descriptive system used by the accrediting agency. For this to occur, a set of combination rules which are equitable and can be justified has to be devised. If grades are used, as is the case with both GCSE and A Level – currently the certificates most likely to be gained by students on modular courses – it will almost certainly be necessary to introduce levels or grades within the assessment of the modules themselves as the first stage in the aggregation process.

A good example of such an arrangement is that adopted by the Associated Examining Board (AEB) in its work with the Somerset LEA, which uses four grades. Similar procedures are used by both BTEC and the Open University. Each module is assessed upon completion and graded and the result reported to the students through the school. Combinations of module grades involving six modules are specified for the achievement of particular GCSE grades and these rules are then applied upon the completion of the sixth module and a GCSE certificate issued. The rules used are known to all parties involved, including the students.

This scheme has a number of major disadvantages which stem not from flaws in the system as such but from the attempt to fit curriculum and assessment strategies into a certificating system which was never designed to accommodate them. The procedures adopted impose a degree of uniformity upon course structures which need flexibility if they are to deliver the elements which increasingly feature in 14–18 curriculum agendas (stress upon skills and concepts, less emphasis upon subjects, a wider range of evidence and increased student autonomy, to name but four). The arrangements work much better with well-defined subject areas, and hence more clear-cut levels of performance, and they can easily lead to over assessment within modules. Nor is it easy to take account through differential weighting of the order or sequence in which modules are taken by different students. The difficulties facing the certificating body in establishing standards between modules which are equally weighted in theory, although not necessarily in practice, tend also to encourage the continuing use of moderation systems which attempt to secure agreement through the scrutiny of products rather than achieving quality control through establishing consensus about procedures and their rigorous implementation.

The way forward

What can be done to resolve these problems? Clearly, greater experience and confidence in operating this and similar systems by both examining boards and teachers, and the development of in-service provision, can help to alleviate day-to-day running difficulties and suggest improvements, for example, in the use of tariff weighting. These will not, however, resolve the fundamental issues created by a certificating system which does not match the curriculum models or learning strategies used and hence tends to distort both assessment and moderation. What likelihood is there in the next few years of changes which will take on board the practical implications for assessment and certification posed by such things as a shift towards criterion referencing, credit accumulation and transfer and modular accreditation?

The policies of central government, which over the past decade has increasingly seen the role of public assessment as central to curriculum control and change, are obviously of crucial importance here. The signs to date are not particularly encouraging. Despite growing centralisation in relation to the curriculum and to testing based upon national benchmarks and criteria, government continues to encourage – at least by omission – a market-led approach to accreditation which operates through a jungle of largely independent, highly selfish and competing agencies. There is little to suggest at present that this situation will change significantly or that opportunities like that provided by the NCVQ framework for vocational qualifications on the one hand and the GCSE (and soon A Level criteria) on the other, will be used to reconcile the current vocational/academic divide at 14–18.

A continuance of this divide, with its endless antagonisms: process *v* product; skills *v* knowledge; profiling *v* grading; thinking *v* doing and theory *v* practice, makes it impossible for institutions or groups of institutions to design coherent curricula for all their students and to have performance described as well as judged. The present government also remains uncertain about, if not hostile towards, a number of

developments which are fundamental to changing the ways in which
the curriculum is managed and performance assessed. These include
modules themselves, the formative use of records of achievement, cross-
curricula initiatives, fewer grades and a genuine rôle for teachers in the
assessment of their own students, as opposed to acting as unpaid
assistants to examining bodies.

Unless attitudes of the kind described in the preceding paragraph
change or turn out to be unjustified in practice, progression, both
individual and through courses, will remain extremely problematic, as
will coherent curriculum planning. There are fortunately a number of
current developments from which to take encouragement. Significant
and substantial initiatives have been set up to address the linked issues
involved in profiling, credit transfer, credit accumulation and modular
accreditation, notably the Northern Partnership for Records of Achievement Unit Credit Scheme, the Oxford Examinations Syndicate (which
is not an examining agency but a forum for all secondary schools in
Oxfordshire) and the Dorset Record of Achievement pilot project.
There has been a marked increase in the use of profiling in relation to
the more formal aspects of the curriculum as part of the certificating
process, mainly by the FE examining bodies. The Certificate of Pre-
vocational Education (CPVE) is, for instance, an example of a very
different approach to assessment and certification. It is worth noting
that this use of profiling forms is one of the four main purposes for
Records of Achievement set down in the July 1984 DES *Policy Statement.*

There is a growing interest from employers in extending the range of
information available from and about students. Higher education is also
beginning to show encouraging signs of interest in the use of
supplementary information about academic performance, as well as
about extra mural activities, and it is clear that this cannot readily be
provided by formal, graded assessment, however well designed. Such
developments could run without difficulty alongside and in harness with
more traditional forms of assessment. Work currently underway between
Somerset and the AEB on a modular 'A' Level curriculum shows how
this might work. 'A' level cores have been developed initially in the
Sciences which have a weighting of 60% together with a number of
satellite modules, each of which carry a weighting of 10%, and four of
which have to be taken by every student. These modules can extend or
enhance the particular core with which they have been developed or
can provide links with other cores. They can also provide different
contexts for learning, for example the workplace or another institution.
The core could easily constitute the graded external part of the
examination, the modules being profiled with student performance being
described or judged on a can do/cannot do basis (neither of which

incidentally is as simple as this description suggests), by teachers and students.

Conclusion

The worrying feature of the initiatives described in the last paragraph is their piecemeal nature. It would be much more logical, for example, for profiling in its widest sense to form the heart of an overall assessment package for all students aged 14–18/19 and ultimately to act as the basis for a 5–19 (and beyond) accreditation package. In practice, given current resources, government policies, community attitudes, the vested interests of the examining agencies and the current debate over teacher conditions of service, pay and appraisal, change is likely to take place extremely slowly and as a supplement to existing practice. Moreover, the pace of change will in the last resort depend upon the establishment of public confidence in what is being attempted.

In order to secure that confidence, much more work is needed upon both curriculum management and upon programmes, particularly those covering the 14–18 age range, which systematically and continuously mesh outcomes, evidence, assessment methods and teaching and learning strategies in the interests of all students. Here the TVEI extension will be particularly helpful. In the construction and delivery of such programmes both modules and accreditation have significant parts to play, but as elements within an overall package and not as absolute solutions in their own right. A key requirement will be the 'establishment' of certificating agencies very different from those which currently provide public examinations in this country, particularly in the school sector. This could come about by voluntary action, but it is significant that in countries like Australia where major changes have taken place in public examinations these have been accompanied by the creation of statutory agencies with different functions and very often different staff. Whether we can establish the degree of public confidence and consensus in this country to make such changes, particularly when they affect those who intend to go into higher education, must be an open question. What is certain is that we cannot as a nation afford a continuation of present arrangements if we wish to do justice to all our young people.

10 Credit banking

Christine Southall

This chapter describes the Module or Credit Bank which has been established in Oxfordshire. The Credit Bank was set up in 1986 by a consortium of 40 Oxfordshire schools and colleges, known as the Oxfordshire Examination Syndicate, in collaboration with the Southern Examining Group. It represents the response of one Local Education Authority to two major developments: the General Certificate of Secondary Education (GCSE) and modular approaches to the curriculum. It is designed to assist locally devised curriculum arrangements to obtain GCSE certification.

Throughout this chapter the word 'credit' is used where the reader might expect the word 'module'. This is intentional. Technically, a credit is what is received on successful completion of a module. The Oxfordshire Examination Syndicate uses the word 'credit' to signify 'module' as it has proved a more acceptable term to parents and students on account of its more positive connotations.

Christine Southall was seconded from Peers School, Oxford, to work on behalf of the Oxfordshire Examination Syndicate in 1986–1987. She is Vice-Principal of Lord Williams's School, Thame, Oxfordshire.

Module or credit banking is a means of achieving a certificate, degree or other qualification by accumulating its constituent parts. Each part or unit is clearly defined and delimited and its contribution to the whole certificate is specified. The unit may be recognised and reported in its own right (unit accreditation) or it may have recognition only as a proportion of the whole. Credit banking operates principally in further and higher education, the Scottish National Certificate and the degrees of the Open University being the best known examples. Credit banking

I would like to thank the following for their help: Bob Moon and Peter Walter of Peers School, Oxford. Bob Eggleshaw, Michael Jones and Nick Young of Wantage School, Oxfordshire; Peter Burke, John Wilmut and Stephen Vickers of Southern Examining Group.

as a means of fulfilling the requirements of the General Certificate of Secondary Education (GCSE) is explored in this chapter.

The credit bank of the Oxfordshire Examination Syndicate

In 1986 representatives from Oxfordshire's Local Education Authority (LEA) approached the Southern Examining Group (SEG) with a proposal that an LEA consortium – the Oxfordshire Examination Syndicate (OES) – should establish and administer a bank of GCSE credits. A definition of terms may be helpful at this point:

A *credit* is a free-standing unit of learning which may be combined with other credits to form an educational programme leading to the award of a GCSE certificate. Each credit is assessed within the time span allocated to it. This is usually in the region of 20 to 30 hours.

A *programme* is a group of five credits which together offer sufficient depth, rigour and quality to qualify for a GCSE title.

A *scheme* is the total set of credits which relate to a GCSE title in the Bank.

The Oxfordshire Examination Syndicate is responsible for agreeing with SEG the GCSE titles and the combinations of five credits which are appropriate for those titles. It maintains, therefore, what is known as a *module map* which indicates the ways in which credits can be grouped to give a GCSE title.

The *Credit Bank* is a bank in two senses. First, it is a bank for students as they receive an interim certificate on successful completion of a credit. Students deposit and accumulate their credits which can be retrieved and submitted for a GCSE award when the requirements for a given GCSE title have been met (ie in the agreed combinations of five). Credits can be banked over a number of years and the Southern Examining Group has not specified a time limit. Indications are that five years is acceptable, with the possibility of an extension period beyond that time. Credit banking holds notable advantages for students: they may accumulate credits beyond the years of compulsory schooling and complete programmes in Further or Adult Education. Students who are dissatisfied with their result on a particular credit may repeat it or replace it with a different credit in order to improve their final GCSE grade. Banking means that individual students may not only defer certification, they may request it earlier; the extent to which modular schemes might lead to premature assessment continues to be debated and is discussed later in the chapter. It is important to note that a GCSE obtained by credit accumulation is indistinguishable at the point of final certification from a GCSE obtained by more conventional means. GCSEs – whether mode 1, 2, 3, modular or non-modular – have all been vetted to ensure compliance with National Criteria. Standards are therefore guaranteed irrespective of the mode of examination and a GCSE Geography certificate, for example, contains no reference either to modes or modules.

Second, the Credit Bank is a bank for teachers and lecturers. Credits accepted into the bank from one school or group of schools immediately become available to all other Syndicate members. The bank provides a means for teachers to obtain GCSE recognition for curriculum components either to reflect particular circumstances and needs or to support new and changing areas of study and methodology. Prior to the advent of modular approaches, teachers seeking certification for school-based curriculum development had to construct entire mode III syllabuses. The Credit Bank enables teachers to submit smaller curriculum units for accreditation.

The origins of the Credit Bank

The LEA's initial proposal to SEG, *Examining the Modular Curriculum. Proposals to the Southern Examining Group for an Oxfordshire Framework*, was warmly received in SEG, which published its guidelines on modular GCSE shortly afterwards. The congruence of the LEA scheme and the SEG guidelines generated optimism in Oxfordshire, fuelled also by the knowledge that similar developments were already well advanced in Leicestershire with the Midland Examining Group. The *ad hoc* working party of the LEA which had made the proposal was replaced by a more formally constituted body, the Oxfordshire Examination Syndicate. The Syndicate is the parent organisation of the Credit Bank. Membership of the Syndicate is open to all educational establishments interested in the furtherance of modular approaches to GCSE. Member institutions may contribute and borrow credits on whatever scale they feel appropriate. Schools and colleges were invited to become members of the Oxfordshire Examination Syndicate and all Oxfordshire secondary schools and most colleges elected to do so at the Syndicate's inauguration in September 1986. This level of response exceeded all expectations.

A number of factors may account for the enthusiastic response to the Credit Bank and these are enumerated below.

1 Curriculum development and structural change in schools

Several schools in the county were attracted to modular approaches. Peers School has a 70% modular offer in years four and five. Wantage

School has implemented a modular structure starting in year three. Oxfordshire was developing a modular double award in GCSE Science. The motivational benefits to students on credit-based schemes were receiving widespread recognition and were seen to be linked to:

- the setting of clear, short-term goals;
- assessment within the time span of a credit;
- assessment against explicit criteria
- assessment closely articulated with learning.

2 TVEI

The TVEI scheme operating in six Oxford schools is modular, with two modular mode III GCSEs on offer and a further non-modular mode 1 GCSE taught in units.

3 GCSE

September 1986 was confirmed as the starting date for GCSE. The advent of GCSE was of major significance. If credit-based approaches were to have a long term future, they needed to espouse the new national examining system. More than anything else credits needed a life *inside* GCSE, not outside it. There were already a few modular mode 1 syllabuses available. On the whole, though, such syllabuses had not relinquished terminal examining in some form. There was a need for modular GCSE schemes with assessment within the time-span of the credit. There are benefits here both for curriculum and for GCSE. Credits accessed into the bank will have been subject to rigorous scrutiny against the National Criteria for GCSE. Credits therefore have the status and credibility that comes from accordance with national standards. A sense of local ownership of the national examining system is achieved. At the same time GCSE is seen to be capable of accommodating school-based curriculum development and assessment is demonstrably curriculum-led. The stated intention of GCSE to make the important measurable and not the measurable important gains ground.

4 Oxford Certificate of Educational Achievement

Oxfordshire is extensively committed to the piloting of Records of Achievement through the Oxford Certificate of Educational Achievement (OCEA). OCEA in Oxfordshire was influential in the establishment of the Syndicate. It embraces the notion of assessment against explicit criteria, against absolute not relative standards. Thus far its aims are consonant with those of GCSE. In addition OCEA actively solicits the student viewpoint throughout the learning and assessment process. The OCEA 'G' component had at one time promoted short-term objectives for students: the 'G' component had grown out of the graded objectives movement, but had subsequently mutated into a wider, less hierarchical but more complex assessment framework. It now appeared to some of those involved in OCEA that the credit, not OCEA 'G', was to be the successor to the graded objective in the promotion of short-term goals. OCEA had much expertise in criterion-referenced assessment. At the same time GCSE was going to make immense demands on teacher time and effort and could threaten to displace OCEA work in schools. If OCEA and GCSE could coexist symbiotically within a credit-based structure, there would be significant gains for both.

The role of the Southern Examining Group

The Credit Bank is based on the premise that some of the functions normally performed by the examining group can be devolved to an LEA consortium like the Oxfordshire Examination Syndicate. This would follow a period of mutual development and presupposes a relationship between the LEA and the examining group which is collaborative and consultative. The Southern Examining Group was proposing just such a *modus operandi* during the winter of 1986. The senior committees of the Southern Examining Group were receiving a clear message from the Chief Executive that the long-term interests of the Group lay not only in the marketing of board-based syllabuses but in the accreditation of school-based curriculum initiatives. The best way of achieving this was through an LEA/SEG partnership. An LEA consortium such as the Oxfordshire Examination Syndicate provided an ideal contact point for the Group to ensure convergence of curriculum, assessment and pedagogy.

The extent to which the Oxfordshire Examination Syndicate may take on the functions of the examining group is not fully worked out. A gradual devolution is envisaged. At the outset the Oxfordshire Examination Syndicate and the Group work together to achieve a system of operating the Bank which is as simple and economical as possible and compatible with the maintenance of standards. Ultimately it is likely that the Syndicate will take over the management of the Credit Bank under licence from the Group. When fully operational the Syndicate will be responsible for the issue of credit results, and the maintenance of all records, monitored only lightly by the Group. The

Group will issue GCSE certificates on receipt of the appropriate information from the Syndicate.

Credit banking in GCSE

A GCSE Credit Bank operates within the parameters of GCSE National Criteria. The latter pre-date widespread interest in modular approaches, as do the Mode 1, 2 and 3 regulations of examining groups. GCSE was designed with two year/180 hour courses as the norm. The relationship of GCSE to credits has been described as 'credit accommodation' as opposed to 'unit accreditation'. This is not just a pedantic distinction but highlights a very real issue within GCSE. This may best be illustrated by contrasting GCSE credit banking with the type which operates in the Scottish National Certificate.

In the case of the latter, Scottish Vocational Education Council (Scotvec) modules are accumulated by the student and contribute towards a Scottish National Certificate. Modules are listed on the certificate, which may contain only one module or dozens! In a GCSE Credit Bank, on the other hand, units are not accumulated to achieve the certificate, but rather, the syllabus requirements for the certificate are divided up to achieve the units. A credit in GCSE is therefore a fraction of the whole GCSE. The question is often asked: how long is a credit and how many credits make a GCSE? This is like asking how many slices there are in a cake. The answer is, of course, that it depends on how many slices you want to cut it into! The Somerset TVEI modular scheme cuts GCSE into quarters, the Oxfordshire Examination Syndicate cuts it into fifths.[1]

How can the task of fashioning one-fifth of a GCSE be accomplished? Each GCSE scheme or title has a number of aims and assessment objectives. The knack (the word is used deliberately, as compliance with GCSE requires all manner of technical ingenuity) is to carve the assessment objectives into fifths and to apportion them to credits. The cake example is useful here and Figure 10.1 offers a tentative illustration of how this operates.

In the first diagram (10.1a) a cross-section of objectives is addressed in the credit; the credits are then truly free-standing and can be stacked in any order in fives to achieve the title. This method lends itself to a humanities title, for example, where there is no hierarchy or sequence of credits.

---

[1] It is not clear how far uniformity is either possible or desirable. The Southern Examining Group is prepared to consider schemes with between three and seven modules.

Figure 10.1

(a)

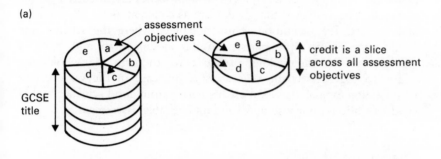

(b)

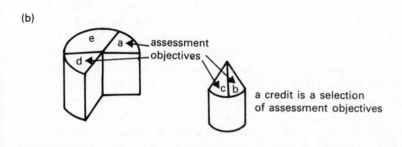

In the second diagram (10.1*b*) a selection of objectives is addressed in each credit. The credits must then be very carefully assembled to achieve the 'whole'. The rules of combination or credit map are essential to show how credits interlock and which permutations are permissible. This approach might lend itself to a scheme in which the later credits contain a design project, for example, which requires greater attention to the application of skills acquired in previous units or in which certain synthetic and evaluative objectives are best left to the end of the sequence.

There are certainly other ways of cutting the cake. Combinations of (*a*) and (*b*) are possible. The overriding principle is that any combination of five put forward for certification demonstrates coverage of the assessment objectives. The carving of knowledge skills and values is not as artificial as it may at first appear. The reality is that in tackling a whole syllabus, teachers are constantly selecting and subdividing. There is simply a more systematic attempt to do so in the credit-based approach.

There is also a fear that the GCSE cake, when sliced, may crumble – the accusation of fragmentation and lack of coherence which surfaces in any teacher audience when modular approaches are discussed for the first time. The answer is that credits are as coherent as GCSE, no more and no less. Fragmentation is not a danger where the scheme (the whole), the credits (the parts) and the module map and rules of aggregation (the interlocking of the parts to form the whole) are addressed together at the outset, as is the case in the Oxfordshire Examination Syndicate. Good credits derive from good schemes with a valid educational purpose and valid and reliable assessment.

The nature of GCSE

It is worth devoting some time, at this point, to acquiring an understanding of GCSE, the nature of assessment in it and the relationship between assessment and certification in GCSE. Assessment in GCSE is directed at the stage of syllabus construction by the statement of aims and assessment objectives. Assessment objectives prescribe the kinds of abilities that candidates are required to demonstrate, eg to know, to evaluate, to look from the perspective of people in the past, to analyse etc. A scheme of assessment defines the assessment components which represent the most effective means of collecting the evidence of those abilities described as assessment objectives. Differentiated assessment opportunities are devised so that a candidate awarded grade G, for example, has performed well on an appropriate task, not badly on a task which was too demanding. Assessment objectives and the criteria for allocating marks must be 'visible' and discernible on the entire continuum that stretches from GCSE National Criteria, through the syllabus of the scheme and the credit descriptor, into the assessment components and the marking schemes or reporting scales. Wherever assessment takes place in GCSE, the assessor asks the same questions:

> Which objective is assessed here?
> To which level can it be assessed here?
> What are the criteria for giving credit?

These are searching, pertinent questions which need to be addressed by every teacher involved in GCSE assessment and they generate much information about an individual candidate's performance.

At the point of certification, however, the assessment information is boiled down and down into a grade. Assessment is elaborate and ambitious in its intention to give all candidates an opportunity to measure their performance against known objectives and agreed standards. Certification remains crude – grades A to G and unclassified. The major defect of GCSE, therefore, is that the certification does not do justice to the quality of assessment envisaged. How has this situation come about? Users (employers, educational establishments) it is argued, require concise indications of a candidate's attainment. Would a publisher, to construct an analogous situation, think it acceptable to distribute the novels of a Nobel prize winner as blocks of compressed paper waste? Of course not, so why apply this reductionist mentality to assessment? The mismatch between process and product is nowhere more acute than in the relationship between assessment and certification in GCSE. This is what is bedevilling the attempt to devise grade criteria; the fairer and more valid the assessment, the greater is the ingenuity required to marry it with reductionist certification.

Interim certification

The tension between assessment and certification has been discussed at some length for the bearing which it has on credit banking. Since interim certificates are to be issued on completion of a credit, there is a risk that certification will interfere with assessment not once in the course of a GCSE programme but five times. The nature of the interim certification is consequently highly significant and was the subject of prolonged debate in the Oxfordshire Examination Syndicate. The following principles were established:

1   GCSE is objectives-led: on the interim certificate candidates are entitled to receive information about their attainment in relation to those objectives. They should be able to make inferences about their learning and their strengths and weaknesses from the credit certificate.

2   The contribution of the credit to the final GCSE grade should be evident from the certificate. The formula for calculating the final grade from the programme of five credits should be public. Thus candidates can look at an interim certificate and deduce that if they obtain the same score on subsequent credits, they will gain a grade C, or that by obtaining a one score improvement on two subsequent credits they will gain a grade B, for example.

3   The aggregation formula for determining the GCSE grade should permit some compensation so that the higher module performances are acknowledged in the final grade. The reason for this is that maturation has been cited as a concern in modular GCSE. A credit acquired in the third or fourth year of secondary school by a 13 or 14 year old has been assessed at 16+ standard and counts

towards the GCSE grade. Students on credit-based schemes have a lower average 'assessment age' than those following syllabuses with a greater emphasis on terminal examining. There is a possibility, therefore, that such students may be disadvantaged by premature assessment.

The aggregation formula should be used to counterbalance this so that the effect of an uncharacteristically weak performance in a single credit can be minimised in the final grade. The case for maturation as a significant factor in candidate performance is not proven and it remains to be seen whether any pattern will emerge of weaker performance in the early credits of a programme.

Having established these three principles, it was necessary to consider what should be recorded on the interim certificate and what is best recorded on the curriculum attainments section of a record of achievement. How much can OCEA accommodate GCSE and vice versa? Similar issues have been faced in the north of England by the Northern Examining Association (NEA) and the Northern Partnership for Records of Achievement (NPRA) in their considerations of the extent to which NPRA units are compatible with GCSE. A first paper to the executive group of OES proposed that assessment objectives or grouped assessment objectives should be listed on the interim certificate and that a score from 1 to 7, effectively a G to A grade, should be recorded alongside each objective. The aggregation formula took the profile of scores across the programme of five on each objective which acknowledged the higher performances. The final accumulation formula had to take into account the relative weightings of the objectives. A five credit, five objective conversion scale looked like this:

$$32-35 = \text{grade A}$$
$$27-31 = \text{grade B}$$
$$22-26 = \text{grade C etc}$$

This proposal was in line with the three principles outlined above. However, the formula and its rationale looked too complicated for public release and the 'assessment' objectives became invisible where the 'certification' arithmetic took over.

By May 1987 the modular approach had become much more firmly embedded in the educational scene, and local pragmatism was quickly being superseded by regional and national solutions to issues encountered by those working on Mode III modular schemes. The Secondary Examinations Council (SEC) had published Working Paper 4 *Assessing Modular Syllabuses*, the Joint Council for the GCSE had discussed issues of mutual concern with regard to modular syllabuses, the Midland

Examining Group had issued a second set of modular guidelines and the SEG was compiling a definitive document on the regulation and operation of modular schemes. The Associated Examining Board had undertaken development work in connection with the Somerset TVEI scheme. The SEG convinced the OES that the best way to ensure that GCSE fulfilled its intention of being criteria-driven was to report results on interim certificates as levels and that levels should not be aggregated arithmetically but by using rules of combination, as follows.

Levels and how they are combined to give a GCSE grade

Credit results are reported on the interim certificate as levels. The levels are 1 to 4 – with 1 as the highest level of attainment that can reasonably be expected on the credit and 4 as the minimum requirement for successful completion of the credit. For each level, level descriptors are written which derive from the assessment objectives. They are written in positive terms and describe in general terms what the candidate knows, understands and can do at each level. The level descriptors are used as the basis for marking coursework and tests either directly or by using conventional mark schemes and matching these with the levels so that scores are assigned to one of the four levels. Interim certificates record, among other things, the credit title and the level attained by the candidate as well as the level descriptor. For each scheme a set of combination rules is devised which compares all possible permutations of levels against the grade descriptions for the scheme and assigns each permutation to a grade. This is a lengthy process requiring thoughtful matching and adjusting of level descriptors in the design stage of schemes and credits. A five credit and four level scheme would generate 56 possible combinations of results ranging from IIIII (grade A) to 44444 (grade G). A decision must also be made about the influence of an unclassified result on the grade.

Contributing credits to the Credit Bank

The administrative structure of the Oxfordshire Examination Syndicate is designed to permit rapid inclusion of school-designed credits in the Credit Bank. A centre wishing to contribute a scheme or credit, sends a notice of intent to OES, which offers assistance from a team of seconded teachers. A list of credits and schemes in preparation is published regularly to maximise the potential for cooperation and shared development. Advisory groups for each GCSE title are established. Their brief is to vet credits against the relevant National Criteria and the regulations of SEG. Advisory groups also invite an injection of curriculum energy from the LEA. It is hoped that the groups will eventually develop positive strategies for combatting gender, ethnic and other forms of bias and contribute expertise in readability and differentiation, for example. The composition of each advisory group is as follows:

- the OES coordinator
- an officer of SEG
- an LEA representative
- a subject specialist who is not a member of the applying institution
- two other members, one of whom is an employer representative

OES also consults advisory groups to evaluate existing credits on an annual basis and to recommend amendments.

Access to credits in the Credit Bank

A full list of credits is distributed to member schools and colleges each autumn term. A short description of each credit is included in the catalogue and the GCSE titles and other certification outcomes for which the credit may be used. Since many credits are valid for more than one title – a Local Studies credit can contribute to a Geography or a Humanities GCSE, for example – entry procedures have been adjusted so that candidates may enter for a credit rather than a title. Clearly, there can also be many routeways to a given title and the best way to hold these is on computer.

Credit descriptors

Each credit is recorded in standard format on a credit descriptor (see Appendix 1 on p 176) the purpose of which is to demonstrate that all GCSE regulations have been satisfied and to assist with the mapping of routeways to GCSE titles. The descriptor is a syllabus and assessment skeleton only, so that individual institutions and teachers can realise the assessment objectives in different ways. The Credit Bank intends eventually to make available teaching syllabuses, support materials and suggested teaching and learning strategies, but must be careful to distinguish between the mandatory and voluntary aspects of a credit when it is loaned to a centre. Guidelines and workshops in credit design are provided by OES.

Moderation

Modular schemes call for revised moderation procedures, particularly in the case of banks issuing interim certification. A situation may arise in which a popular credit is 'borrowed' by several centres. Centres do not have to synchronise credit start and completion and all want a moderated result (interim certificate) for candidates as soon as possible after completion. The Southern Examining Group moderates centre-assessed components by inspection. The following moderation procedure was agreed:

An SEG moderator is appointed for each scheme in the bank. Centres notify OES of their intention to offer a credit during an academic year. Agreement trials are held between participating centres, the moderator and teachers seconded to work on the scheme. Syndicate-based in-service activity ensures that the credit descriptor, assessment instruments, reporting scales and level descriptors are understood. Seconded teachers 'link' with the moderator, the advisory group and centres. Figure 10.2 shows a model for the moderation of credits. The frequency of application of such a model should decrease over time, to be reviewed in the first years of operation of the Bank.

The long-term policy of SEG is for teacher accreditation. Teacher accreditation is the authorisation of teachers to undertake with only a low level of monitoring any of the following: syllabus construction, assessment, awarding grades. The centre-based assessment work in

---

Figure 10.2 Centres A, B, C, D, E, F offer credits under this title in the course of an academic year. The external moderator inspects A, C and F. A teacher from centre A moderates centre B's candidates. A teacher from centre C moderates D's candidates, and so on.

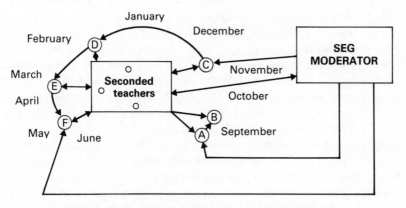

GCSE makes this the only feasible long-term option for GCSE. The OES, with its secondment provision (3 full-time equivalent secondments and 10 × 36 day secondments for 87/88), is able to promote precisely the kind of assessment in-service activity that is needed for teacher accreditation.

Conclusion

The concept of credit banking is an exciting one. I have encountered very few people inside or outside education who have not appreciated its prodigious potential. Students can bank credits and build programmes of study regardless of age. Modular curricula give students the opportunity to attain a long term target like GCSE by making a series of short-term commitments and in many cases determining their routes to that target. Credit banking offers a further benefit. Its intention is simple and powerful: students receive a credit reporting not only their present attainment level but also how that relates to their final grade. The formula for combining credits to give a GCSE grade is public information.

Some progressives in education have been too quick to condemn GCSE. I have not minimised its flaws in this chapter. However, those who have not looked beyond the grades should reconsider. Modular structure and modular banking, combined with an assessment system for GCSE that is sensitively differentiated, where targets are explicit and it is clear what constitutes attainment of a target, will lead to real improvements in educational practice and in the attainment levels of individuals. The National Criteria for GCSE are regarded by some as a means to greater curricular proscription and circumscription. But they also hand over assessment to public ownership. The publication of the 'rule book' can be seen as an opportunity for locally devised initiatives and diverse curricular perspectives to obtain GCSE status.

In Oxfordshire the notion of credit banking received support and enthusiasm from many quarters. The New Learning Initiative (NLI, Oxfordshire's version of LAPP) recognised that it had a useful contribution to make to GCSE. GCSE requires assignments and assessment components on which those receiving foundation grades can register positive achievement. By actively engaging in the design of such components for the Bank's credits and ensuring their readability and accessibility, the NLI could accomplish within GCSE something of lasting benefit for the young people who are the focus of that initiative. A local nature reserve plans to accredit its conservation course through the bank and teachers of health and fitness and sport science also intend to construct a modular scheme. Other LEAs are seeking similar partnerships with the SEG. While different banks within SEG may well remain separate for the purpose of administration and moderation, they can collaborate on particular titles or set up reciprocal arrangements to exchange and share credits. This will necessitate some degree of standardisation on matters such as the essential features of a GCSE credit and the number required for certification.

In its first year the Oxfordshire Examination Syndicate focused attention on understanding the nature of GCSE and how it could be modularised, administrative arrangements, aggregation and moderation. There is still much to refine and decide: what is the optimum achievable degree of criterion-referencing? How can the issue of interim certificates be managed smoothly and economically? The LEA and the SEG show continuing support for the scheme and a willingness to work to improve it. Perhaps the day is not so far distant when the effective secondary school is no longer the school with the highest number of A–C grade GCSE passes. A school's effectiveness will be judged on the extent to which its students improved their performance between their first interim certificates and their final GCSE grades.

The following appendixes are examples of:
1 A credit descriptor
2 A specimen credit

Appendix 1   Credit descriptor

OES A.1.

OXFORDSHIRE EXAMINATION SYNDICATE	SOUTHERN EXAMINING GROUP

GENERAL CERTIFICATE OF SECONDARY EDUCATION

	CREDIT DESCRIPTOR		
Credit Title			
Credit Code		Scheme Title(s)	Scheme Code(s)
Preferred entry level			
Rules of Combination/Module Map			
Aims of Credit			
Assessment Objectives			
Content and Context			

	Objectives	Relative Weighting %
Weighting of Assessment Objectives		

	Assessment Component	% Allocation	Duration (of Test)	Timing
Scheme of Assessment Summary				

Statement of Differentiation	

	Assessment Component				Total
Specification Grid Showing Relationship Between Objectives and Assessment Components	Assessment Objectives				
	Total				

Grades Available	

Appendix 1 (cont.)

LEVEL DESCRIPTORS
Level 1
Level 2
Level 3
Level 4

OES A.1

	Enclosed/to follow: 1. Specimen test items and assignments. 2. Marking criteria showing the levels of response on each assessment objective. 3. Student record card. N.B. Moderation and aggregation are standard throughout the Oxfordshire Examination Syndicate.
	This credit has been designed by _____ _____ _____ Institution(s) It has been checked against OES _____ Head of Faculty/Department guidelines by and submitted by _____ Head of Institution
For OES use.	Date Received _____ Date approved _____ Date accessed _____ Credit code allocated _____ Prohibited combinations _____ Mapped _____ Notification of modifications sent — date _____

Appendix 2 Specimen credit

OES A.1.

OXFORDSHIRE EXAMINATION SYNDICATE		SOUTHERN EXAMINING GROUP

GENERAL CERTIFICATE OF SECONDARY EDUCATION

	CREDIT DESCRIPTOR		
Credit Title	In depth study – Nazi Germany		
Credit Code		Scheme Title(s) HUMANITIES	Scheme Code(s)
Preferred entry level	Candidates may take this unit at any stage when constructing a course in History or Humanities.		
Rules of Combination/Module Map	As for the scheme as a whole. Only one In Depth Study may be offered as part of a course of five Units leading to a certificate in History or Humanities.		
Aims of Credit	To acquire knowledge and understanding of the Nazification of Germany in the past linking, as appropriate, with the present. To ensure that the candidates' knowledge and understanding is rooted in an understanding of the nature and use of historical evidence about Nazi Germany. To develop essential study skills such as the ability to locate and extract information from primary and secondary sources; to detect bias; to analyse this information and to construct a logical argument. To promote an understanding of the nature of cause and consequence, continuity and change, similarity and difference. To stimulate interest and enthusiasm for a study of the past, providing a sound basis for further study and for an informed and balanced approach to economic, political and moral issues.		
Assessment Objectives	1. (a) To recall, evaluate and select knowledge relevant to the context and to deploy it in a clear and coherent form. (b) To make use of and understand the concepts of cause and consequence, continuity and change, similarity and difference. 2. To demonstrate the skills necessary to study a wide variety of historical sources, such as primary and secondary written sources, statistical and visual material, artefacts textbooks and orally transmitted information. 3. To demonstrate the ability to look at events and issues from the perspective of people in the past.		
Content and Context	The context of Post 1st. World War Germany. The economic, political and social effects of defeat – Weimar Republic. The growth of extreme political parties and the role of an individual or individuals in this i.e. Adolf Hitler. The world recession and its social, economic and political effects on Germany. The rise of Hitler, his motivation, impact and factors influencing this. The Nazification of Germany and the methods and tactics used to create a totalitarian dictatorship. The impact of Nazification on the state, institutions, sections of society, families and individuals.		

OES A.1 HUM N.G.

Weighting of Assessment Objectives	Objectives	Relative Weighting %
	1a	25
	b	25
	2	30
	3	20
	TOTAL	100

Scheme of Assessment Summary	Assessment Component	% Allocation	Duration (of Test)	Timing
	COURSEWORK	70%	–	During
	TEST	30%	50 minutes	End

Statement of Differentiation

Coursework differentiation will be achieved by presenting candidates with tasks appropriate to their individual levels of ability.

Unit test differentiation will involve:

(a) differentiation by outcome, related to stimulus material.

(b) structured questions.

Specification Grid Showing Relationship Between Objectives and Assessment Components	Assessment Component / Assessment Objectives	COURSEWORK	TEST		Total
	1a	15	10		25
	1b	15	10		25
	2	25	5		30
	3	15	5		20
	Total	70	30		100

Grades Available	FULL RANGE

OES A.1 HUM N.G.

Bibliography

Adams R H and Wilmut J *The Somerset TVEI scheme. An approach to modular assessment.* Paper to BERA Conference, 1985
Cambridgeshire TVEI (1986) *Modular 'A' Level Guidelines.*
Moon Bob 'A modular framework'. *Forum* 27 (2) 1985
Moon Bob *The Modular Curriculum: Remaking the Mould* Harper and Row, 1987
Oxfordshire Examination Syndicate. *The Credit Bank, Guidelines for Users and Designers of Credits* Oxfordshire County Council 1987
Scottish Information Office *The 16+ Development Programme* Fact Sheet 31, 1985
Southern Examining Group *Guidelines for the Preparation and Submission of Modular or Unit based Curriculum Schemes* 1986
Turner J *Designing the Modular Curriculum* Part 1. GCSE Assessment. 1986
Walter P J *An investigation into the aggregation of grades as proposed for GCSE.* Paper to Oxfordshire Examination Syndicate. 1986
Watkins P *Modular Approaches to the Secondary Curriculum.* Longman for the School Curriculum Development Committee, 1987
Wilmut J and Owen S J *Assessment and Certification for a Modular Curriculum* Associated Examining Board 1985

11 Profiling through computers

Geoffrey Molyneux

Havant College is a sixth form college of some 750 students, serving south east Hampshire. It has six main 12–16 contributory schools, but draws from schools over a wide area, with significant intake from the private sector. In 1986 over 60 schools were represented within the intake. Some 180 students take one-year courses to improve on previous 16+ grades or take 'new' one-year courses such as secretarial subjects and the Certificate of Pre-Vocational Education (CPVE). The main body of students is engaged in 'A' level courses.

As one of the second round of TVEI scheme approvals the college has played a significant role in developing the philosophy of TVEI in conjunction with the six local 12–16 schools and the local FE college. As part of the TVEI scheme, new courses have been developed and enhanced, and interest in profiling – a TVEI commitment – sharpened. As part of the curriculum all students are expected to take part in some non-examination activity. This may take the form of community service, sport, cultural activity, artistic work etc. In addition a new Group Activity Time (GAT) has been developed, with emphasis being placed on student-centred group activities, based on modules spread throughout the timetable.

As Director of Studies at Havant College, I have responsibilities for the curriculum and, from September 1984, was closely involved in negotiations with the 12–16 schools' Heads and the Head of the General Studies Department of the FE College, designing the TVEI submission.

It was obvious that in the hasty negotiations and rapid implementation that followed, mistakes would be made and schools would have to learn as they went along, a difficult task made even more so by low teacher morale at a time of dispute. My college, together with the FE college, had two years to plan for our part of the 14–18 continuum; our first intake of students was to enter in September 1986. From an organisational point of view, each school and college appointed TVEI coordinators, and working parties were set up in key areas, each with a coordinating headteacher. These working parties covered areas such as *business studies, electronics and computing, CDT, the world of work, profiling and life skills* and *in-service training*. Havant College was represented on all of these committees.

Aside from this formal work within TVEI, the College began a City and Guilds 365 Vocational Preparation scheme – a well-resourced, well-financed, idealistic plan based on a model observed at Banbury College of Art and Technology. Within it, staff had their first experience of profiling.

The City and Guilds 'tick box' system of profiling was an opportunity for some staff to learn the pitfalls and strengths of the approach and have a basis for informed comment on TVEI profiling development. By May 1985 the Joint Board responsible for CPVE had produced its draft profiling bank statement system and this was discussed at a residential CPVE staff conference, funded by TVEI, in June 1985. The statements were published later in the year, substantially unchanged. Staff were apprehensive about the time factor involved in the CPVE bank statement system and our first profiling, attempted with the actual statements, bore out our first thoughts. After talking to several colleges involved in CPVE and TVEI profiling, it became apparent that the use of the computer to assist with profiling ought to be possible, and that it would speed up the process.

The first computer profiling system at Havant College

As Director of Studies and CPVE Coordinator, I persuaded a student to write a program that in essence reproduced the Joint Board profiling system. The aims of our system were:

- to familiarise students with profiling and, in a sense, with how the course was being assessed;
- to encourage staff to profile meaningfully, with individual students using the computer to record assessments *and* produce a summative record at the end of every assessment;
- to encourage good and simple record keeping with the minimum of paperwork.

The program, based on a BBC model B, single 40 track disk drive and 80 character printer (Epsom FX or similar) enabled us to print a profile which stated: the time span of the profile; the college name; the individual student's name and date of birth – all on a single disk, for up to 150 students. The menu driven system had sections for adding and deleting students, printing the list of students on file by name and date of birth. It also had a section for entering assessments based upon the bank statements against individual students' names. In addition, it had sections for displaying the CPVE core areas, and the factors within each CPVE area, together with the ability to print individual student profiles (see Figure 11.1).

Each profile is sub-divided into *areas, factors* and *descriptors.* The broad use of these *descriptors* can be further illustrated by reference to one of the early banks developed for Group Activities (see Figure 11.2).

Profiling practice

Before using the system for actual CPVE profiles, staff and students are encouraged to use a bank of artificial situations not related to the particular student concerned, where students and staff, each with a disk and computer, profile the evidence presented and discuss the assessment made. This enables the users of the system to realise the subjective nature of all interpersonal assessments. 'Real' profiling obviously involves all sorts of pressures which are absent when profiling an artificial situation.

The profiling practice exercises consist of a variety of exercises involving specific core factors. The student is, for example, presented with a piece of work involving percentages, which is marked correct. The student then has to decide what, given the core descriptors relevant to percentage, is the most appropriate descriptor statement relevant to that particular percentage work. Students faced with several similar exercises involving aspects of numeracy soon begin to profile quite accurately and appreciate the nature of profiling and the descriptor bank system.

Using profiling practice exercises in numeracy may be relatively simple, but more evaluative judgements may be involved in profiling. Other exercises cover personal and career development, with students given situations which they have to relate to factors within the Personal and Career Development section of the program, profile, and then discuss with staff.

Students are also asked to profile a sample work diary in terms of certain specified factors. A role play exercise, with students taking on different roles within a situation, is profiled by watching students. The students taking on the acting roles then discuss the assessments with

Figure 11.1   JOINT BOARD CPVE BANK STATEMENTS
DIAGRAMMATIC APPROACH

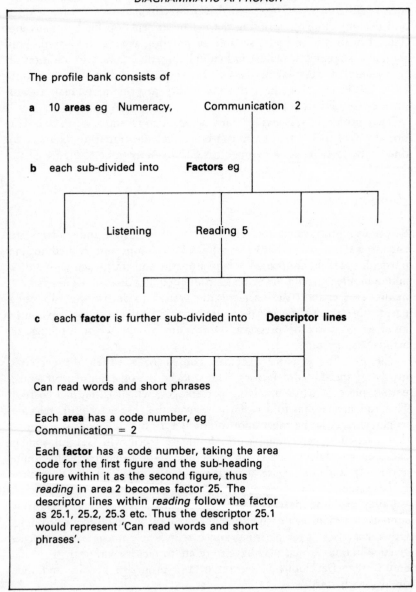

The profile bank consists of

a   10 **areas** eg Numeracy,   Communication 2

b   each sub-divided into   **Factors** eg

Listening   Reading 5

c   each **factor** is further sub-divided into   **Descriptor lines**

Can read words and short phrases

Each **area** has a code number, eg
Communication = 2

Each **factor** has a code number, taking the area
code for the first figure and the sub-heading
figure within it as the second figure, thus
reading in area 2 becomes factor 25. The
descriptor lines within *reading* follow the factor
as 25.1, 25.2, 25.3 etc. Thus the descriptor 25.1
would represent 'Can read words and short
phrases'.

Figure 11.2

UCCA − GENERAL

MAIN PROFILING TEXT

AREA 0: Industry, determination and perseverance

FACTOR 01: Industry

01.1: A hardworking student, always putting in the maximum effort one could expect.

01.2: A hardworking student, usually working at maximum capacity.

01.3: A student who generally works hard.

01.4: A student who sometimes works hard.

01.5: A student who is capable of working hard.

FACTOR 02: Effective working

02.1: A student who manages an efficient working approach.

02.2: A student who usually manages to develop a sound working approach.

02.3: A student who may work effectively.

FACTOR 03: Signs of motivation

03.1: Is strongly motivated to succeed.

03.2: May be motivated to succeed.

03.3: Sometimes shows signs of motivation.

FACTOR 04: Determination and perseverance

04.1: A student who has shown determination to succeed in the face of difficulties.

04.2: A student who has persevered when faced with a challenge.

04.3: A student who has shown some signs of perseverance when faced with difficulties.

AREA 1: Powers of analysis, expression and argument

FACTOR 11: Analysis

11.1: A clear thinking student who has shown a perceptive approach to a variety of issues.

11.2: A clear thinking student who has shown an analytical approach to problems.

11.3: A student capable of understanding clearly stated theories.

11.4: A student with the ability to retain facts and principles.

FACTOR 12: Oral expression

12.1: A student who always expresses clearly and fluently relevant details.

12.2: A student who usually expresses clearly and fluently relevant details.

Figure 11.2 (cont.)

12.3: A student capable of expressing clearly and fluently relevant details.

12.4: A student usually capable of expressing details clearly.

12.5: A student sometimes capable of expressing details clearly.

FACTOR 13: Written material

13.1: Written work is always well organised, neatly presented and clearly expressed.

13.2: Written work is usually well organised, neatly presented and clearly expressed.

13.3: Written work is sometimes well organised, neatly presented and clearly expressed.

FACTOR 14: Coherent argument

14.1: A student who has shown evidence of the ability to develop arguments along clear logical lines.

14.2: A student who has shown some evidence of being able to develop arguments along logical lines.

14.3: A student capable of understanding a logical argument.

14.4: A student who has shown some awareness of logical argument.

AREA 2: Imagination, Creativity and Independence of Mind

FACTOR 21: Imagination/creativity

21.1: A student who has shown evidence of original independent thought.

21.2: A student capable of creative independent thought.

21.3: A student capable of developing an hypothesis.

FACTOR 22: Independence of mind

22.1: A student who constantly, yet constructively, questions ideas, facts and theories.

22.2: A student who shows healthy scepticism.

22.3: A student who sometimes takes a critical approach to issues.

22.4: A student capable of evaluating some issues critically.

AREA 3: Personal qualities, initiative, reliability and responsibility

FACTOR 31: Social interaction

31.1: Plays an active and sensitive part in all aspects of group work.

31.2: Takes active part in all aspects of group work.

31.3: Takes active part in some aspects of group work.

FACTOR 32: Self-discipline/maturity

32.1: A student who has shown considerable self-discipline and maturity.

32.2: A student who has shown some considerable self-discipline and maturity.

32.3: A student who has shown some evidence of self-discipline.

FACTOR 33: Reliability

33.1: A very reliable and responsible student.

33.2: A reliable and responsible student.

33.3: A generally reliable and responsible student.

FACTOR 34: Initiative

34.1: A student who has shown a high level of personal initiative.

34.2: A student capable of taking personal initiatives.

34.3: A student who works well with staff guidance.

those who have been doing the profiling. At each stage, printed copies of the profile exercise can be discussed at length.

Further profiling practice exercises cover assessing responses to questions and assessing individual students' performance in discussing strategies for dealing with different hypothetical, but possible, situations in which students or their friends may find themselves. At all stages the computer provides an easy means of recording responses and provides a checklist of possible responses without the necessity for long and involved writing – which may be time-consuming and/or beyond the capabilities of some students.

After completing a number of profiling exercises, the students are familiar with the system, and can easily prepare evidence to back up selected profiling bank statements when negotiating with staff at official CPVE profiling sessions. At each official profiling session, students and staff cover a limited number of factors particularly relevant to recent activities within the CPVE course. At the end of each profiling session the student receives a copy of the profile in hard copy form, ready for renegotiation at a later date. The disk retains the record ready for use at the next profile session with arrows indicating the last profile descriptor used against every factor previously discussed. The disk at this stage is retained by members of staff to avoid loss and corruption of the data.

The second computer-profiling system

Experience with the first CPVE profiling disk led me to develop a more general computer-assisted profiling program. As a result, after considering the requirements of profiles in general, and the TVEI scheme locally, it was decided to produce a program capable of being used in a variety of contexts, and which would counter one of the key criticisms of the Joint Board Descriptor Bank system.

At several CPVE meetings staff commented on the weakness of some Joint Board descriptors, and said that they would like to use different words and phrases with the system. No descriptor bank will ever be perfect and one person's view of the meaning of a particular descriptor will often differ from that of another person. This, of course, is true of almost any statement involving value judgements – whether it be in a descriptor bank or not. Nevertheless, in developing a new general purpose profiling disk the key requirement was to have flexibility in creating the descriptor bank, and to allow for changes in the descriptors as we developed experience in using the system. A second key feature in developing the general purpose profiling disk was to profile more than the core competencies of the CPVE system and to indicate a *context* in which the profile was being developed. Third, it was considered important to retain simplicity while accommodating as many students as possible on one 40-track disk. Figure 11.3 outlines the structure of the system. Figure 11.4 is an example of a student profile.

Since BBCs are the most widely available machines in schools we decided to stick to the BBC format and also to single disk drive – which again, is most widely used. By now it was obvious that the work involved in developing the disk and system and the potential market for a computerised profiling system justified attempting to produce something that would be of interest to a publisher, rather than just applicable to one college's needs.

The TVEI scheme within local schools seemed an obvious starting point. Each school had its own particular characteristics and needs in terms of a profiling system and the TVEI panel was working against the odds to provide a comprehensive system. As an outsider with no brief, using CPVE experience, I considered that with every profile it ought to be clear in what *context* the profile was taking place. Space was created on the disk for inserting up to 10 contexts. This seemed adequate to deal with up to 150 students, given that the system required one statement bank per disk.

Figure 11.3 General purpose disk system

Main Menu
    1 Edit students
    2 Print students
    3 Enter assessment
    4 Print assessment
    5 Print profiling text

To avoid the corruption of data files it is impossible to change a descriptor once it has been assigned to a student. If you wish to change any descriptor you must delete it from any student record then simply type into the appropriate section of the program. The data bank covering

      CONTEXTS

      COURSE ACTIVITIES

      NON-COURSE ACTIVITIES

      EXAMINATION LEVELS

      EXAMINATIONS

      PROFILING TEXT

can all be changed at will, with the above restriction. The text and student files can be copied. The profiling text uses the 10 core areas, core factors, 5 descriptor lines system type approach of the CPVE system. The descriptor bank can be inserted hierarchically or in random order, according to the user's needs. In all, 450 descriptors may be used. Using a coding sheet it takes less than one and a half minutes to enter a full student record which, when printed out, runs to three sides of A4 (see Figure 11.4).

The *contexts* of the profile might be:
  1 A first-year student
  2 An electronics module
  3 A fourth-year TVEI student
  4 A student engaged upon a CPVE course
  5 A third year Mathematics student
  6 A student engaged upon a Modular GCSE course
and so on.

This assumes that the statement bank has appropriate descriptors within it to deal with the contexts outlined. Within Havant College one of the contexts covers 'A student engaged upon student organised group activities' and a descriptor bank has been developed from the UCCA confidential requirements and the reference requirements of major firms (see Figure 11.2).

It is of course impossible to provide opportunities for every student to show such qualities as initiative, determination, creativity, and so on, but students who are aware of the desirability of these qualities

Figure 11.4 An example of a student profile

Forename   : Joe
Surname   : Bloggs
Sex   : M
DOB   : 10.06.68
Group   : 4PW
Context   : A student engaged upon a GCE 'A' level course

COURSE ACTIVITIES

Has undertaken 3 weeks work experience.
Has played an active role in a Mini-Co project involving setting up and running a small company.
Has learnt to operate and use a word processor for general purposes.

NON-COURSE ACTIVITIES

Is a member of one or more local societies or clubs.
Has taken a part-time job at the weekend or in the evenings.
Has taken an active role in student committee work.
Is a member of a college club or group.

EXAMINATIONS.

Code	SUBJECT	LEVEL	RESULT
MA	Mathematics	'O' level	A
CH	Chemistry	'O' level	A
PH	Physics	'O' level	A
HI	History	'O' level	B
TD	Technical Drawing	'O' level	C
EN	English	'O' level	U
MA	Mathematics	'A' level	
PS	Physics	'A' level	
ES	Engineering Science	'A' level	
EN	English	CEE	

PROFILE:

Personal and career development

Can make the most of opportunities for development of own interests. Can produce a realistic career plan.

Industrial, Social and environmental studies

Can recognise the structure and organisations of an identified workplace. Can cope with own financial and legal responsibilities. Can describe the responsibilities of local, national and international government. Can describe the role of financial, social and legal institutions. Can appreciate the need for conserving the environment.

Communication

Can listen and respond to information presented in familiar situations. Can speak effectively, maintaining the confidence of the listener in a variety of situations. Can make requests and give instructions when appropriate. Can hold a social conversation with friends and colleagues. Can read and understand straightforward instructions and messages. Can convey straightforward information and ideas in writing. Can recognise ambiguous statements. Can recognise and use a few words of a second/foreign language.

Social skills

Can co-operate with others in a group task. Can operate effectively in familiar group situations. Can recognise the worth of other people's opinions. Can adapt behaviour in informal and formal roles. Can recognise when people are placed in categories.

Numeracy

Can carry out simple calculations involving money. Can use percentages to compare data. Can use the conventions of algebraic representation. Can solve multi-stage problems using various mathematical techniques. Can read graduated dials and scales. Can make reasonable estimates of size and quantity. Can use simple statistical and graphical techniques to analyse data. Can apply simple geometric techniques to solve problems. Can interpret charts, diagrams and drawings.

Science and technology

Can recognise the impact of science and technology in society. Can analyse problems capable of scientific or technical solution. Can set up, carry out and record experiments systematically, accurately and safely. Can apply basic scientific facts, laws, principles and generalisations in solving a problem.

Information technology

Can recognise the developing impact of IT on individuals and society. Can use a VDU/terminal to retrieve information from an IT system. Can write, debug and run a simple computer program based on a given specification. Can give examples of the application of IT in everyday life.

Creative developing

Can justify opinions on a range of product designs and creative activities. Can recognise a range of cultural activities drawn from own and other cultures. Can identify opportunities for creative activity in a variety of situations. Can make an original contribution to a creative group activity.

Practical skills

Can match own abilities with those of skilled workers. Can work safely with a range of materials and machines to an agreed standard. Can perform tasks requiring accuracy and manual dexterity safely to an agreed standard. Can adapt practical skills to new situations with guidance. Can evaluate own performance of practical skills without assistance.

Problem solving

Can identify problems which require attention. Can assemble relevant information from several sources. Can select and try out alternative approaches to solving a problem. Can assess own results when guided. Can confidently apply problem solving techniques to achieve personal goals.

once they are made explicit in the profiling bank, and in negotiation with staff, begin to realise that education is about a lot more than completing an assignment on time and appearing attentive. It would be quite possible to use the context section to name particular activities involved in the Group Activity Time, for example:

1   A student involved in planning all aspects of modern languages trips/exchanges abroad.
2   A student involved in promoting all aspects of International Year for Shelter of the Homeless, 1987.
3   A student involved in planning an Inter-Rail trip around Europe
    . . .

A second major feature of the General Purpose Profiling program is a section for *Course and Non-Course Activities*. The CPVE profile does not cover these, yet it is generally agreed that a full profile should cover the whole student. Being limited to ten course activities is sometimes a disadvantage; this depends on the context in which the student is being profiled. In the context of a modular course such as the Group Activities Time above, ten course activities are quite sufficient. The program also limits the bank of descriptors for non-course activities to ten, but again this is usually quite sufficient for most purposes – outside jobs, activities in clubs, representation of school in sports might be covered in the non-course activities section.

The next section of the program covers *Examinations* and allows the user to insert against each student up to 20 examination subjects (chosen from 88 available) with up to 10 different levels per subject. There is also space for recording a result, if required.

The remaining section, and by far the largest section of the program, concerns the *Profiling text*. After building up a bank of descriptors the user is able to profile the student in up to 10 *areas*. Each area is divided into nine factors and the *factors* are then further sub-divided into five *descriptors*. Each of these descriptors may be up to four lines long, covering 320 characters. Thus it is possible to hold 450 bank statements each up to four lines long. When profiling the student the bank statements are codified and staff use a grid to report the statements attributed to each student, which are then centrally keyed into the program and hard copies obtained.

Assessment of value

In this form the program has been used within the college with Group Activities Time students, TVEI students and CPVE students. Outside the college the program has been used in over 100 schools and colleges throughout the country in a variety of ways, and with students in middle schools, schools for the handicapped and the whole gamut of secondary education.

Schools that have been using the system for some time were circulated with a questionnaire, designed to provide evidence for further development of the system and to ascertain the possible strengths and drawbacks of computer-assisted profiling. Analysis of the returns suggests that users felt that the program was easy to understand and led to:

- a saving of time;
- a simplification of record-keeping;
- increased standardisation of record-keeping.

Most users thought that it was helpful in that it:

- created discussion with students;
- increased student motivation;
- helped assess the value of the course;
- helped introduce new technology to staff and students;
- helped achieve criterion referenced assessment;
- brought an awareness of the whole student.

From the survey, users seemed quite happy with the basic structure of the program, although it was suggested that the course activities section ought to be extended to give a greater variety of descriptors. Users were quite satisfied with the space for descriptors and the number of descriptors available; the inability to use the system on Econet was regretted and this has been rectified in the most recent disk.

Difficulties with implementing computer-assisted profiling

In considering what have been the greatest stumbling blocks to the introduction of computer-assisted profiling within their own institutions, respondents were in much agreement. *Most* difficulties centred on hostility to the descriptor bank system; the time needed to implement the system with students; and the lack of time/personnel available to input material. *Least* difficulties seem to be associated with the concept of negotiation; satisfaction with pre-existing systems; willingness on the part of students to be involved in computer-assisted profiling; and willingness of junior staff to take on what is seen as new work. Attitudes towards *other aspects* of the difficulty or otherwise of introducing computer-assisted profiling surveyed varied considerably, and included:

- staff hostility to profiling;
- staff hostility to computer profiling;
- the time needed to introduce the system to members of staff;
- the reluctance of senior staff to take a lead in using the system;
- lack of finance for software;
- lack of finance for hardware.

In all cases there are conflicting accounts. What does seem to be a common factor among users is concern about the time involved in using the system and the descriptor bank system, yet there was general satisfaction with the system itself. This is the basis of the inherent conflict between computer-assisted profiling and other means of assessment, certainly as far as this system is concerned.

In trying to use existing technologies, for instance the BBC, retain simplicity, and cover a large number of students, the system inevitably must have its weaknesses. The descriptor bank, although quite large, is limited, and its value is obviously dependent upon the quality of thought that has gone into its construction. There is no real substitute for the continuous prose individual statement tailored for each and every student, and some staff, quite rightly, wish to protect their right to provide this service for students. However, a study of a vast quantity of reports over many years suggests that statements for the vast majority of students do recur, and are repeated yearly. There should be a case for both systems, the computer dealing with the routine statements whilst leaving room for individual comment and personalised commenting.

The third profiling system and future development

The systems described so far have been developed to tackle the current situation and are very flexible. However a new and as yet untested program has been developed which is more flexible and faster than the current system. Using the existing framework, the new program will work on all BBC machines and networks and may be used to simply produce profiles from the key descriptor bank. This program is a response to demands for a program that simply produces a profile against a name without having to deal with dates of birth, sex, tutor group, context, course activities, non-course activities, examinations and so on. It will, of course, deal with all these things but the re-programming has added flexibility and speed, particularly valuable when inputting a vast quantity of coded material.

For some time to come those involved in profiling courses will continue to discuss the formative and summative nature of profiles and those involved in computer-assisted profiling will discuss the nature of descriptor banks. As staff become more familiar with developing descriptor banks and more aware that profiling is a motivator for both students and staff, then the value of computer assisted profiling will be fully recognised. One of the strategies for encouraging such development seems to be to provide as much correct evidence of existing descriptor banks as possible. Staff in secondary education often feel more confident in their own subject area, and so encouraging them to develop profile descriptor banks related to their own subject areas might be a good way of developing such banks. Key common cross-curricular skills are probably best left until staff feel confident about handling their own subject areas. A starting point for such subject descriptor banks might be the aims and objectives contained in syllabus documents. Within Havant College such a process has begun in most subject areas. Using a modular approach with limited clear aims and objectives, ought to enable the development of accurate and carefully thought out descriptor banks.

While computer-based descriptor banks are important, the real value of profiling lies on the formative side with its emphasis on improving performance and the assumption that if there is a positive descriptor bank then there will be improved self-worth. The computer provides the mechanism by which records of the profile can be kept and if necessary passed on to others. Undue stress on the summative side of computer-assisted profiling, trying to get the computer to actually produce final reports just as good as those produced by teachers, may result in designing systems that lack real flexibility and delay the use of formative profiling. The systems described above simplify record-keeping, and encourage the development of profiling but should not be seen as a total substitute for teacher reports.

12 Consortia issues

Adrian Booth, David Darwood and Julie Wright

Coventry has a unified comprehensive school system incorporating all LEA, Roman Catholic and Church of England Schools in a 11–18 structure. All of these schools are of recent construction or remodelling, and are generally purpose-designed on single sites. The LEA schools are so disposed throughout the city that each serves its own local community. The development of comprehensive education was completed in Coventry in 1975 and since that time nine schools have been designated community colleges. In essence these operate as very large community centres within which there is a secondary school.

In 1982 the Education Committee issued a consultative document entitled Comprehensive Education for Life. *The background to the document was the significant decline in the birth rate and the changing needs of the community caused by unemployment and new technology. The purpose was to provide a flexible framework within which the education service could be responsive to changing needs and circumstances within the community. The document produced various policy principles including the notions that:*

- *education is a life-long process;*
- *education is for all up to 18;*
- *access to educational opportunities should be flexible;*
- *a system of modular based courses or credits should be developed from the age of 14 which can be extended and built up to 18 and beyond.*

It was clearly recognised that open access to education throughout life required a system of modules or credits which are interchangeable between levels and systems including the recognition of the less formal and non-vocational provision. Following the publication of Comprehensive Education for Life *various developmental initiatives have addressed themselves to flexible learning opportunities via modularity.*

In 1982 a Humanities Reference Group was established to produce a matrix of Humanities modules for 14–16 year olds and to provide modular courses in History and Geography for Joint Certification at 16. Two years later Coventry launched a pilot TVEI project which incorporated a core of technical and pre-vocational modules. This development, unconstrained by traditional curriculum or departmental boundaries, has offered enormous possibilities for radically liberalising the curriculum.

Other initiatives in Coventry have similarly been exploring the practical implementation of policy principles espoused in Comprehensive Education for Life *in a way that is complementary to modular developments and encourages consortia working. The low attainers project, for example, has developed shared modular provision at the city's Edgwick (TOPSHOP) site. Students on the project experience a variety of vocational and practical activities on 'day-release' from school.*

The OCEA (Oxford Certificate of Educational Achievement) scheme has been centrally concerned with profiling and assessment. This scheme has caused the traditional relationship between teacher and learner to shift from a didactic non-negotiable relationship to an active partnership between teacher and student. The lessons offered for the nature of self-assessment, negotiating curriculum pathways, criteria-based assessment, records of achievement and collaborative staff working have been significant for the further development of the modular curriculum in Coventry.

At the same time the city's commitment to 11–18 comprehensive schools in the face of falling student numbers at 16 has led to consortia arrangements for the city's 'A' level students. Although 'A' level provision is not yet modular the experience of providing guidance and counselling and of tracking youngsters receiving their curriculum in more than one institution has proved important for assessing the type and nature of 16–18 provision in TVEI.

In Coventry the TVEI pilot scheme involves four institutions: three comprehensive schools and a college of further education. An essential element is the collaboration of these institutions in the promotion of a modular curriculum. To meet this end 'curriculum groups' were established in the following areas:

Business studies	Microelectronics
Computing	Product development
Graphic design/Photography	Technology
Home economics	Equal opportunities.
Media studies	

Each group has representatives from all TVEI institutions, a member of the Advisory service and the Curriculum Development Officer from the central TVEI team. In some cases representatives from Industry/ Commerce are also involved.

The curricular model

The purpose of the groups was originally concerned with the development of curriculum materials, assessment tasks and the promotion of active learning styles. However, they soon took on a far wider role. Meeting for half-day sessions every one or two weeks they provide on-going INSET for the members and are able to identify wider INSET needs, particularly those involving the training and up-dating of staff in new technology being introduced into schools and the use of new assessment and moderation procedures. The groups ensure a cohesion and uniformity of approach between the institutions and identify good practice as well as shortfalls in the scheme. They are able to respond to comments from their colleagues within the schools as well as from the students themselves. This formative evaluation proves invaluable in the development of the modules, allowing weak areas to be 'weeded out' or amended and successful areas to be extended and built upon.

This model for curriculum development also gives a sense of 'ownership' to the staff, which has accounted for its success. The groups have become powerful pressure groups for change allowing new modules to be developed, identifying specific resource needs and acting as an early alarm system as and when things appear to be going wrong. Minutes of meetings are circulated to all TVEI institutions and individual members of the groups are expected to report back to their school/ college coordinators. Furthermore the membership of the groups helps dissemination across the LEA – to the Officers of the Authority through the TVEI Coordinator; to the Chief Inspector via the Advisers; and to the Heads and classroom teachers within the schools via the teacher representatives.

It is important to note that the curriculum groups are not just subject specific, they are expected to work on whole-curriculum developments such as experiential learning, supported self-study, profiling, equal opportunities and links with industry. Figure 12.1 illustrates the curriculum development system in Coventry TVEI, and Figure 12.2 the programmes offered for 1987.

Institutional co-operation

An interesting aspect of co-operation centres on the role played by the

Figure 12.1 Curriculum development in the Coventry TVEI scheme

Curriculum groups

Business studies
Computing
Equal opportunities
Graphic design/Photography
Home economics
Media studies
Microelectronics
Product development
Technology

Dissemination

To: TVEI teachers
Managers of TVEI
Non-TVEI schools via
Advisers and INSET

Structure

- Representatives from TVEI schools and college
- Curriculum Development Officer
- Advisers
- TRIST members
- Half a day a week available for each group

Functions

- Develops curriculum materials and assessment tasks
- Provides on-going INSET for members
- Identifies wider INSET needs
- Identifies good practice
- Identifies resource needs across project
- Ensures cohesion across project
- Consultation with industry
- Evaluates
- Regular reporting to Project Leader and School Coordinator

Influence

Pressure group for change

- on curriculum organisation
- on teaching/learning strategies
- sounding board for new ideas/developments
- early warning systems for problems

FE College. The involvement of the College is essential to the overall development of the scheme. It offers support in three practical ways.

1   It provides facilities for staff and students, particularly where modules need the support of more sophisticated facilities. For

Figure 12.2 Programmes for 1987

PROGRAMMES FOR 1987

The assessment of each candidate will be carried out by teachers in the centre. Each candidate may study up to two programmes of five modules and will be assessed on the work completed in each of these modules. Students will select modules progressively. Counselling during the course will lead them to compose one or two of the programmes outlined below. Guidance will aim to support vocational options and to balance them.

Each programme = 5 modules = 1 certificated title   * New modules starting September 1987

Computer Literacy

Four Computer Literacy modules plus
One module from
: Microelectronics 1 or 2
: Information Processing
: Word Processing

Microelectronics and Control

Three modules from Microelectronics (4)
A further two from
: Control Technology (4)
: Other Microelectronics modules
: Product Development
: Computer Literacy 1

Design Studies

Textile Design
Graphic Design
A further three from
: The Fashion Industry
: Photography
: Technical Graphics
: Product Development
: Computer Literacy 4
(Communications)

Modern Business Systems

Modern Office Practice
Two modules from Modern Business Systems (2)
A further two from
: Information Processing
: Word Processing
: Product Development
: Computer Literacy 1
: Modern Languages (3)
: Marketing

Food Technology

Food Technology
Food and Related Services
A further three from
: Marketing
: Photography
: Word Processing
: Modern Business Systems (2)
: Biotechnology
: Product Development
: Computer Literacy 1

Services in the Community

Two modules from Services in the Community (2)
A further three from
: Food Technology
: Food and Related Service
: Biotechnology
: Product Development
: Computer Literacy 1
: Leisure and Recreation

Information Processing

Computer Literacy 1 or Product Development

Information Processing
A further three from

: Computer Literacy Module (3) or (4)
: Word Processing
: Technical Graphics
: Mass Media (2)
: Modern Office Practice

Studies in British Industry

Three modules from Understanding British Industry (4)

A further two from

: Understanding British Industry (4)
: Information Processing
: Word Processing
: Marketing
: The Fashion Industry
: Product Development
: Computer Literacy 1
: Leisure and Recreation

Media Studies

Mass Media 1
Graphic Design
A further three from

: Mass Media 2
: Marketing
: Photography
: Product Development
: Computer Literacy 1

Technological Studies

Three modules from Control Technology (4)
Plus either
or two form:

: Technology Project (equivalent to 1)
: Technology Project (equivalent to 1)
: Other Control Technology module
: Microelectronics (4)
: Technical Graphics
: Food Technology
: Biotechnology
: Product Development
: Computer Literacy 1

NB *Disqualified combinations of programmes*

The following combinations of programmes are disallowed by the Examination Board:
a) Computer Literacy and Information Processing
b) Media Studies and Design Studies
c) Services in the Community & Food Technology

NB The numbers in brackets refer to the number of sub-modules available under each modular title.

example the college contribution includes experience of CNC lathes for Control Technology modules, CAD machinery for a variety of 14–18 courses and the electronic office within the *Modern business systems* modules.

2   It delivers particular modules providing both the staff and the facilities, eg *Modern office practice; Modern business systems;* and *Food technology.*

3   In cases where INSET has not yet prepared staff, college lecturers have the expertise to teach certain modules, either in schools or in the college.

TVEI is concerned with the notion of progression from 14 to 18. The involvement of the college in planning with schools is clearly important in helping students identify potential routes which they might follow after the 14–16 phase. The college also gives students the opportunity to involve themselves in the atmosphere of an FE institution, and is able to offer a version of 'vocationalism' which is immediately realistic and practical.

Consortia working is enhanced by the organisation of modules in half-day blocks. This not only facilitates more varied teaching approaches and active learning styles but also permits collaboration with FE and industry, as well as facilitating out of school visits. Although the schools do not, as yet, have completely common timetables many of the modular programmes are offered on the same day so as to allow movement of students between institutions as and when necessary. While students are not expected to move in large numbers from one institution to another there has been a need for such consortia arrangements in the delivery of specific modules. This might be necesary where the cost of equipment prevents replication in all centres or where the level of expertise is lacking in one centre. In this way institutional collaboration is able to facilitate broad curriculum objectives for each student.

Records of achievement

An essential element of modular schemes in Coventry is recognition of the need for students to review and reflect on experiences in the modules and record personal views and possible applications of learning. One school in particular has had considerable experience in this field and a member of their staff worked in the other TVEI pilot institutions to replicate good practice. This ensured that the process of developing, reflecting and recording would remain integral to each module.

Supported self-study

In September 1986 TVEI funded the appointment of a central coordinator for supported self-study and personal recording. Her brief was to coordinate the implementation of pilot schemes of supported self-study in the three TVEI schools and the college, including the provision of professional support and in-service training for teachers, advising on suitable resources and developing the necessary tutorial support for such a project.

Each institution within the consortia selected its own coordinator, who was given .2 of a timetable in which to support the development of materials and tutoring skills. Funding was made available for resources and two subject areas in each school chosen. These were:

Computer literacy modules	A marketing module
English	Geography
Food and related service	Travel and tourism
Modern languages	History

With regular support from the central coordinator these subject areas began to look for resources and appropriate structures suitable for the 14 to 18 age group. A framework evolved through which advice was sought from advisers, curriculum development groups, supported self-study coordinators, subject teachers and the TRIST team. By drawing upon this expertise across the consortia and city the quality and quantity of the resources was increased. The importance of tutorial support was uppermost when planning curriculum and again a common framework began to evolve, drawing on the expertise of the consortia. It soon became apparent that developing materials in such a way raised awareness of the existence of supported self-study developments and requests to see and use materials came in. The exchange of packages across consortia necessitated the collection and storage at TVEI central office and it is hoped that in future all members of consortia will hold such materials in their resource libraries.

The TVEI modular approach has created opportunities for schools to experiment with mixed-age provision. In one school this has meant fourth and fifth year students timetabled together, in another, fourth and lower sixth form students. This necessitated the need for clear and concise instructions for students and initial tasks suited as much to the fourth former as the sixth former. The determining factor is that the teacher knows which enrichment materials to give to which student, and in which situation. Additionally, it is hoped that anyone wishing for any reason to 'catch up' on part of a course can use these materials.

The importance of support from tutors is paramount in supported self-study and the next stage will be to provide INSET for teachers in the consortia who wish to develop their skills in this area. Because the central coordinator attends supported self-study meetings in schools and publishes a regular bulletin distributed to all interested teachers in Coventry schools, the work of the pilot schools has a wide audience and details of successful innovation often result in a request for materials.

The common aim highlighted in supported self-study encourages all involved to keep in mind the important goals of pupil autonomy and active learning, a central aim for Coventry's TVEI. To really succeed in this aim it is necessary that schools and colleges re-examine their library and study provision. The project's next goal is to support schools in the re-organisation of libraries into resource centres capable of providing study facilities using all media. Some supported self-study funding has gone towards technological provision to enable students to use reference tools which they will need in a technological world.

Problems of consortia

Inevitably there are difficulties arising from consortia even where institutions are willing partners in cooperative activity. Essentially a Coventry comprehensive school is the pastoral base for its own students up to the age of 18 and beyond. With the school being the clear focus for guidance and counselling there are bound to be tensions when students are studying their chosen curriculum in more than one institution.

The operation of the TVEI modular scheme at 14–16 involves only limited movement of students between institutions. At maximum a student would only be at another school or college for two half-days a week at any one time. Travelling, even in a geographically compact city like Coventry, can present difficulties and can be time-consuming.

There can, however, be more fundamental problems in ensuring the effective working of a modular system based on consortia. The compatibility of learning styles between, for example, schools and colleges is not always evident, despite the workings of curriculum groups and consortia management. TVEI has encouraged youngsters to negotiate their learning and routes through modules. This process can be undermined when students meet a system in another institution which appears less flexible and offers less responsibility to the learner.

Consortia can only be as effective as their management. If time is not invested in the necessary preparation and co-ordination then problems can arise, forcing schools and colleges to revert to autonomy and self-reliance. Indeed the very idea of consortia challenges an institution's autonomy and freedom to determine its own curriculum and styles of learning. The purposes of consortia need to be clearly delineated in setting up modules for collaborative working. At a time of falling rolls and greater demands to fit new subjects on to the curriculum, consortia can offer realistic solutions. The principle of offering flexible access and opportunities for following a richer and more varied curriculum within a modular system can provide the necessary motivation in making consortia work.

The way forward

The lessons learnt from the pilot stages of TVEI with regard to consortia and modular development will prove invaluable as and when moves are made towards a full modular curriculum.

The prospect of full-time education/training for all up to 18 makes it essential to plan a sequence of educational experiences for each individual through to 18. The present significance of 16+ will therefore change. As the Education Committee's *Comprehensive Education for Life* document states:

> It is clear that the majority of youngsters would not want a continuation of the present schooling process. Many youngsters are bored in the last two years of secondary school: others take the examinations at 16+ without much enthusiasm. Both these groups, which together constitute over 50% of the age group, require a fundamentally different approach. Current work (eg at School TOPSHOP) is showing the value for *all students* of work experience, life skills and personal programmes where positive self-esteem, status and achievement are promoted.

It is concluded that provision up to 18 will need to concentrate on preparing the young for independent living in an increasingly complex adult society. The content of programmes should include life, social and personal skills as well as vocational skills. Direct experience through personal and group activity is needed as well as book learning. These programmes should start at age 14 and allow for sequential and progressive development for each individual, which could encompass a mixture of academic, personal, work-related, full and part-time experiences, including encounters with employers. The youngsters should be accorded as nearly as possible adult status – adults with 'L' plates, rather than pupils. It is therefore proposed that:

> *A system of modular based courses or credits be developed from age 14* (the present age of choice for examination courses) *which can be extended and built upon to age 18* and including the present examinations in

academic subjects. This could be likened to an à la carte menu of education.

This will inevitably mean new and more flexible forms of accreditation. In conjunction with MEG Coventry has succeeded in gaining accreditation for some 36 modules encompassing a variety of technical and pre-vocational experience. Although free standing the modules can be clustered to provide coherent packages leading to GCSE. The next step is to negotiate a system of unit accreditation for students from the age of 14 offering the acquisition of credits across a range of academic and vocational subject areas enabling progression, transferability and the ability to bank credits. Such a scheme could embrace those in full-time and part-time education, those on work-related training programmes and YTS students.

Work has already been done in other areas on the modularisation of 'A' level courses that will allow students to cross and experience the inter-relationship between traditional subject boundaries. A system of modular accreditation at this level would allow courses to be packaged leading to a fusion of vocational (B/TEC) and 'A' level subjects. This would realise the notion of breadth and balance, as well as depth, through to 18 and allow for more flexible learning opportunities by establishing transfer between routes with credits.

For such developments to occur there has to be a clear and coherent curriculum framework for all institutions dealing with students from 14–18. This has major implications for the organisation of 11–18 education and management at institutional and consortia level.

As *Education for Life* states in reference to 'A framework for modular programmes 14–18:'

> We envisage that the programmes which will be needed to support our proposals for 14–18 year olds will need to be developed within a framework constructed from a variety of activity components. This will not be easy because, as has been indicated, this must include and give status to areas of experience and activity beyond the traditional subjects. Not all the components will be available at or managed from the 'home base'. As now, under consortium arrangements some components will only be available at certain schools or FE colleges. Through the four year period, increasing use will need to be made of opportunities provided by bodies outside the education service: particularly by employers (ie work or work experience) and under MSC programmes. All these and other components will need to be available as building blocks in the kit.

13 Modules in management

David Warwick

Modules are not ends in themselves. They need always to be viewed against a wider perspective and within the context of the purpose they were created to serve.

Their application to management is no exception. Here, the perspective needs to be that of a single institution or, possibly, a close-knit consortium; the context in which they have most to offer would seem to be that of staff development. It is necessary, then, to look first at just what it is that the school as an organisation sets out to achieve, after which the role that modules may play in this whole process can be more thoroughly examined.

The tasks of management

Early managerial research – more specifically into the process of leadership – concentrated upon characteristics exhibited by those who had manifestly made their mark in business or in commerce. It was hoped that an aggregation of such qualities would provide a blueprint whereby their successors might be trained. This biographical line had a pedagogic counterpart in the study of the charismatic headteachers of our nineteenth century public schools – the Arnolds, Butlers and Things of the educational world. The exercise, however, proved fruitless, giving credence to the idea that leadership was – after all – a holistic concept. The successful were 'born to greatness' and no amount of categorisation could assist those who had it 'thrust upon them'.

Far more promising than an examination of the leadership styles of the good and the great has been some analysis of the actual tasks they are called upon to perform. Here a second, somewhat more lowly, strand within our educational history has significance – the Bells and Lancasters of the elementary sector. Their thinking had, perforce, to be dominated by issues of size, structure, organisation and system.

Both elements came together in the pioneer work of Carroll Shartle who, in the late 1940s, identified two major dimensions which needed to be kept in balance and within which managers needed to excel. These were: *Consideration* (the ability to deal fairly and effectively within individuals or groups) and *Initiating Structure* (establishing and maintaining an appropriate organisational framework).[1] Similar findings emerged from Parsons,[2] who labelled them *expressive* and *instrumental*; from Getzels and Guba,[3] to whom they were *ideographic* and *nomathetic* dimensions; and from Blake and Mouton,[4] who produced a grid plotting the extent of *employee-centred* and *production-centred* leadership. In 1975 Yukl[5] added a third dimension to the duality – *decision-centralization*, which serves to indicate the degree to which a leader influences a group's decision. Tannenbaum and Schmidt[6] have plotted the nature of this intervention on their celebrated *continuum* of 1958.

This is a very broad canvas on which to sketch the tasks of management, but at least it is a beginning. The next step is for each institution – be it school, college, hospital, factory, supermarket, etc – to scale down the process enormously. The needs of each will differ and a whole range of purely parochial considerations will come into play, but two factors at least remain constant. Any organisation has to be thought of in terms of divisions that are both vertical and horizontal; the administrative levels and lateral sections through which its aims can best be met.

Vertical and horizontal divisions

A straightforward approach to the levels of responsibility within any organisation is to regard these are being threefold: *executive, tactical* and *operational*. In a school, for example:

- *executive* decisions relate to overall aims and long-term policy;
- *tactical* decisions are concerned with the influence of such aims on sectional planning;

---

[1] See, Halpin, A, *Theory and Research in Administration*, Macmillan, New York, 1966, pp. 97–8.
[2] Parsons, T, *The Social System*, Free Press, Glencoe, 1951.
[3] Getzels, JW and Guba, EG 'Social Behaviour and the Administrative Process', in *School Review*, 65, pp. 423–41.
[4] Blake, RR and Mouton, JS, *The Managerial Grid*, Gulf Publishing Co, Houston, 1964.
[5] Yukl, G, 'Towards a Behavioural Theory of Leadership', in Houghton, V, *The Management of Organisations and Individuals*, Ward Lock, London, 1975.
[6] Tannenbaum, R and Schmidt, WH, 'How to Choose a Leadership Pattern', in *Harvard Business Review*, 51 (3), 1973.

- *operational* decisions are vital for the translation of institutional policy into classroom practice.

The interrelationship of all three areas may be shown diagrammatically, as in Figure 13.1.

Lateral divisions will again differ from institution to institution according to local needs, the variation here being from the large-scale (Faculty/House/School) to the more precisely defined (Department/Year/Form), and from the highly participative (Working party/Matrix) to the more rigidly regulated (Line and branch/Hierarchy). It can be seen that, quite irrespective of the actual form they take, these vertical and horizontal divisions form a close relationship one with the other.

Individual and organisation: a symbiotic relationship

Viewed in this way an organisation is a coherent whole, with each of the components having its part to play in the translation of aims into action, of policy in practice. This concept has never been better

Figure 13.1

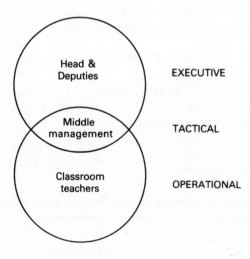

expressed than it was – in its political context – by the eighteenth century orator, Edmund Burke:

> Parliament is not a congress of ambassadors from different and hostile interests; which interests each must maintain as an agent and advocate, against other agents and advocates; but parliament is a deliberative assembly of one nation, with one interest, that of the whole; where, not local purposes, not local prejudices ought to guide, but the general good, resulting from the general reason of the whole. You choose a member indeed; but when you have chosen him, he is not a member of Bristol, but he is a member of parliament.[7]

Once appointed, the Head of History, of Physics, of Granville House, the School of Creative Studies or the Upper Sixth, the co-ordinator of TVEI or Chairman of a working-party on Community Links – all have sectional interests to uphold. But each also has far more important responsibilities, and these are to the school or college as a whole. Again, the duality – or the creative tension – that lies at the heart of management is revealed. To return once more to Shartle's premise (see p 208), each post-holder at every level needs to have *consideration* for all those within his group, but he also has a duty to the *structure* from which his authority derives.

It used to be assumed that such responsibilities were, at each level, self-evident and so little attempt was made to spell them out in writing or even to describe them verbally to newly appointed members of staff. More recently, though, as schools have increased in size, the influence of industry has been more widely felt, managerial training has been made available and teachers more professionally 'extended'[8] – the preparation of *job descriptions* has become more common. These usually state *to* whom the person is responsible, *for* whom and *in respect of* which areas of work.

It is important that such documents are jointly agreed and regularly reviewed. Just as structure can give the individual a framework within which to innovate, such ideas also need to be fed back into the system. The relationship which exists here is a symbiotic one, central both to job satisfaction and organisational growth.

Contingency planning

Alongside the job description, especially in larger organisations, should go the *succession plan*. This is merely a process whereby all contingencies,

---

[7] Burke, E, *Speech to the Electors of Bristol*, 3rd November, 1774.

however wild, are considered and some time set aside for discussing them.

What, for example, happens if Joe goes under the proverbial bus, Mary requests maternity leave, the Geography Department suffers a sudden decline in numbers, or the Head of Mathematics unexpectedly decides to take early retirement? The options are various – promotion of the next teacher in line, advertising the position, switching someone over from another area of the curriculum, closing the Department, amalgamating two or more areas – but these are decisions which should not be taken in a hurry. Each has implications for the institution as a whole and they all require some element of planned professional development if they are to succeed.

At first sight the task may seem enormous. If, however, the overall aims of the organisation have been clearly established and are currently being translated into practice in the ways indicated above, such contingency planning will not be seen as a series of 'one off' decisions. Rather, broad strategies emerge that encompass a large range of possibilities. Furthermore, the organisation will move from one which is continually having to reconsider its options in the light of changing circumstances to one which is in a proactive state of readiness for all eventualities.

This is particularly relevant to schools and colleges at times of demographic decline or geographic mobility; when they are subject to falling rolls and fluctuating demands upon various sections of their curriculum. Succession plans may, at their worst, amount to little more than a series of increasingly untenable fall-back positions but, even so, they are a major advance on the organisational drift and curricular uncertainty that so often preceded them.

Audit and appraisal

The *job description* and the *succession plan* are great advances on what has gone before, but something even more direct is required if they are to be really successful. Specific targets need to be set, precise activities identified – a *skills audit* conducted for every position within the organisation. In this way not only will those in post have a much clearer idea of their role and thus be able to develop it in accordance with their own individual strengths, but new possibilities are opened up in the field of in-service education and training – especially if this is coupled with a cross-institutional approach to succession planning.

This whole area is, of course, a controversial one. The very title – *staff appraisal* – under which it has come to be known, has guaranteed the hostility of the teaching profession, whilst pronouncements from politicians from the Secretary of State downwards have done little to avert their suspicion. Here, most of the emphasis seems to have been upon the exposure of weaknesses and ineptitude, the ousting of incompetents from our schools. Little is heard of the positive features of the process, and certainly no attempt has been made to link appraisal – if we must call it this! – to other aspects of management.

In reality this regularly scheduled meeting of section heads with those for whom they are responsible is the focal-point of the symbiotic relationship between individual and organisation referred to above (see p. 209). It ensures that the former sees his work in relation to all else that is going on and that the latter is strengthened by the continual infusion of new ideas. These may, through appraisal interviews, be fed back into the system, while assistance in their furtherance is guaranteed through succession planning and an appropriate form of staff development.

More particularly, staff appraisal involves:

- a *two-way process*, in which the roles of both parties and their mutual relationship are openly discussed and, if necessary, redefined;
- the setting of jointly-agreed *targets* for the coming year;
- an examination of those *agreed* at the *last meeting* in relation to organizational policy in general;
- a discussion of prospects for *advancement* within the organization or the profession in general against a background of the skills audit of all positions.
- an opportunity to plan the provision of suitable *training* as and when requested.

The link between *staff appraisal*, the *skills audit* and *in-service education and training* is an important one.

In-service education

Whatever training is required usually devolves upon a specific department established for this purpose, or is bought in from external agencies. Similarly, within the educational system, it is common practice to invite teachers at certain stages in their careers to attend Local Authority programmes. These are normally run by the local Inspectorate.

In-service education of this kind, being pitched at specified levels in the hierarchy, includes all those skills and competencies looked for in those seeking promotion to the next. As such, it often fails to respond adequately to individual need. Within a single course, for example, one teacher may excel in communication but be hopeless at time-management, a second might be really good at planning and preparation but fall down badly on the skills of leadership, a third could have experience in organisation but be unfamiliar with and therefore uncertain of the whole area of professional counselling. In the same programme, certain areas may appear to some to be elementary, simplistic and tedious, to others they are complex and badly in need of further development.

In more general terms, it can be seen that such training brings pressure to bear upon the individual to conform either to the school or to the company 'norm'. This is acceptable up to a point – the juncture at which creativity and initiative are stifled. Furthermore, the blending of training and of assessment in such courses is not a happy one. It does not lend itself either to the open expression of opinion, or to a readiness to make the kind of mistakes from which learning can ensue. If, as is almost universally the case with local education authorities, the programmes are conducted by those upon whom one's future career prospects depend, the temptation to conform, take the party line or merely to remain silent, must be almost overwhelming.

What is really needed is something far more responsive to individual need: an approach which, albeit within the context of an overall system or single institution, begins where people are, is directly applicable to their everyday working lives, delivers what is wanted in weeks rather than months and is capable of endless modification. Traditional forms of in-service work cannot meet such exacting specifications. Immediacy, relevance and specificity are essential ingredients, and some form of modular approach is indicated.

Modular transactions

If it has taken some time to arrive at this point, it is for the reason given at the beginning of this chapter – that modules should never be considered in isolation. They always form part of some larger process. Here, their importance lies not as a theoretical model that someone outside the organisation has decided will be helpful to those toiling at specified levels within it. Rather, modules arise naturally from the managerial pattern already described.

For each of the skills that have been identified, or for coherent groups of them, short, highly participative units of training may be developed. These will take the form of one, two or three day mini-courses, half-day workshops, interactive videos or tape/slide sequences, planned visits or interviews, extended simulations/case studies, or a combination of any of these approaches. The *goals* of each are precisely spelt out, prepared beforehand and 'banked' in readiness for use at short notice. They need to be infinitely adaptable within their limited remit as the approach differs each time they are used. Such a unit has the merits of being:

> *positive* – as it begins where the individual is, or wants to go
> *direct* – as it focuses on skills related to this
> *brief* – as these skills are isolated for individual attention
> *immediate* – as such a response is readily available
> *practical* – as it relates positively to the work being done
> *functional* – as direct feedback is received

Modules of this kind place the individual at the centre of the staff development process, permitting personal and professional growth to occur at his own pace; in the very best educational tradition, learning to occur as and when he is *ready* to receive it. Discrete yet interrelated units such as those described above also enable the institution more readily to determine its own destiny and to involve all its employees in doing just this. If the *organisation* and the *individual* are key elements in a symbiotic relationship, then it is through modular transactions that such osmotic transferences occur.

Modular planning

Modules prepared for these purposes should have as wide an application as possible. One of their great benefits is that they promote the professional development of both the agile-minded and his equally reliable but more ponderous colleague without necessarily favouring one above the other. Much, in fact, is to be gained from such a cross-fertilisation of ideas and practice between those of varying age, responsibility and length of service. Each module will have its own tightly specified set of objectives but, within these, experience can inform youth and enthusiasm question custom.

Although wide in their application, modules will vary considerably both in form and in function. Indeed, under this approach to in-service education, length of unit, size of group and basic approach are all determined by specified objectives, rather than vice-versa. This is partly a result of the direct, practical nature of the work being done and partly due to a concentration on specific skills.

Some modules, then, may consist of inter-active video material which focuses sharply on a series of tiny but important skills – *using a telephone, eye contact, terminating an encounter*, etc. These will be designed for use by individuals and the length of time devoted to each will be infinitely variable. As well as forming part of the staff development programme, such modules should be freely available in the Staff and Departmental libraries. It can be seen how they may be utilised at a variety of levels and can form supplementary material for larger units.

Other modules are basically experiential by design and therefore are appropriate for groups of five or six only. *Interviewing skills*, for example, may make extensive use of CCTV, whilst *Professional counselling* is likely to contain a large amount of role-play material. The length here is likely to be two to three days full-time, although such units are often 'stepped'. In other words, between each full-day session they provide periods of about a week's duration for structured observation, discussion within Departments, viewing of video material or further consideration.

Larger numbers may be accommodated by modules which draw their strength from the interaction of sub-groups. *Leadership styles* or *Delegation*, for instance, may consist of up to 12 or 15 participants, with sets of three to five operating in rather different ways to make the point. Plenary sessions may then be devoted to an exchange of experiences and reactions to them. These units are usually self contained and each lasts for two or more days.

It may be decided, of course, that within such a scheme not every module can be made available to all those who wish to attend it, although care has to be taken to retain as much of the 'open access' policy as possible. Certain units may be deemed to be rather specialised, relating as they do to specific areas within the organisation. Those on *Chairing a meeting; Decision making in groups; Team building* and *Time management* may be equally applicable across a wide spectrum of middle management, or for those aspiring to it. *Profiling procedures, The parental interview* or *Reference writing*, tend to relate particularly to one area of the school, whilst *Working with a secretary, Staff appointments* and *The Governors' meeting* might be reserved for Heads and their Deputies only.

Various different types of modules can, in fact, be identified for use within a management training scheme:

Free standing [open to all] eg *The use of TTNS; Job application; Time management*
Inter-related [closely linked] eg *Presentation skills; Report writing, preparing an agenda; 'selling' the school*
Sequential [to be taken in correct order] eg *Assessment procedures 1,2,3* etc

Stratified [taken only at appropriate level] – see examples above
Spiral [same material covered in greater depth at different stages]
eg Interviews and interviewing; Decision making; Presenting your
case; Outside agencies
Refresher [up-dated and repeated at regular intervals] Research
findings, School/College policy
Stepped see above

Just how far this process of modular differentiation should go is for
each school, college or company to decide. A lot will depend upon the
precise balance which is required between the pre-structuring of the
pathways to promotion and the encouragement of personal initiative
and ambition. This once more reflects the larger duality between
individual and organisation already noted, and places great responsibility
on those who prepare the modules. Too great an emphasis in one
direction could lead to an over-formalised programme and the stifling
of individuality; too much attention to the other might result in the
fragmentation of staff development policy within the institution or over-
indulgence of personal whims.

Attention also needs to be given to the manner in which modules are
brought to the attention of all those likely to require them, the
communication of their precise content and the provision of advice or
guidance over their selection. Here much reliance has to be placed upon
managers at each level within the organisation and, although staff
development should be on-going throughout the year, the *appraisal
interview* is likely to play a central part within it. The concept of
readiness has already been borrowed from the world of the classroom
to epitomise the transition of in-service education along modular lines.
Further pedagogic terms may now be applied to the handling of the
advisory part of the process:

1   Transactions conducted during the appraisal interview, including
    the selection of appropriate modules, have already been described
    as two-way, reciprocal ones. They are open to *negotiation.*
2   Future professional development may thus be jointly planned
    through an aggregation of modules and plotted by means of open
    profiling.
3   In order to do this, each module needs to be clearly *specified.*

Modular specification

An accurate description of each module which is on offer will be
required both by those who may wish to attend it and those with

responsibility for guidance in such matters. To avoid any ambiguity over content or approach, and to assist those preparing the material, a common *specification sheet* is helpful. Such sheets enable the essential features of each module to be set out in a format that is easy to understand and which facilitates the combination of various units, in a variety of patterns, according to individual need.

A typical format could be that shown in Figure 13.2.

Figure 13.2

TITLE _____ REF. NO. _____

LENGTH _____ PREPARED BY _____

OBJECTIVES _____

APPROACH _____

LINKS WITH OTHER MODULES _____

COMMENTS _____

DATE _____ SIGNED _____

The final entry enables the module's contribution to the staff development programme to be evaluated. Each time it is activated, feedback is received not only from those teaching it, but also those attending it and their line managers. In this way each module is continually being revised and up-dated, whilst – within the Department – assistance can be given in the translation of the insights gained into daily practice. Information thus garnered within the profile also provides the basis for future staff development.

Intensive in-service education, albeit of the traditional kind, will probably be required prior to the introduction of any such scheme. The main features of this programme serve also to summarise the modular contribution to staff development. They will consist of:

- the *preparation* of modules which precisely match the requisite skills at each level and within each section of the organisation;

- the *running* of such short, participative units;
- precise *specification* of their content;
- the *communication* of information regarding this throughout the institution;
- two-way *negotiation* regarding selection of modules and feed-back relating to them;
- open-ended *profiling* based upon modules attended and those which are available;
- continuous *modification* of individual modules.

Crossing the boundaries

Industrial concerns may well be able to mount such programmes on their own premises and within their budget and, under the new INSET regulations, most secondary schools should be able to do so also. Smaller schools, and in particular those at primary and middle level, may have to look elsewhere for alternative arrangements. Here, *consortia* of schools is one solution, another is to rely upon the local teachers' centre or the LEA advisory service to provide for such needs. If this is done, the schools involved must remain closely involved at all stages in the planning and implementation of the scheme or there could be little to distinguish it from what has gone before.

Elements in the consortia solution are, in any case, likely to prove necessary. Even given the small numbers involved with each module, it may not always prove possible to find sufficient teachers within a single institution once a particular unit has been requested. It would then seem logical to combine forces with other schools to meet a jointly-felt need. On the other hand, some modules could prove to be so popular that undue pressure is felt by specific schools in certain areas. Again, an exchange of ideas could lead to the running of different modules at different centres. The problem here, of course, is that the wider the consortia net is spread, the more likely it is to provide just the elements of staff development that are required but the further the process becomes removed from the specific needs of each individual school. A careful balance has to be struck between these two requirements.

All this assumes that it is only *educational* institutions that are involved in such managerial processes; that the problems explored in this chapter are the province of teachers alone. But is this really the case? Are there not in close proximity to each and every school other establishments tackling issues that have a remarkably similar look about them? Is, for example, a *meeting* conducted differently in a school, a hospital or a university? Does *staff appraisal* vary all that much when handled in industry and in education? *Time management* in factories, offices, cathedrals or classrooms – are new approaches required in each? Is there a marked change between the way trade unionists and teachers write their *reports*? And are *appointments* made after a radically different fashion by solicitors, the armed services, commerce or headteachers?

The answer to all these questions is probably a qualified 'no'. These various organisations may differ considerably in their aims and approach, but the method whereby they arrive at these aims, the means by which they achieve their goals, the structures they establish for this purpose and the way in which they evaluate their success are all very similar. The overall context may vary but individual processes and procedures do not. Certainly, when one concentrates on the specific skills required and the levels at which these operate across large enterprises of all kinds – be they educational, industrial, ecclesiastical or military, to do with the creation of wealth or the welfare of the citizenry – remarkably little variation is perceived.

Changes of emphasis there will be and institutions of different kinds will obviously stress different aspects of their work. This, however, should be a growth-point when managerial processes and staff development are considered across organisations of all kinds. To do so would strengthen the work of each individual concern. Not only this. The essence of any analysis, such as the one conducted in this chapter, is the generation of new, mutually-acceptable syntheses. To apply the technique in macro within an even broader context could provide some coherence within an increasingly specialised and fragmentary society.

14 Modular INSET

Michael Phillips

The West Sussex Institute of Higher Education was formally constituted in 1977 by uniting the Bishop Otter College, Chichester, and the Bognor Regis College. In 1985 a formal association was made between the Institute and the Graylingwell School of Nursing, which is housed on the Bishop Otter site.

The Bishop Otter College was founded by William Otter, Bishop of Chichester, in 1839. This Anglican college was established to train teachers who could relate their professional studies to Christian values.

The Bognor Regis College was established in 1947 and is based on a handsome terrace of Georgian mansions built in 1790 by Sir Richard Hotham as a home for the Prince Regent, his daughter Charlotte and members of the aristocracy.

The West Sussex Institute of Higher Education is primarily concerned with initial teacher training, but also with numerous INSET activities – Mathematics being the largest and involving 35 LEAs and the DES. Special educational needs is also involved in the expanding INSET programme.

Besides initial teacher education and INSET, the West Sussex Institute offers a wide range of first degree programmes, including sports studies, history, geography, English and religious studies.

The old concept of INSET delivered in traditional didactic style is unsuited to the current demands from teaching. INSET must now be seen as on-going, as a form of professional and educational development which begins soon after qualifying and is career-long. INSET needs to strive to bridge the gap between Higher Education and schools. Initial teacher training needs to be more the responsibility of schools in general and teachers in particular. Newly-qualified teachers need to understand that their professional duty is to be continuously up-dated and that this is the responsibility jointly and collaboratively of Higher Education, the LEA and teachers themselves.

But teachers are traditionally suspicious of change. Evolution rather than revolution has governed the nature of educational change. Over the past decade, the rate of change has increased and the nature of change has altered. No longer, it seems, do Education Acts and government initiatives appear after a period of debate and so take effect within an informed climate of opinion. In the past, there was not necessarily agreement but at least ·there was understanding.

Past and present

Professional autonomy features highly among the differences between changes past and present. Past changes involved teachers and their LEAs in the management of the change processes. In recent times the control of change has been taken, to a great extent, away from teachers, schools and LEAs and, increasingly, has been prescribed and controlled by central government. Parent power has caused teachers to become more accountable to parents. The movement towards vocational education has caused the world of industry and commerce to become more involved in the education of young people. The education system itself is moving rapidly towards accountability and market forces are creating a 'quality control' type of influence upon the ways schools, teachers and LEAs operate.

This increasing pace of change, centrally dictated and externally prescribed, with its inbuilt demand for accountability, is exposing a need for teachers to acquire swiftly a new set of skills. If teachers are to be members of the change processes (and for change to be successful they *must* be part of the process), then there are resource implications. Teachers need to be change agents, not simply promoting changes but managing them – monitoring, assessing, evaluating and planning with proactive professionalism. Out of this 'need' the main resource implication emerges: the need for *time* – time to acquire new sets of skills. It is not good enough to 'teach' them, they have to be learnt and sharpened. In-service opportunities need to be available which allow teachers to follow courses which are professionally orientated. Newly acquired professional skills demand that teachers are offered INSET which matches knowledge and theory to practice.

INSET tutors themselves must have a depth of knowledge and sets of skills which enable them to engage INSET teachers in the process of change. If teachers are to become extended professionals, the tutors must be extended professionals too. These tutors must have classroom credibility, with recent and relevant as well as successful experience and be part of a continuous updating process.

Location is also a resource requiring careful consideration. INSET cannot afford to be distanced from the workplace if it is to consider, research and analyse the changing nature of the curriculum and the professional skills required to manage and deliver it. Yet, to perceive the only location for INSET as the workplace is to encourage a rather myopic view of current professional needs. INSET needs to make use of a combination of on- and off-site locations in order to encourage wide-ranging and far-sighted professional development.

Just as teachers are under pressure to respond effectively and appropriately to the needs of a changing technological society, so too are INSET providers. Both are being subjected to similar, centralist demands. The traditional form of INSET is faced with a dilemma which may be described – in simplistic terms – as government and other agencies knowing what they want but the education system being unable to provide it as swiftly as required. The constraints lie in present resources: time, money and above all expertise.

INSET and teacher control

Teachers increasingly complain that they are forever being told what they ought to be doing but that no-one seems able to tell them *how* to do it. Expertise, it is often assumed, lies somewhere 'out there' and teachers could do the job if only they could get their hands on it. It seems to me that there is no one magical outside agency to which techers or others can go to obtain the elixir of eternal professionalism. In order to begin to meet the requirements of teachers in this time of 'revolutionary' change, teachers themselves need to be involved increasingly in the creation of their own expertise through professional development.

The implications of this self-generating body of knowledge and expertise begin to shift the traditional concept of INSET from one that is prescribed and the responsibility solely or partly of individuals outside the classroom – advisors, Higher Education tutors – to a concept of INSET which is interactive and involves the teachers themselves in conception, inception and delivery.

If effectiveness is a prerequisite of INSET then teacher involvement with LEA, school and outside agencies will ensure that INSET is real, relevant and professionally pertinent. In cost effective terms the return on the investment will be quicker if teachers obtain a greater 'ownership' of their own professional development and the nature and content of INSET is negotiated tri-partitely – by school or LEA, teacher and provider. Such INSET is more likely to be sharply and professionally focused.

This concept of INSET – by no means new (see Stenhouse, 1975) –

begins to address the issue of professional autonomy raised earlier. Teachers need to be consulted about the demands being made upon them. It is hoped that appraisal will contain the mechanism whereby teachers can clarify and articulate their needs. Teachers' representatives at Professional Centres and within professional organisations need to be involved in negotiations with providers and, where appropriate, outside agencies including representatives from industry, in order to plan content, modes of 'delivery' and INSET routes.

Ownership of this nature will address the need to create pools of expertise both in and outside teaching and so begin the process of re-skilling. It will raise the morale and status of teachers. It will involve teachers in developing professionalism and creating some control over their own professional destiny. It is my opinion that this can best be achieved through modular forms of INSET, such as those being developed at the West Sussex Institute of Higher Education.

The West Sussex Institute of Higher Education has for some time taken part in Southampton University's regional credit award transfer scheme. A number of establishments of higher education offer, like WSIHE, a diverse range of certificated courses on a modular pattern. By selecting certificates on offer from various places of higher education and at the university, a student can create a study route to suit individual needs, as long as the cluster of four certificates makes up a compatible, coherent and rational range of studies. The certificates – referred to as modules – are therefore 'stand alone' certificates, enabling teachers to space out their study time over a period of up to five years. Teachers can pick a route and pace of study to suit their needs. Each module can be studied in its own right. Four certificate modules successfully studied lead to the award of the Diploma of Advanced Educational Studies (DAES); studying two further modules leads to the award of an MA.

The four special needs certificates on offer at WSIHE are as follows:

Module 1, Certificate 1: the approaches to the education of children with special educational needs

This is specifically designed to be 'taught' off site, enabling the LEA to contribute up to 50%, usually to the intervention aspects of the module. This certificate lends itself well to investigative research and combines practical skills with the development of research techniques, which enable teachers to expose issues to be explored further in the following curriculum module.

Teachers returning to study after a lapse of some years are provided with support in order to allow them to acquire study skills. A combination of tutorial and seminar work as well as non-assessed assignments allow teachers to progress through this course gaining in skills and confidence.

Module 2, Certificate 2: The curriculum

This module combines a theoretical and practical focus on a range of curriculum issues. Once again teachers begin with their own school and classroom from which emergent concerns are considered, analysed and further actions are decided upon. As previously explained, a deliberate attempt is made to broaden the teacher's perceptions and knowledge.

Module 3, Certificate 3: Theoretical studies

This is usually 'taught' on site or at an outpost centre and it engages teachers in the study of theoretical aspects of special needs, with a practical, action research focus. Teachers will have studied the previous certificates with the cyclical blend of theory and practice, so the concepts and knowledge required to be studied in depth in this certificate will already have been introduced. There ought therefore to be a good basic understanding of the pedagogical, psychological and sociological areas of study and investigation.

Module 4, Certificate 4: Integrative studies

Certificate 4 is the independent mode of the DAES INSET package. This can involve the teacher in in-depth action research 'in the field'. Ideally the subject of study emerges out of the work already undertaken in previous modules. Indeed, it may well be that issues and concerns illuminated previously and data already gathered provide the impetus for the in-depth study. A tutor is assigned to each teacher and, via a process of negotiation between school, LEA, teacher and tutor, a suitable form of professional study is decided upon. The independent mode involves core groups where ideas are discussed and studies are planned under the guidance of a tutor, leading to seminar sessions and individual tutorials.

Modular design

Each module covers 80–100 hours of taught or supervised time, each hour generating at least two further hours of research and study. Normally they are designed with five or six sections indicating the route through the module. Both LEA representatives (and these may include teachers, headteachers and LEA tutors at this stage); and HE tutors are involved in this type of sequential design. The next phase may involve all concerned in the planning in more detail of course content and structure. Certificate (module) 1, for example, may at this stage be divided into 'mini-modules', maybe four in all, each one of a particular investigative nature. It is at this stage, also, that the delicate balance between open-ended investigations, which reveal issues requiring analysis and study, and the timing of the 'taught' elements essential to the introduction of wider issues are discussed. Planning will centre around the need to reflect upon and analyse emergent concerns, to introduce research methodology and methods and to introduce, for study and discussion, a range of relevant philosophical, ideological and political issues as well as ideas associated with methodology and pedagogy. This does require a responsive and flexible type of proactive planning because, ideally, the need to study these areas and the relevance of these concerns grows out of the investigational work of the teachers.

Figures 14.1 and 14.2 illustrate examples of course outline proposals. Figure 14.2 shows, in a simplified form, Module 1 broken down into *mini-modules*.

The examples of course content proposals are designed to cover between 20 and 30 days of INSET contact time. The formats contain phases – the final one intending to indicate rather than dictate types of outcomes and to provide summative evaluation in order to expose issues and study areas needing to be addressed in the next module. Thus, module 1 can be fused to module 2 in a way which ensures that emergent needs are studied and investigated in a coherent and relevant fashion. Each module incorporates forms of evaluation ensuring that continuity is rationally planned and is both academically and professionally rigorous and relevant.

Management

Modular action research-type INSET which involves the school and senior teachers to a significant extent needs to allow teachers to acquire negotiation, consultative and other change agent skills. From module 1 these are taught, learnt and reflected upon and, as the teacher moves through the modules, these skills are further developed. Certificates 2 and 3 generate 5000-word research projects; Certificate 4 is an independent mode certificate, culminating in a 10 000 word piece of research.

The modules offered operate a permeation policy. The concerns are

Figure 14.1 Module 1 SEN GRIST INSET

INDUCTION	ORIENTATION	PRINCIPLES OF ID	INTERVENTION	POLICY FORMATION OF SEN TEACHER
DATES				
Course introduction Expectations – aims objectives, procedures Library visit Library based investigation Study skills Head/Senior teacher involvement To ensure school focus – Assignments negotiated with senior school colleagues.	Group orientation and data collection - skills within group - professional requirement of participants - needs of work place - Collecting field data upon which to build course Education Act 1981 and beyond - Setting all of above in context - Policies and approaches - Introduction of permeating issues 1 identified by LEA 2 identified by group 3 others negotiated with WSIHE What should/ought an SEN policy contain? - a focus on the main purpose of the course	Making sense of assessment - Norm-v-criteria references - Informal assessment - profiling - record keeping - understanding current school/LEA tests Assignment Early Identification - 0–2 - 2–5 - purpose of assessment and screening - formative, summative - monitoring, recording, reporting (further consideration of issues raised earlier) Report writing - How to approach report writing - Writing for professionals e.g. FAI, Advisers, SPS - Investigate above through case studies ensuring confidentiality	Intervention in learning and behaviour - theory > practice - class based investigation - organisation and management of learning and behavioural difficulties Behaviour analysis and change - school based assignment using behavioural techniques - Precision teaching/Data Pak - Parental involvement Assignment evaluation - An evaluation of assignments Disability and access - environmental, managerial and curriculum concerns	Management models and the whole school approach role of SEN teacher in ID, assessment, intervention - data collection - change agent skills - Incremental management Outside agencies - inter-professional considerations - liaising and collaborating with other professionals Headteacher involvement - writing the policy, outlining strategies - Pro-active management - time-tabling - Special school links Assignment INSET needs in school course evaluation

Figure 14.2

INDUCTION	ORIENTATION	PRINCIPLES OF IDENTIFICATION AND INTERVENTION	POLICY FORMATION AND THE ROLE OF THE SEN TEACHER
MINI-MODULE 1	MINI-MODULE 2	MINI-MODULE 3	MINI-MODULE 4
Current legislation, DES reports, HMI documents, LEA policy – course style, teacher involvement, school involvement, objectives.	School investigation, introduction of further research skills, data collection, writing up and presenting findings	Using information obtained during induction and data collected during mini-module 2 teachers embark upon on in-depth investigation researching own and other schools, other research and literature, using information and skills introduced on course.	To reflect upon emergent issues and collected data and analyse gathered information. Investigate own and other schools and decide how the SEN teacher can best operate and the type of policy information required.
Non-assessed assignments – introduces study skills expectations	Assessed assignments	Some non-assessed assignments leading to assessed research assignment.	Assessed assignments ISSUES FOR PART 2

PERMEATING CONCERNS

ETHNIC DIVERSITY   GENDER   POLICY FORMATION   DEVELOPMENT OF RESEARCH SKILLS   SCHOOL INVOLVEMENT   MICRO-TECHNOLOGY

CHANGE AGENT SKILLS

Figure 14.3

CERTIFICATE (Module) 2 – 'Curriculum Studies'

Weeks	1	3	5	4	2	
	INTRODUCTION	ORIENTATION	CURRICULUM STUDIES	PROVISION, ORGANISATION MANAGEMENT	POLICY	OUTCOMES
	AIMS OBJECTIVES ASSIGNMENTS Nature Purpose Need for coherence, (each assignment phasing into another – illuminative exploration) DUAL FOCUS – Each area to be studied based on common theory concerns etc. but where necessary course splits * OS – MLD } (DF) SLD } HEAD TEACHER SENIOR TEACHER INVOLVEMENT	WHAT IS 'A CURRICULUM?' PROCESS v PRODUCT Curriculum theory INTRODUCTION OF CURRENT CONCERNS Research Literature 5-16 documents LEA DES (DF) SCHOOL BASED INVESTIGATION Data gathering Inventory DATA DISSEMINATION Emergent concerns Curriculum foci Research ASSIGNMENT – based on data and identified concerns To complete for approval research assignment Completion deadline agreed	CURRICULUM MODELS (non-prescriptive) Intro. Whole School Approach NEEDS RELATED CURRICULUM I.D. Assessment (DF) Provision Testing ASSESSING THE CURRICULUM Techniques and Approaches School investigation CURRICULUM ACCESS Modification/ LANG AND LIT. NUMERACY (DF) COMM. SKILLS e.g. Maths across the curriculum, augmented communication, Cockcroft Report, 5-16 documents, lang. development, cloze procedure, IRI SCHOOL INVESTIGATION ASSIGNMENT – 2 Curriculum focus	WHOLE SCHOOL APPROACH Illumination of managerial/ organisational environmental/structural professional issues (DF) LEARNING STYLES and TEACHING STYLES (DF) CLASSROOM MANAGEMENT (DF) RESOURCE BASED LEARNING Planning, providing organising, delivering and evaluating (DF) PROFILING (DF) TIME TABLING (DF) CURRICULUM ISSUES Special School → OS ↓ Lang Units → OS ↓	POLICY FORMATION This began in Cert. 1 and has been a high profile permeation feature of this course. The theme is POLICY: STRATEGIES and PRACTICES CONSIDERATION OF DATA (DF) Seminar Tutorial CONSIDERATION OF POLICIES (DF) Policies of schools participants & others County ASSIGNMENT STUDY Writing the policy, specifying strategies outlining practices. Include FIRST STEPS, include DATA/INFO. upon which this is based EVALUATION	POLICY DOCUMENTS CURRICULUM MATERIALS and PACKAGES ASSESSMENT and EVALUATION PROCEDURES e.g. profiles Research assignment well underway – most data collected Tutorials organised IDENTIFICATION OF SCHOOL'S CURRENT NEEDS INSET PLANS PROFESSIONAL REQUIREMENTS TO BE MET IN CERTIFICATE 3

Permeating issues Ethnic diversity Gender Policy formation Research Curriculum materials Vocational Education Micro-technology
and concerns Change agents skills Ordinary School–Special School Collaboration Research skills

*(DF) = opportunity for course to divide to consider issues pertinent to OS and MLD, and SLD settings.

itemised at the foot of each certificated module and each item must be seen to be addressed during the course. Throughout the INSET courses, teachers' representatives meet formally as a Programmes Board and the course is discussed. Clearly, an item of importance on the agenda must be the permeating concerns, how they are being addressed and how the permeation process is being managed. The tutors and LEA representatives meet on a Management Board during each certificated module and discuss concerns and ideas arising out of the INSET offered or raised by the Programmes Board. These meetings are a requirement of WSIHE and during the Special Needs courses the meetings take place at least twice per module.

Each module has co-ordinating tutor with a team of contributing tutors. It is this co-ordinator who calls the meetings, organises tutorials and seminars and conducts the formative and summative evaluations ensuring quality control.

Such a form of management which involves the teachers ensures the ownership of INSET as previously discussed and ensures also that, in the planning of other certificated modules, ideas, issues and concerns arising out of the INSET currently in operation can be placed within the course outline of the next certificated module. This creates coherence and ensures a professionally cohesive rolling programme. For teachers who come on and off the modules the INSET is, of course, more problematical. However, it is possible to use teachers who have studied previous certificates to induct new members.

Developmental programming

This form of developmental modular INSET emphasises that the tacit, pedagogical knowledge of teachers is important and that practical, professionally-grounded theories are a rich foundation upon which to base class-focused research. Essential to such programmes is the concept of 'the teacher as researcher' being able to reflect, record and analyse in order to investigate in precise terms what is happening to children when they learn. Also stressed is the importance of collaborative work and the crucial importance of the 'supportive professional', whose task it is to help the teacher reflect upon his/her learning as well as that of the pupils.

The kind of programme described here is a form of anthropological in-service education, developmental and evolutionary, which, through modules, can be designed in investigational phases, each phase planned in the light of previously analysed knowledge, skills and actions. It is also illuminative, each phase highlighting issues and concerns to be analysed, acted upon and studied further during the next phase or within the next module. This unfolding, analytical yet practical form of INSET allows teachers to focus progressively upon pertinent and relevant issues. It also enables teachers to develop as extended professionals by increasing awareness and by developing research skills enabling them to be more professionally proactive. An important characteristic of this form of INSET is that it causes participants (both tutor and teacher) to define and refine their thinking.

This professionally-focused 'bottom up' INSET is unlike the traditionally delivered 'top down' type of in-service education in that at no point does it distance the teacher from the classroom. It creates, by its very nature, opportunities for providers to work collaboratively with teachers and so become participant observers of the INSET process. For those INSET tutors like myself who have spent most of their careers in the classroom, this is a welcome feature ensuring continuous up-dating. It guarantees that HE INSET providers have at least some knowledge of, and insight into, the current needs of teachers while ensuring some level of external and available expertise.

Action research – effective learning

A parallel can be drawn between the professional development of teachers incorporating action research, and child-centred education. Learning takes place through experience and discovery. It is most effective when the learner is involved in his/her own learning processes at a pace decided by the learner. Learning involves creating hypotheses and via a process of discovery and problem solving the learner experiments, tests solutions, records and shares findings. It is acknowledged that learning is deemed to have taken place when the learner can generalise from his/her learning and experiences. As part of this learning process the virtues of collaborative work are frequently stressed. All these are features of the type of INSET being developed at WSIHE. It seems strange to me that so much INSET concerned with improving the quality of learning for pupils still persists with the view that INSET is something that needs to be delivered as produce to the supermarket shelves.

In common with other places of Higher Education, WSIHE has moved away from the type of in-service education which sets prescribed outcomes for pre-planned routes. The Stenhousian model of INSET highlights instead concerns associated with the quality and process of learning for both teacher and taught. The modular INSET of WSIHE's Special Needs team is seen as 'needs related' promoting professionally orientated INSET which investigates the dynamic relationship between learning and teaching, teacher and taught, parents, pupils and teachers, centralised demands and school needs. Class focused modular INSET involves teachers in developing an awareness of the needs of all those directly and indirectly involved in the education of pupils. A high priority is placed upon teachers acquiring and demonstrating consultancy and negotiation skills, observation and research skills, skills in identification of needs and provision for them, planning and evaluation as well as management skills. Modular INSET of this nature sensitises teachers to the needs of those whose prime concern is not education, and alerts teachers to giving priority to the process of learning rather than to the mechanical concerns of mere product.

Product versus process

It could be argued that an investigative form of modular INSET built upon the principles of Lawrence Stenhouse is both 'fuzzy' in design and unsure of outcomes. If one of the INSET intentions is to enable teachers to respond positively to the complexity of demands from a variety of forces and, moreover, to do so in a child-centred manner and in a way which broadens and develops professionalism, then I see no fundamental conflict. Conflict can arise if outside forces dictate the nature of the 'journey' teachers must take in order to meet the complexity of demands. Teacher orientated modular INSET which prioritises processes and perceives the journey as one of practice and professional discovery does not regard objectives as unimportant. There is a need for careful, sensitive and rigorous course planning. The INSET planning phases shown in detail in Figures 14.1–14.3 (pp 226–28) comprise *introduction, orientation, management and intervention, evaluation and outcomes* for one module. Such a structure enables teachers to negotiate their initial area of inquiry and then to engage in a process of progressive focusing upon areas to be investigated. Course structure needs to ensure that, as participation is an on-going and integral feature of the entire modular INSET experience, it does in fact happen.

Evaluation and assessment

It is my contention that INSET which employs 'action research' engages teachers in relevant concerns and, rather than lacking evaluation and objectives, is continually setting professionally important and realistically attainable goals. Action research involves both formative and summative evaluation procedures and so has built-in quality control. Prescribed outcomes often cause course participants to focus upon issues which may, in the planning stages, seem important, but as this type of INSET progresses, the emergent issues and concerns, truly important within the context of the teacher's needs, are missed or denied the attention they deserve.

The action research model is inextricably concerned with the classroom, child-centred issues and professional skills and knowledge. It is my contention that this form of modular INSET is most effective, due to its practical focus.

Centralism, parochialism and action research

One of the criticisms of class or school-focused modular in-service education is that, rather than extending and broadening the perceptions, knowledge and skills of teachers, it concentrates on a set of myopic concerns. Rather than encouraging 'professional peripheral vision' it involves teachers in, and so promotes, a narrow focus upon parochial concerns.

When designing and managing modular INSET, the special needs tutors at WSIHE attempt to create 'school focused' rather than purely 'school based' INSET. This is a deliberate attempt to move teachers away from narrow concerns associated with a particular location to an exploration and study of broader and more far-reaching issues. The type of interactive INSET being developed at the Special Needs Centre at WSIHE begins by involving teachers and tutors in class focused investigations in order to raise awareness of wider issues, which are then studied, thus creating a far better informed, and so more effective, classroom practitioner. School based INSET tends to lock teachers into a constricted form of development.

Another criticism is that the centralist control of INSET denies providers sufficient opportunities to involve teachers in devising, at the inception of their INSET, the type of professional development they require.

The GRIST (DES Circ 1986) arrangements allowed the Special Needs modular courses to expand rapidly. The arrangements insist that courses must be geared to the 'designated' teacher responsible for special needs. Centralist forces have therefore dictated the focus of concern but not the journey.

Management and evaluation skills are developed and the processes and functions of systems within an organisation are studied. It is from this focus that the INSET agenda widens and engages teachers in the exploration and investigation of issues arising out of management concerns. In fact, rather than limit the areas of inquiry, it encourages the study of change agent skills. It encourages teachers – in our case special needs teachers – to study the ways their schools function and so gain an introduction to management skills in general. The modular course allows the teachers to acquire skills and insights which match the requirements of a particular system, but the tutors deliberately encourage the development of a wider professional perspective and a study of other – perhaps non-educational – settings.

By addressing the centralist concerns in this way, parochialism can be avoided. In my view it is perfectly valid to address centralism, with its systems developmental demands, by applying action learning and the 'teacher as a researcher' model. To do so via a problem-solving, investigative approach, with the assistance of a supportive professional, can ensure a breadth and depth of investigation alerting the 'systems managers' and class teachers to wider ranging issues beyond those of the classroom and school. Such an approach can illuminate for further analysis the need for new and particular skills, approaches, strategies and methodologies within both the organisation and the curriculum. It will, as a natural process, expose for further consideration the dynamic relationship between the two.

Closing the dilemma divide

It can be argued, therefore, that an action learning and research modular approach has the capacity to contain within it a range of conflicting interests and demands.

1 The teacher can be involved in the planning and evaluation of the INSET investigative route.
2 The teacher can obtain a significant degree of 'course ownership'.
3 The requirements of central government and LEA can be met without diluting the range of INSET experiences or limiting the range of study.
4 The needs of the school can be met alongside those of the teacher.
5 The time between the teacher beginning the course and being able to make use of the skills and knowledge is in most cases a matter of weeks.
6 The school's, government's, LEA's, teacher's and pupils' needs can be investigated, studied and met without being constrained by centralism or parochialism.
7 Tutors working with teachers acquire fresh insights and teaching experiences.

8   There is cyclical concern whereby practical experience informs theory – theory informs practice.
9   Throughout the modules there is an insistence on practical and academic rigour which is never far from class or school reality.

Modular INSET is capable of meeting both centralist and professional needs in such a way that the two are not perceived as incompatible. A modular type of INSET which offers forms of 'continuing education' within a range of investigative study options can go a long way to resolving many of the tensions. It may be that modular INSET is more able than other forms of more traditional in-service education to respond to these conflicting demands and to do so without losing Stenhousian principles. It is the flexibility of this eclectic type of INSET, with its host of options, which allows it to close the 'dilemma divide' of conflicting interests and ideologies.

Bibliography

DES Circular No 6/86
DES Circular No 1/88
Rudduck, J and Hopkins, D *Lawrence Stenhouse: readings from the work of Lawrence Stenhouse* Heinemann, 1985
Stenhouse, L. (ed) *Curriculum research and development in action* Heinemann, 1980

Notes on Contributors

Adrian Booth

Adrian graduated in Politics and History at Lanchester Polytechnic and, from 1975–83, taught History in a Coventry comprehensive school, latterly as a Department head. In 1984 he was appointed as TVEI Co-ordinator for the Coventry pilot project, and in 1987 to take on the Project Extension. His publications include numerous contributions to journals and to books on the teaching of politics, language, learning and TVEI developments.

Susan Bourne

Educated at Blackheath High School, with an English degree from Reading University and a PGCE from Bulmershe College, Susan has taught both at primary and secondary level in state and independent schools since 1963. Her most recent appointments have been at Great Hollands Primary School, Bracknell; Ravenswood SSN Independent School and, from 1978, at New Scotland Primary, Berkshire. She has been associated with the Fulmer Research Project and is a member of the County Primary Science and Technology Committee. Susan is married with three grown-up children.

Terry Brown

Married with four children, Terry graduated at Swansea University in Zoology, then pursuing doctoral research at Edinburgh University. He began teaching in 1967 at Cheshunt School, Hertfordshire, becoming Deputy Head at Codsall High School, Staffordshire, in 1973, and Head of King Edward VI, Stafford, nine years later. He has been involved in a wide range of in-service and staff development teams, especially in the area of personal and social education. Terry's main interests are cooking and reading (science fiction and thrillers).

David Darwood

Following graduate studies at University College, Swansea, and post-graduate study at Warwick, David began teaching in Birmingham before taking up the headship of a History Department in a Coventry comprehensive in 1973. He went on to become a Senior Teacher prior to a one-year secondment to Leicester University and, in 1985, was appointed to his present position as Curriculum Development Officer for the Coventry TVEI project. David is married, with one daughter, his interests including theatre, golf and gardening.

Richard Dunn

Richard was born in County Durham and educated at King James I Grammar School, Bishop Auckland. He has been Head of Creative Studies and Director of Studies at Melton Mowbray Upper School, Leicestershire, and in 1984 took up his present appointment as Deputy Headteacher at Hemsworth High School. Married with two teenage daughters, Richard's interests are sport, music and work. He has recently successfully completed an MEd Degree at Leeds University.

Ted Goodhew

Born in Bermondsey and with two degrees and a PGCE from Reading University, Ted began his career teaching History, Economics and Sixth Form General Studies at Greenford Grammar School, Ealing. He went on to become Head of History and of Sixth Form at Waingels Copse Comprehensive in Berkshire before two years as an advisory teacher (INSET) for the county. He was appointed Deputy Head (Curriculum) at the Turnpike School, Newbury, in September 1987. As well as articles in *The Times Educational Supplement* and *Pastoral Care in Education*, Ted has co-authored *Guidance and the Changing Curriculum* with Bill Gothard for Croom Helm.

Michael Jones

Mike, who was educated at Carisbrooke High School on the Isle of Wight, started teaching in 1964. He was Deputy Head of Wanstead High and became the first principal of Bretton Woods Community School in 1976. From there he moved to Oxfordshire, where he currently holds the principalship of Wantage School, an 11–18 comprehensive with 1900 students. Mike is a member of the MCC, Chairman of the Oxfordshire Examination Syndicate, an external examiner at Worcester College of Higher Education and has contributed articles to the educational press as well as a chapter in *Teacher Training and Special Educational Needs*.

Henry Macintosh

A graduate from Edinburgh University, Henry taught History at secondary and primary schools before taking up a senior lectureship in

Modern Studies at the Royal Military Academy, Sandhurst. Between 1964 and 1970 he was Deputy Secretary of the AEB and, from 1971 to 1986, Secretary of SREB. Currently he is Consultant on Assessment and Accreditation to the TVEI Unit of MSC and Treasurer of the *International Association for Educational Assessment.* He has published and lectured widely on educational and assessment issues.

Clive Marshall

Educated at Calder High and Bridlington schools, Clive began his career in the National Provincial Bank but, following National Service in the Royal Air Force, trained as a teacher at St John's College, York, and worked for some time in secondary modern schools in that city. In 1972 he moved to Hemsworth High, where he is currently Head of Drama and of the Faculty of Creative and Physical Studies. Clive was awarded an MA in Theatre and Media Production from the Department of Drama at Hull University in 1985. His personal interests are in theatre and opera. He is keen on all sport and plays the trombone, is married and has two young children.

Geoff Molyneux

Educated in Suffolk and graduating in Economics at Hull University, Geoff taught in comprehensive and grammar schools before becoming Director of Studies at Havant Sixth Form College. His interests centre around sport, travel and politics.

Mike Phillips

Born and educated in Southampton, Mike was trained at Bishop Lonsdale College, returning south to teach English in Southampton and Eastleigh secondary schools. He then read Educational Drama at Newcastle University and was appointed to a Departmental Headship at Brune Park, Gosport, in 1971, and at Kirkley High School, Lowestoft in 1974. Whilst here he was awarded a further professional qualification at the Cambridge Institute and went on to gain his Masters Degree in Special Needs at the University of East Anglia. In 1985 Mike was appointed Senior Lecturer in Special Needs at the West Sussex Institute of Higher Education and co-ordinator for In-Service BEd Hons Degree in 1986.

Bruce Pyart

Born at Haverfordwest and with higher degrees in Education from Cardiff and the Open Universities, Bruce has taught music at Haverfordwest Grammar School, Holy Trinity School, Welwyn Garden City, Cefn Hengoed School, Swansea, and has been Deputy Head at

Grango School, Wrexham. He was appointed Headteacher at Ysgol Emrys ap Iwan in 1985 and was TVEI Evaluator for Clwyd LEA and Lancaster University. His interests include gardening, reading and music.

Susan Pyart

Susan was born in Whitehaven and has taught Physics at Tasker's Grammar School, Haverfordwest, Townsend Comprehensive, St Albans, and Christ's Hospital, Hertford. She has been TVEI co-ordinator for Darland School, Rossett, and is currently TVEI Evaluator for Clwyd LEA and Lancaster University. Her publications include *Modules in Action, Evaluation of a Modular Curriculum*, and *Writing Modules: a Teacher's Guide* (with Alun Owen) – all available from *Ysgol Emrys ap Iwan Publications*.

David Sharp

Born and educated in Kingston-upon-Hull, David was awarded an external degree from Portsmouth Polytechnic and his PGCE from Newcastle University. As he says, he 'worked his way up through the ranks' at Hemsworth High, as assistant teacher, Head of Economics, Head of Humanities, examination officer and now Deputy Head. He has taken an active part in running economics and INSET groups in the area, is a parish councillor and a school governor. David is married with two young daughters.

Sidney Slater

Currently Headteacher at Park Hall School, Solihull, and formerly Headteacher/Assistant Principal, Abraham Moss High Street, North Manchester College, Sid is Editor of *The Journal of Evaluation in Education* and has co-directed a number of national conferences. He has also lectured widely in the areas of curriculum, management and industry/education links. He contributed a chapter on *Curriculum Innovation and Evaluation* in *Action Research in Classrooms and Schools* (eds. Cassidy and Cuff, Allen and Unwin, 1986) and he also has a chapter appearing in *The Practical Guide to Staff Appraisal in Schools* (ed Dr L. Bell, Routledge & Kegan Paul).

Christine Southall

Christine Southall has just taken up the post of Vice Principal of Lord Williams's School, Thame, after ten years at Peers School, Oxford. Here she taught German and Russian, going on to take responsibility for the sixth form and to become Director of Studies. Christine has also taught in primary schools, has contributed material to *Open University* courses, has written a chapter with Pat O'Shea in Bob

Moon's *The Modular Curriculum: Remaking the Mould* (Harper and Row, 1987) and is currently co-editing a curriculum handbook with Bob Moon for publication in 1988.

David Warwick

Following national service in the Royal Air Force, Fighter Command, David took a combined first degree in Theology and Teaching Certificate at the College of S. Mark and S. John, Chelsea, and between 1961 and 1967 taught in secondary modern and comprehensive schools in Hampshire and Bristol. He was then a Senior Lecturer in Education at St. John's College, York, and a lecturer at University of Lancaster. In 1974 he was appointed Vice Principal, with responsibility for curriculum and staff development, at the first of Surrey's open-access sixth form colleges (Farnham) and was seconded for three years in 1985 as Surrey Co-ordinator of the School Curriculum Industry Project. From September 1988 he is to be Director of Project INOTEL (Industry and Teacher Education Liaison). David has an Advanced Diploma in Management and an MA in Education, both from London University, and a PhD from Lancaster. He has written or edited 28 books, is a tutor in Curriculum and Management for the Open University, external examiner at Kingston and Portsmouth polytechnics and holds consultancies at universities in North America and Europe. Married for 27 years, David has two grown up sons, his interests including writing, the theatre, science fiction and Victorian social history.

Glinys Weller

A member of the Executive Committee of the *National Association for Remedial Education* and an editorial adviser for the journal *Support for Learning*. Glinys is a director of curriculum at Greendown School, Wiltshire, having previously taught Humanities at Codsall Comprehensive, Staffordshire, and at Whitstone School, Shepton Mallet, and concentrating on Special Needs at Devizes School, Wiltshire.

Geoffrey Wilby

Born in the Hemsworth area and educated at Normanton Grammar School, Geoffrey was awarded a BSc Honours degree in Physics at Reading University, where he also gained his PGCE. Hemsworth High is his third school and, as Head of Science, he took a leading role in the development of modular programmes and a scheme of unit accreditation. Geoffrey is now a member of the senior management team. He enjoys outdoor activities, plays the guitar and is married with two young children.

James Williams
A physicist by training, and currently a director of curriculum at Greendown Community School, James previously taught at Thomas Audley School, Colchester, and Berkeley Vale School, Gloucestershire.

Julie Wright
Julie came late into teaching, previously working as an Estate Sales Promoter and travelling widely in America and Europe. She took an English degree as a mature student at Warwick University and taught her subject within a secondary school prior to joining the Coventry TVEI Project as Co-ordinator for Supported Self-Study.

Index

AEB, 157, 159, 171
Accountability, 82, 137, 221
Accreditation, 2, 49, 61, 86,
  148–52, 155–60, 161–80
Active Tutorial Work, 124
Adult Education, 162
Advisers, 35, 37, 42, 197, 212–13,
  217
Aggregation, 157–8, 169–70
Aims, 5, 6, 11, 13, 17, 28, 44,
  70–1, 83, 135, 208, 219
Appraisal, 137, 154, 160, 211–13,
  216, 218, 223
Art, 14, 91, 98
Assembly, 72, 126
Assessment, 5, 30, 44, 74, 80, 83,
  95, 127, 128, 134, 157,
  192–3, 198, 213, 231–2
Aspects of Secondary Education, 2

BTEC, 155, 157, 206
Benchmark testing, 156, 160
Bernstein, B., 102
Biology, 24, 33, 54, 60
Blackburn, K., 122, 129
Booklets, 18, 21–24
Budget, 17, 20
Burke, E., 210
Business studies, 133, 134, 197
Button, L., 124

CBI, 139, 153
CDT, 29, 91, 182
CGLI, 10, 155, 182
CNAA, 151
CPVE, 4, 90, 155, 159, 182, 183,
  187, 188
CSE, 2, 11, 16, 102
Callaghan, J., 139
Careers, 106, 108, 109, 111, 123,
  125, 127, 133, 145, 153, 183
Certification, 168–70
Chemistry, 54, 60
Child care, 33

Collaborative Writing Project,
  54–5
Colleges of Further Education, 54,
  181, 197, 199–202
Communication, 36–7, 61, 71, 72,
  131, 156, 213, 216, 218
Community, the, 35, 43, 44, 56,
  100, 126, 130, 133, 210
Community studies, 17, 132
Comprehensive Education for Life,
  205
Computers, 7, 18, 27, 63, 72, 103,
  109, 127, 128, 141, 181–95,
  197, 203
Concepts, 13, 80, 83, 136
Co-ordinators, 37, 72, 77, 105,
  106, 108–9, 127, 131, 135,
  198, 203, 229
Consortia, 148–53, 163, 196–206,
  218
Counselling, 60, 71, 114, 123,
  133, 134, 141, 204, 213, 215
Coventry LEA, 196/7
Creative studies, 14–15, 43, 52,
  72, 76, 81, 93, 210
Credit bank, 92, 98, 161–180
Credits, 86, 158, 162, 177, 206,
  223
Criteria referencing, 87, 156, 163,
  164, 166, 193
Critical incidents, 124
Curriculum:
  balanced, 12, 14, 42, 88, 91, 132, 206
  changing, 42–3, 54–8, 220
  core, 42, 48, 50, 53, 90–100, 131, 132
  cross, 4, 12, 15, 72, 75–8, 82, 131–4,
    135, 159, 195
  development, 11, 32, 40–1, 144,
    163–5, 199, 229–30
  hidden, 126, 135, 152
  national, 3, 137
  negotiated, 28, 44, 47, 49, 59–61, 71,
    74, 82, 92, 95, 103–121, 127,
    145, 187, 193, 223, 224, 225,
    231

pastoral, 122–36
planning, 6, 11–12, 18, 33, 46–50,
　　77–82, 143–5, 214–6
　whole, 1, 43, 49, 90, 139, 198, 224,
　　228
DES, 54, 138, 155
DTI, 139
Decision-making, 14, 29, 31, 42, 57,
　　105, 106, 114, 124, 125, 208–9,
　　215
Delegation, 66, 215
Deputy Head, 56, 72, 77–8, 143, 215
Descriptors, 172–3, 175/6, 183, 194
Design, 14, 72
Differentiation, 4, 87, 91, 158, 168, 174,
　　215
Diploma, 223–9
Double Certification, 56, 164
Drama, 75–6

Economics, 13, 16
Economy, the, 138–40
Edgebarrow Comprehensive, 28
Education Acts, 137, 138, 139, 221
English, 52, 65, 67, 72, 86, 91, 138, 203
Environmental studies, 12, 71, 77
Equal opportunities, 127, 197
Evaluation, 7, 14, 17, 18–19, 28, 32, 38,
　　65, 94–8, 217, 231–32
　formative, 7, 60, 159, 195, 198, 229,
　　230
　summative, 7, 182, 195, 225, 229, 231
Examinations, 5, 15, 43, 88, 123, 132,
　　134–5, 141, 157, 192
Expressive arts, 44
Extra-curricular activities, 137, 138, 139,
　　221

Feedback, 26, 33, 36, 62, 145, 156, 217
French, 75–6
Fulmer Research Institute, 31–2, 37
Further Education, 54, 91, 159, 161,
　　181, 197, 199–202

GCE, 2, 102
　A Level, 148–50, 153, 157, 206
　A/S Level, 155
GCSE, 4, 10, 25, 44, 46, 48, 59, 62, 63,
　　86, 87, 92, 93, 105, 109, 134, 141,
　　155, 157, 158, 162–80, 206
GRASP Project, 30
GRIST, 232
General studies, 181
Geography, 13, 16, 54, 93, 133, 138,
　　163, 172, 203, 210
Goals:
　long-term, 5, 20, 38, 56, 66, 70–1

short-term, 4, 27, 44, 95, 100, 114,
　　132, 156, 164, 214
Government, 35, 156, 158, 160, 221,
　　222, 233
Governors, 35, 46, 138, 215
Graphics, 71, 197
Great Debate, the, 139
Greendown School, Swindon, 69–70, 134
Group work, 29–31, 32, 71

HMI, 2, 3, 91, 138, 151
Hamblin, D., 124
Hargreaves Report, The, 130–2, 134
Havant College, Hampshire, 181
Headteacher, 6, 43, 46, 77, 215, 225
Health education, 126, 127
Hemsworth High School, Yorkshire,
　　9–10
Higher Education, 150, 159, 161, 220,
　　222
History, 13, 16, 54, 93, 133, 138, 156,
　　203, 210
Home economics, 32, 197
Homework, 110, 124
House system, 42, 122, 129, 209
Humanities, the, 13–14, 16, 52, 54, 65,
　　72, 75, 87, 91, 93, 98, 133, 134,
　　172

ILEA, 131, 135
INSET, 79, 158, 182, 198, 202, 211,
　　212–13, 217, 220–33
Industrial:
　action, 56/7, 160
　advisers, 29, 148–52, 198
　liaison, 29, 31, 43, 44, 54, 64, 115,
　　137–53, 159, 169, 210, 218–9,
　　221
Infant schools, 37
Information technology, 133, 134, 141
Interpersonal skills, 109, 114
Interviews, 118–9, 130, 215

Jackson, K.F., 40
Jamieson, I., 140
JIIG CAL, 128
Job description, 77, 78, 210
Joint Board, 182, 188

King Edward VI School, Stafford, 42

LEA, 63/4, 67, 138, 165, 172, 212, 220,
　　222–3, 229, 233
Land Rover Ltd, 142–5
Latin, 138
Leadership, 207–8, 215
Learning:

active, 4/5, 18, 21, 66, 127, 132, 134, 198, 202, 204, 218
experiential, 15, 44, 71, 130, 215, 230
individualized, 14, 30, 71, 155
progression, 5, 13, 159, 215
Life skills, 42, 46, 49, 50, 132, 134, 182, 205
Literacy, 28, 70

MEG, 44, 48, 58, 66, 163, 171, 206
MSC, 54, 64, 139, 144
Management, 29, 42, 56–9, 72, 77, 113–4, 129, 146–7, 155–7, 204, 207–9, 225–9, 232
Manufacturing technology, 141–2
Marland, M., 122, 124/5
Materials, 17, 20, 32, 66, 71, 82, 88, 143, 198
Mathematics, 26, 35, 36, 52, 67, 72, 86, 91, 94, 138, 210
Media, the, 71, 72, 92, 105, 140, 197
Meetings, 16, 17, 32, 63, 79, 212, 215, 218
Methodology, 1, 13, 17, 21–4, 32, 49, 56, 59, 61, 62, 71, 82, 91–2, 97, 98, 127, 137, 156, 202, 225
Mini-Enterprise, 28–31, 35, 86
Moderation, 158, 173/4
Modular:
 banking, 3, 92, 129, 161–80, 214
 choice, 52, 59, 60
 flexibility, 17, 26, 32, 68, 87, 100, 128, 133, 206
 grouping, 3, 155, 157–8
 planning, 2, 11–12, 18, 29, 33, 42–68, 77–82, 93, 143–5, 214–6
 preparation, 21–25, 58, 217
 proforma, 77, 80, 108, 117, 120–1, 217
 scheme, 27–34, 44–5, 57, 81, 127–34, 149, 200–1, 226–8
 specification, 7, 157, 216–8
Modules:
 advantages of, 35–41, 44, 58, 82
 categories, 3, 5, 6, 74/5, 92, 106, 215
 combinations, 5, 74, 105
 core, 6, 128, 141, 159, 224
 defined, 3–7, 26, 154
 designing, 34, 84, 224
 length, 12, 16, 32, 46, 74, 91, 132, 154, 214, 224
 levels, 5, 86, 133, 171, 215
Monitoring, 7, 26, 35, 103, 127, 165, 221
Moon, R., 8, 161
Moral education, 71, 126, 133
Motivation, 4, 11, 12, 29, 30, 38–9, 44, 82, 98, 131, 152, 192
Music, 15

NEA, 54, 170
NPRA, 159, 170
National Criteria, 156, 163, 166, 171, 174
National Westminster Bank, 29
Needs, individual, 5, 35, 71, 87, 103, 125–6, 128, 213, 223
Newman, G., 102
New Scotland Hill Primary School, Berkshire, 26
Numeracy, 28, 70, 183

OCEA, 90, 92, 159, 161, 164–5
OES, 162–5, 170, 171
Objectives, 5, 7, 61, 81, 83, 86, 135, 169, 214
Open University, 154, 157, 161
Options, 42, 46, 60, 91, 123
Ownership, 15–17, 57, 59, 138, 164, 198, 222, 229, 233

PE, 72, 76, 81, 91, 93, 138
PSE, 56, 105–6, 127, 130–2, 134, 141
PTA, 31
Parents, 7, 28, 30, 33, 35, 36–7, 49, 60, 61–3, 74, 95, 105, 106, 108–9, 114–5, 116, 123, 131, 138, 215, 221, 231
Parents' evening, 61, 65, 108
Park Hall School, Birmingham, 137
Pastoral work, 42, 103, 122, 124, 204
Peers School, Oxford, 132, 163
Personal development, 72, 122, 128, 134
Physical Science, 18
Physics, 54, 141, 210
Political education, 71, 126, 127, 133, 225
Polytechnics, 150–2
Practical Curriculum, The, 39
Practical work, 12, 20, 27, 31, 44, 52, 133, 223
Primary education, 26–41, 82, 91
Problem-solving, 18, 28, 70, 71, 133, 152, 233
Professionalism, 220–23, 229, 230–1
Profiling, 5, 56, 74, 80, 113, 141–2, 148, 158, 160, 181–95, 215, 216, 218
Promotion, 212–13, 215

Quadrivium, 1
Questionnaires, 18, 193

ROSLA, 123
RSA, 92, 155

Reading, 40–1
Records of achievement, 56, 132, 155, 159, 193, 202
Religious education, 93, 104, 131
Research, 207–8, 222, 223, 225, 229–30, 232–3
Residential education, 126, 130, 133, 141, 144
Resources, 16, 17–18, 27, 28–9, 63–4, 203, 204, 221, 222
Role Play, 183, 215
Rolls, 28, 44, 78, 210

SCDC, 58
SCIP, 139
SEB, 75, 89, 162–4, 165–6, 171–2, 173
SEC, 170
SILO, 139
School:
    climate, 67, 103
    liaison, 27, 29, 31–2, 35, 37, 43, 54, 60, 91, 198–202
    organisation, 52–4, 123, 125, 208–10
Schools Council, 39, 139
Science, 12–13, 32, 43, 49, 52, 72, 86, 89, 91, 94, 138, 139, 159, 164
Scottish National Certificate, 161, 166
Self-directed study, 4, 71, 203–4
Simulation, 214
Situational analysis, 20, 36
Sixth form, 4, 90, 124, 141, 203, 210
Skilbeck, M., 11
Skills, 12, 13, 28, 29, 33, 39–40, 80, 83, 125, 127, 157, 211, 212, 213–14, 220, 225, 229, 233
Socialisation, 7
Social studies, 16, 72, 126, 128, 135
Special needs, 29, 72, 87–8, 126, 223–4, 229, 230, 232
Sport, 74
Staff development, 137, 152, 207, 211, 212–19
Staffordshire Education/Industry Project, 64, 67
Stake, R., 7
Steering group, 141, 143
Stenhouse, L., 222, 230, 231
Study skills, 4, 124, 152, 223

TRIST, 203
TVE(I), 4, 44, 46, 56, 57, 64, 81, 88, 102, 133, 137, 140, 144, 145, 160, 164, 166, 171, 181, 188, 196–206, 210
Teacher centres, 37, 145, 223
Teacher education, 220
Technology, 12, 28, 43, 70, 72, 139, 141, 142–5, 193, 197, 203, 222
Timetable:
    blocked, 7, 34, 52, 62, 73, 98, 202
    modular, 16, 50, 95, 103
    planning, 34, 44, 49–52, 98
Trident, Project, 139
Trivium, 1
Tutorial:
    guidance, 5, 60, 98, 110–13, 125, 204
    work, 49, 91, 93, 125, 126, 128–30, 132, 135, 203, 229
Tutor, the, 61, 74, 108, 122–3, 125, 221, 224, 231, 234

UBI, 139
UCCA, 185–7
Unemployment, 12

Vertical streaming, 100, 203
Videos, 18, 27, 213, 214
Visual aids, 24
Vocational education, 3, 43, 105, 108, 123, 125–6, 158, 205, 221

Wantage School, Oxfordshire, 90, 165
Warwick, D., 3, 6
Watkins, C., 126, 127
Welsh Joint Board, 115
West Sussex Institute of Higher Education, 220
Work experience, 126, 130, 133, 145, 205
Working parties, 56–8, 209
Worksheets, 18, 27
Workshop, 143, 213–14

YTS 206
Yateley Industries, 29
Year system, 42, 123, 129, 209
Ysgol Emrys ap Iwan, Abergele, 101